Library of Congress Cataloging-in-Publication Data

Hayes, Timothy.
    The research driven investor : how to use information, data, and analysis for investment
success / Timothy Hayes.
    p. cm.
    ISBN 0-07-135462-X
    1. Investments. 2. Investment analysis. I. Title.

HG4521 .H43 2000
332.6—dc21

00-040109

raw-Hill

A Division of The McGraw·Hill Companies

AGM/AGM   0 6 5 4 3 2 1 0

or this book was Stephen Isaacs, the editing supervisor was Ruth W. Mannino, and the
as Tina Cameron. It was set in Century Schoolbook by Judy Brown.

becor/Martinsburg.

y of Ned Davis Research.

provide accurate and authoritative information in regard to the subject matter
erstanding that neither the author nor the publisher is engaged in rendering legal,
service. If legal advice or other expert assistance is required, the services of a
ould be sought.

*Declaration of Principles jointly adopted
ommittee of the American Bar
tion and a Committee of Publishers*

cial quantity discounts to use as premiums and sales promotions, or for use
e information, please write to the Director of Special Sales, Professional
a, New York, NY 10121-2298. Or contact your local bookstore.

d-free paper containing a minimum of 50% recycled de-inked fiber.

The
Research Driven
Investor

The Research Driven Investor

How to Use Information, Data, and Analysis for Investment Success

TIMOTHY HAYES

Copyright ©
permitted un
distributed in
permission of th

1 2 3 4 5 6 7 8 9 0

0-07-135462-X

The sponsoring editor
production supervisor

Printed and bound by Qu

All charts and tables courte

This publication is designed t
covered. It is sold with the un
accounting, or other professiona
competent professional person s

—From a
by a C
Associa

McGraw-Hill books are available at sp
in corporate training programs. For mo
Publishing, McGraw-Hill, Two Penn Pla

This book is printed on recycled, ac

McGraw-Hill McG

New York   San Francisco
Caracas   Lisbon   London   M.
Montreal   New Delhi   San Juan
Sydney   Tokyo   Toronto

To Karin, Max, and Alex

CONTENTS

PART TWO

DEVELOPING A VIEW OF WHERE THE MARKET IS HEADING

Chapter 3

How Stock Market Indicators Can Help You   43

Chapter 4

Developing Indicators   51

Chapter 5

Trend-Sensitive Indicators   79

Chapter 6

Valuation and Long-Term Sentiment   131

Chapter 7

Shorter-Term Sentiment   161

Chapter 8

Monetary and Economic Indicators   191

ACKNOWLEDGMENTS

My first acknowledgment goes to Ned Davis, who has maintained an environment conducive to independent research. Ned's market philosophies and modeling concepts are behind many of the market tools featured in these pages.

Regarding the preparation of this book, I would like to thank Sam Burns for creating several of the indicators and tables while providing overall assistance; Sara Morano for her work with the nine-indicator model and other aspects of the book; LeeAnn Tillis for preparing the manuscript and many of the tables; Emily Snyder, likewise for her work with tables; and the Ned Davis Research graphics team for their help with the charts. I would also like to thank Neil Leeson of Spyglass Trading, who conducted much of the research for Chapter 2, reviewing Web sites and software packages.

Acknowledgments are also due to everyone at Ned Davis Research who has had a partial or complete role in the creation of indicators and systems shown in this book. This list includes NDR analysts as well as those involved in computer programming and data management.

Finally, I would like to thank my family for their patience and support during this project.

The
Research Driven
Investor

The days of easy stock market profits are over. After a year-to-year rise of 34 percent in 1995, the momentum of the Standard & Poor's 500 has gradually receded, as the index gained 31 percent in 1997, 27 percent in 1998, and 20 percent in 1999. It would not be surprising to see the major market averages continue to revert toward the market's normal rate of growth for this century, an annual rise of 9 percent since 1926. And the corrective process could take several years, perhaps including one or more years of negative stock market returns. At the same time, volatility has continued to rise, with averages of 1998 and 1999 volatility reaching levels last seen during the nerve-wracking years of 1987 and 1974, and during the tumultuous 1930s.

From the investor used to reaping profits by responding to the hot stock story of the moment, to the investor accustomed to earning double-digit returns via the passive strategy of indexing to the market via mutual funds, the continued return to reality means that greater care, effort, and oversight will be required for investment success. A proactive, research-based approach is needed, an approach that (1) gauges downside risk and upside reward, limiting losses and maximizing profits by identifying the stock market's turning points within the longer-term uptrends, downtrends, and trading ranges; (2) focuses on the developing market themes, leading to the selection of mutual funds and individual stocks likely to outperform the broad market; and (3) determines the desirable degree of exposure to equities relative to bonds, cash, and markets in other regions of the world.

This book will help you develop this proactive approach to investing, explaining how to develop an accurate market outlook, discussing the issues essential to an effective investment strategy, and walking you through an array of reliable investment tools—how to develop them correctly and how to use them for maximizing stock market profits. The book explains how you can capitalize on the breadth of available information sources, data sources, and analysis packages to be your own investment advisor.

Part One presents the framework for getting started, with Chapter 1 discussing the "top-down" approach to market analysis. This chapter addresses why it's essential to start with an assessment of the economy, both global and domestic, and the impact on market psychology and resulting investor actions. The chapter explains why it's so advantageous to begin your analysis with the broad market outlook, then narrowing this outlook down to general market themes, asset allocation considerations, the identification of the strongest market sectors and industry groups, and finally, the most attractive

1

stocks within those favored market segments. Chapter 2 provides an overview of the information and raw materials that you will need at the outset, listing various sources for market news, data, and analysis available via the Internet. By the end of Part One, you will have a good idea of how to implement a top-down approach to research and where to go for the data and information that you will need for getting started.

In Part Two, the book moves into the specifics of forming an outlook on the market, starting in Chapter 3 with a discussion of how data and indicators can help you, but also how they can deceive you if handled in the wrong way. Chapter 4 follows with a look at various techniques for developing indicators and quantifying their ability to provide input as you develop a market view. The chapter discusses the issues to address when working with data, and how to identify the specific events and indicator developments with significant implications for the market's future course.

Chapter 5 is the first of four chapters explaining how to build and use various types of indicators. This chapter focuses on the kind of indicator that receives a great deal of attention throughout the book—the tape or "trend-sensitive" indicator. While demonstrating that the process of developing and updating trend-sensitive indicators is relatively straightforward, the chapter discusses how essential it is to keep your equity exposure consistent with the market's underlying technical health. The chapter not only reviews a wide range of tape indicators, but also discusses their differing uses and relevance at differing points in the market cycle.

Chapter 5 is then followed by two chapters on sentiment indicators. These chapters discuss the key market influence of investor psychology, explaining contrarian investing and demonstrating how to develop indicators based on reversals from extremes in market sentiment. Chapter 6 considers long-term indicators based on liquidity, supply and demand, and valuation, including a look at valuation models for gauging risk and reward. And Chapter 7 looks at shorter-term sentiment indicators based on market opinion surveys and the trading activity of various groups. The chapter also discusses contra-trend indicators that identify the overbought conditions prevalent at market tops and the oversold conditions found at market bottoms.

The fourth of the chapters on indicators for assessing the stock market as a whole, Chapter 8 focuses on why Fed policy is such an important influence on the stock market, featuring indicators based on interest rates and money supply growth. The chapter also illustrates how to develop and use indicators based on inflation measures and other economic data.

In Part Three, the book addresses the questions surrounding what to do once you have used your market indicators to develop a view of where the market is heading. Chapter 9 discusses the major asset allocation considerations of stocks versus bonds and cash, growth versus value, small caps versus large caps, and the sectors warranting attention given the status of the market cycle. Chapter 10 hones in on the question of what to buy, discussing top-down stock screening techniques that can be used not only for trading ideas but also for perspective on the market's health and changing internals. The chapter completes the allocation discussion with attention to global market sectors and the consideration of relative strength among markets in the various regions of the globe.

The final chapter uses current conditions as an example of how the top-down approach can be used to assess the current outlook, featuring a model comprising nine of the indicators featured in the book. The chapter discusses the importance of remaining aligned with the composite model message in detecting changes in the risk/reward balance, changes that are crucial to your investment decisions.

Throughout, the book features the graphics unique to Ned Davis Research, graphics widely recognized among market professionals. In most cases, these charts show a market index in the top clip and an indicator in the bottom clip, with a horizontal time scale and vertical scales for the index and indicator values. The charts typically include parameters indicating levels that, when reached, have significant implications for the market outlook. Many of the charts include buy and sell signals, with the indicator's track record summarized in the upper-left-hand corner. In most cases, the results include at least several years of real-time performance—that is, they are based on actual signals as well as hypothetical trades. Alternatively, many of the charts include a box indicating how the market index has performed with the indicator in different modes. You will also find numerous tables developed from the Ned Davis Research database.

When coming away from this book, you should have a new way of looking at the stock market as a vehicle for building wealth. And you will have specific guidelines on how to go about obtaining necessary data and analytical tools, how to work with the data properly, how to build effective indicators, how to combine the indicators into a model, how to interpret the indicator and model readings, and how to use the input in developing a market outlook, an outlook guiding the decisions of whether to buy, what to buy, what to sell, and how to allocate your assets. In an increasingly volatile market and difficult environment for profiting in stocks, this book should prove not only useful but necessary.

PART ONE

The Optimal Strategy for Stock Market Profits

CHAPTER 1

Thinking Big—The Top-Down Approach

In order to beat the market, you must first understand it. And to gain that understanding, there are two approaches you can take—bottom-up or top-down. For the vast majority of individual investors, the top-down approach is preferable.

If you think of the market as a mountain, then the bottom-up approach examines the boulders at the base. Those are the thousands of individual firms that make up the broader stock market. By getting to know the composition of these companies, the Wall Street bottom-up analyst may draw conclusions about the market as a whole. If the analyst uncovers promising earnings among the bulk of the companies under study, he or she may consider the earnings outlook to be favorable for the market in general. The shared elements of the many boulders at the base of the mountain would be considered representative of the entire mountain.

The top-down analyst would point out that the bottom-up approach does not account for changes in the investment climate. If the weather warms, chunks of ice may slide to the bottom of the mountain, alongside the boulders. The bottom-up analyst might conclude that these are aberrations, or simply companies with poor earnings prospects. No broader cause would be assigned to their initial appearance. But if enough of the ice blocks appeared amid the boulders, if firms with poor fundamentals had become as numerous as the promising firms, then the bottom-up analyst would have to conclude that something about the mountain had changed.

Early on, the top-down analyst might warn the bottom-up analyst that falling ice could be expected, because of the warming weather. For example, the top-down analyst may observe that inflation is heating up, which in turn could be expected to send interest rates higher and most stocks lower. The bottom-up analyst would argue that regardless of whatever else lies at the base of the mountain, there will always be solid boulders, or good stocks to buy and hold for the long term. This is the fundamental approach espoused by Graham and Dodd (1934) and used with success by Warren Buffett (1985), Peter Lynch (1994), and others. Their success is attributable to experience, skill, and excellent sources of information.

But for the vast majority of investors, lacking the tools and experience needed to effectively evaluate a company—the metallurgical tools needed to analyze the composition of a boulder—the top-down approach is preferable for several reasons.

First, it lends itself to market timing and asset allocation. When the climate is turning hostile for the market as whole, the top-down investor reduces exposure to the increasingly risky market.

Second, it lends itself to the broad array of style and theme investing options. When inflation is rising, the top-down investor may look to mutual funds and stocks that tend to rise when inflation is rising, such as gold funds or energy stocks.

Third, it generally is easier than bottom-up analysis. The information available to the top-down analyst is far more expansive and readily available than the information needed by the bottom-up analyst. The top-down analyst requires accurate economic data and stock market data, information disseminated broadly and efficiently via the media and numerous data providers. The bottom-up analyst relies heavily on the financial statements and annual reports released by individual firms. The analyst must scour the financial statements and their footnotes for evidence of write-offs or accounting gimmicks that can affect a firm's reported earnings.

The bottom-up analyst must also be confident in the assessment of management's intentions and future actions. Unexpected merger and acquisitions news, for example, can have a dramatic impact on a firm's valuation. Climbing with a bottom-up approach is generally more hazardous and difficult than descending with the top-down approach.

STARTING FROM THE TOP

In its most comprehensive application, a top-down approach would descend from matters as broad as society's survival, to demographics, to economic analysis, to global asset allocation, to broad domestic market analysis, to domestic asset allocation, to industry analysis, and finally, to individual stock selection. Starting with the very broadest of perspectives, the initial concern would be the fundamental question of society's survival. Given that the sun isn't ready to burn out quite yet, it can safely be said that at this point, the human race warrants a bullish outlook.

So the analysis would quickly move to the next level down, which deals with demographics—population issues such as global migration trends, birth rates, and average age. While these issues can be complex, especially on a global scale, Harry S. Dent, Jr., and other futurists have attempted to apply demographic trends to the future performance of the economy and the U.S. stock market. Dent (1999) has pointed out that the U.S. Census Bureau expects the U.S. population of 45- to 54-year-olds to rise until about 2009, leading him to believe that consumer spending will remain strong and that the U.S. stock market will continue rising toward a peak of 41,000. His rationale is illustrated in Figure 1–1, which moves U.S. births ahead by 46 years and then plots it against the S&P 500, adjusted for inflation.

After addressing demographics, the top-down approach moves to the question of the economy, on global, regional, and individual country bases. Within a major global demographic trend, such as the aging of the baby boom population, several economic cycles will occur, though not necessarily at the same time in each region and each country. Since World War II and the subsequent population boom, the United States has experi-

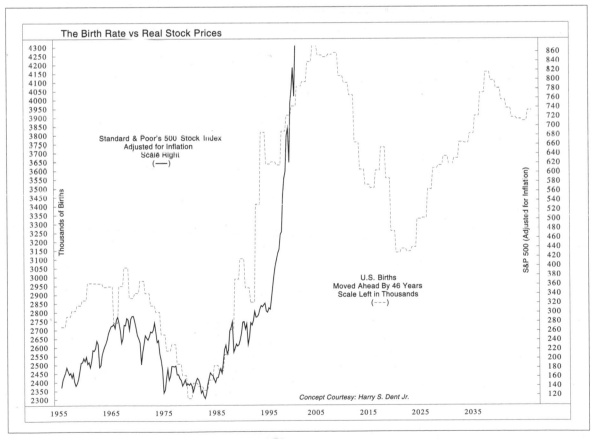

Figure 1–1

enced nine economic expansions and nine recessions, as defined by the National Bureau of Economic Research.[1] Over the same period, Japan experienced four economic expansions and five recessions, almost never occurring in tandem with the U.S. equivalents, as shown in Table 1–1.

In developing an economic viewpoint, then, the global economy must first be considered in terms of the relative economic strength among regions and the specific countries within those regions. In 1999, global economic growth generally improved from the weakness of the previous year, but the major regions stood at different points in the economic cycle. The contrast between Japan and the United States was especially glaring. While Japan was emerging from a painfully protracted economic slump, the United States was in the mature stages of its longest expansion ever.

Many factors come into play, including interest rates and inflation. But in general terms, when one country is gaining economic momentum relative to another, the stronger country's currency will tend to strengthen versus the weaker country's currency, and the stronger country will attract investment flows, to the benefit of its financial markets.

For the global equity investor, the most attractive market is one that has turned around and is moving higher in anticipation of improving economic conditions ahead,

T A B L E   1–1

Recessions and Expansions—United States and Japan

Start	Finish	Start	Finish
Recessions in the United States		*Expansions in the United States*	
August 1957	April 1958	April 1958	April 1960
April 1960	February 1961	February 1961	December 1969
December 1969	November 1970	November 1970	November 1973
November 1973	March 1975	March 1975	January 1980
January 1980	July 1980	July 1980	July 1981
July 1981	November 1982	November 1982	July 1990
July 1990	March 1991	March 1991	?
Recessions in Japan		*Expansions in Japan*	
September 1957	March 1958	March 1958	September 1994
September 1994	March 1995	March 1995	March 1996
March 1996	September 1996	September 1996	September 1997
September 1997	December 1998	December 1998	June 1999
June 1999	?		

Note: Table starts with first recession since 1955. U.S. economic turning points based on monthly dates identified by the National Bureau of Economic Research. Japan economic turning points based on recessions defined as two consecutive quarterly declines in seasonally adjusted gross domestic product.

timing and trend analysis to be conducted most effectively, it is essential to
the time frames and risk/reward parameters. Using a top-down approach,
start with the very long-term trend, the kind of trend that culminated with
ad market tops in the late 1920s and late 1960s, and the major bottoms in the
the 1970s. But for timing and allocation purposes, the very long-term turn-
are useful only for the die-hard buy-and-hold investor. Few investors would
to sit through the major declines that can occur within these trends, such as
rash that took the Dow Industrials down by 36 percent.
useful for timing purposes is the identification of the cyclical bull and bear
at occur within the long-term moves, such as the 31 bear markets listed in
These cyclical moves are based on criteria developed by Ned Davis Research
eria based not only on magnitude, but also on duration, as explained in the
note. Although the drop that included the 1987 crash lasted only 55 days, it
a bear market since it exceeded the 30 percent minimum required for de-
g 50 to 145 days. The decline of 1983–1984 took the Dow Industrials down by
cent, but the slide qualifies as a bear market since it lasted more than 145
ration for declines ranging from 13 to 30 percent. But even if the Dow Indus-
meet the magnitude or duration requirement, a decline can still qualify as a
if the Value Line Composite drops by 30 percent, as occurred during the
0 and 1998.
se, all bear markets are preceded and followed by bull markets, listed in Ta-
rules of magnitude are the same for the NDR-defined bull markets as they
ears, except the duration requirement is 155 days instead of 145 days. The
counts for the normal tendency for bull markets to last longer than bear
s can be seen in Figure 1–2, which illustrates the Dow Industrials with all
d bear markets.
tification of bull and bear markets can lend perspective to shorter-term
stance, the 7 percent drop from April to June of 1999 turned out to be an in-
rm correction within the longer-term bull market. The longer-term inves-
illing to sit through such a decline as long as the indicators pointed to the
f the longer-term uptrend. But the shorter-term investor would want to
rly to avoid the decline and would therefore stay focused on short-term in-
own in Table 1–6, the median for the largest bull market correction has
ent. Similarly, Table 1–7 indicates that the median for the largest bear
as been 12 percent.
gnitude and duration parameters can identify turning points in hind-
verages can be used to describe the direction of market trends over vari-
s. A moving average is the average price of an index over a specified time
arket index's short-term moving average is falling but the long-term

doing so with a strengthening currency. A foreign investor in that market will benefit from the rising market as well as the strengthening currency.

But economic strength is not always a good thing. Late in an economic cycle, interest rates and inflation tend to trend upward, with negative implications for future economic performance. In anticipation of that future weakness, the stock market will tend to weaken, and the market downtrend will be well under way by the time the economic data confirm that a contraction has started. At that point, interest rates will usually be moving lower again, as will the currency if the rates are dropping faster than they are in other major economies.

The key point to remember is that stock market performance tends to lead economic performance. The relationship is not precise, as shown in Table 1–2, which compares postwar bear markets with recessions. Because stock market cycles are shorter and more nu-

T A B L E 1–2

Bear Markets versus Recessions

Bear Market Dates		Recession Dates	
Start	End	Start	End
05/29/1946	05/17/1947	11/30/1948	10/31/1949
06/15/1948	06/13/1949	—	—
01/05/1953	09/14/1953	07/31/1953	08/31/1954
04/06/1956	10/22/1957	08/31/1957	04/30/1958
01/05/1960	10/25/1960	04/30/1960	02/28/1961
12/13/1961	06/26/1962	—	—
02/09/1966	10/07/1966	—	—
12/03/1968	05/26/1970	12/31/1969	11/30/1970
04/28/1971	11/23/1971	—	—
01/11/1973	12/06/1974	11/30/1973	03/31/1975
09/21/1976	02/28/1978	—	—
09/08/1978	04/21/1980	01/31/1980	07/31/1980
04/27/1981	08/12/1982	07/31/1981	11/30/1982
11/29/1983	07/24/1984	—	—
08/25/1987	10/19/1987	—	—
07/16/1990	10/11/1990	07/31/1990	03/31/1991
07/17/1998	08/31/1998	—	—

Notes: Bear market dates are based on NDR criteria.
Recession dates are as defined by the National Bureau of Economic Research.

merous than economic cycles, there's truth to the quip, restated based on the data in the table, that "the stock market has led 17 of the past nine recessions." The table shows that economic expansions were oblivious to the bear markets of 1962, 1976–1978, 1987, and others in which the market's fears proved to be overdone. But regardless of the actual economic outcome, it's the expectations that drive market performance, and a challenge for the top-down investor is to gauge those expectations accurately.

In 1999 and early 2000, U.S. interest rates were rising and the stock market was starting to anticipate future economic problems, performing worse than in previous years, and worse than the benchmark indexes of most other major markets. In contrast, the Japanese market was anticipating a continued recovery from its prolonged economic malaise, performing far better than the U.S. market. Both markets were driven by expectations, a topic I will address in greater detail during the discussion of market psychology, sentiment, and market valuation in Chapters 6 and 7.

FROM THE MACRO TO THE MARKET

After addressing demographics, the state of the global economy in general, and the current phase of the domestic economy, you can start your assessment of the financial market outlook. The most ambitious and comprehensive task is to gauge the relative risk and return of different asset classes in different markets. For example, if the U.S. economy has peaked and has started to contract with falling inflation, yet the Japanese economy has reached a stage of rapid growth with inflation and interest rates that have started to move higher, it is likely that Japanese stocks will be outperforming U.S. stocks. It is also likely that Japanese bonds will be underperforming U.S. bonds, since bonds tend to correlate inversely with inflationary economic growth. And the merits of each of the stock and bond market alternatives would appear attractive or unattractive relative to cash, or the risk-free rate of return in each country.

It's possible, then, that in assessing the investment outlook for both countries, the investor might conclude that Japanese stocks held the most promise, followed in order by U.S. bonds, U.S. cash, Japanese cash, Japanese bonds, and U.S. stocks. Numerous factors come into play, such as the investor's tolerance for risk, investment goals, time horizon, liquidity, transaction costs, and the available vehicles for investment. But when the U.S. market is unattractive relative to other investment alternatives, you will need to consider allocating assets into other investments such as bonds and cash, and you will also need to consider global diversification. I will discuss asset allocation in more detail in Part Three, encompassing Chapters 9, 10, and 11.

For most investors, the top-down approach will include a great deal of attention paid to the broad stock market outlook. In Part Two, I will discuss the applicable analytical techniques in terms of the U.S. market. But the techniques can also be applied to markets throughout the world, at least to the extent that data are available.

Whether the market is in the United States or the Far anywhere else, two factors are responsible for bull and bear m market peaks at the maximum point of greed and bottoms at Stated differently, a peak is the extreme of investor optimi treme of investor pessimism. These universal truths of sto ceive attention at various points throughout the book. I will ences to the interest rate sensitivity of stock market inve Chapter 8 will discuss monetary conditions and how to gau the stock market.

But there's another truth as well, one that best lends it sis, but also to profitable investing. Addressed in Chapter 5 move in trends. That sounds simple enough. But getting t Ned Davis (1991) has discussed how we all make our ow things as we want to see them. An investor who is levera look at charts and data and see a strong and healthy up short might look at the exact same information and see why objective indicators and models are so important, as

The pure bottom-up investor will pay little attention or her mind it is inconsequential. But effective trend ana vestor's most important advantage over the bottom-up will be invested when the market is in an uptrend and o the bottom-up investor will be exposed throughout. Wit points and the appropriate market exposure, the top turns. Table 1–3 uses data starting in 1928 to show that 500's returns have expanded at a pace of 12 percent p cent per annum absent its 50 best days.

TABLE 1-3

Gain per Annum (%) of Standard & Poor's 5 and Worst Days (01/04/1928–03/15/2000)

	Day	
	10	20
Best	4.7	3.6
Worst	7.9	9.0
Best and worst	6.4	6.3
Buy/hold gain per annum	6.2	

For establish you could major br 1930s an ing point be conten the 1987

More markets t Table 1–4. (NDR), cri table's foot qualifies a clines lasti only 16 per days, the du trials fail to bear marke bears of 199

Of cour ble 1–5. The are for the b difference a markets. Th of the bull a

The ide moves. For in termediate-te tor would be continuation take action ea dicators. As s been –11 perc market rally

While ma sight, moving ous time frame period. If the

T A B L E 1–4

NDR-Defined Bear Markets (06/17/1901–12/29/1998)

Beginning		Ending			
Date	DJIA	Date	DJIA	% Gain	Days
06/17/1901	57.33	11/09/1903	30.88	−46.1	875
01/19/1906	75.45	11/15/1907	38.83	−48.5	665
11/19/1909	73.64	09/25/1911	53.43	−27.4	675
09/30/1912	68.97	07/30/1914	52.32	−24.1	668
11/21/1916	110.15	12/19/1917	65.95	−40.1	393
11/03/1919	119.62	08/24/1921	63.90	−46.6	660
03/20/1923	105.38	10/27/1923	85.76	−18.6	221
09/03/1929	381.17	11/13/1929	198.69	−47.9	71
04/17/1930	294.07	07/08/1932	41.22	−86.0	813
09/07/1932	79.93	02/27/1933	50.16	−37.2	173
02/05/1934	110.74	07/26/1934	85.51	−22.8	171
03/10/1937	194.40	03/31/1938	98.95	−49.1	386
11/12/1938	158.41	04/08/1939	121.44	−23.3	147
09/12/1939	155.92	04/28/1942	92.92	−40.4	959
05/29/1946	212.50	05/17/1947	163.21	−23.2	353
06/15/1948	193.16	06/13/1949	161.60	−16.3	363
01/05/1953	293.79	09/14/1953	255.49	−13.0	252
04/06/1956	521.05	10/22/1957	419.79	−19.4	564
01/05/1960	685.47	10/25/1960	566.05	−17.4	294
12/13/1961	734.91	06/26/1962	535.76	−27.1	195
02/09/1966	995.15	10/07/1966	744.32	−25.2	240
12/03/1968	985.21	05/26/1970	631.16	−35.9	539
04/28/1971	950.82	11/23/1971	797.97	−16.1	209
01/11/1973	1051.70	12/06/1974	577.60	−45.1	694
09/21/1976	1014.79	02/28/1978	742.12	−26.9	525
09/08/1978	907.74	04/21/1980	759.13	−16.4	591
04/27/1981	1024.05	08/12/1982	776.92	−24.1	472
11/29/1983	1287.20	07/24/1984	1086.57	−15.6	238
08/25/1987	2722.42	10/19/1987	1738.74	−36.1	55
07/16/1990	2999.75	10/11/1990	2365.10	−21.2	87
07/17/1998	9337.97	08/31/1998	7539.07	−19.3	45
Mean				**−30.9**	**406**
Median				**−25.2**	**363**

Notes: A bear market requires a 30 percent drop in the Dow Jones Industrial Average after 50 calendar days or a 13 percent decline after 145 calendar days. Reversals of 30 percent in the Value Line Composite also qualify. This applied to the 1990 and 1998 high and low. (The table uses corresponding high and low dates and values for the DJIA). The NYSE was closed from 07/31/14 to 12/11/14 because of World War I. The DJIA was then adjusted to reflect the composition change from 12 to 20 stocks.

T A B L E   1–5

NDR-Defined Bull Markets (9/24/1900–3/24/2000)

Beginning		Ending			
Date	DJIA	Date	DJIA	% Gain	Days
09/24/1900	38.80	06/17/1901	57.33	47.8	266
11/09/1903	30.88	01/19/1906	75.45	144.4	802
11/15/1907	38.83	11/19/1909	73.64	89.7	735
09/25/1911	53.43	09/30/1912	68.97	29.1	371
12/24/1914	53.17	11/21/1916	110.15	107.2	698
12/19/1917	65.95	11/03/1919	119.62	81.4	684
08/24/1921	63.90	03/20/1923	105.38	64.9	573
10/27/1923	85.76	09/03/1929	381.17	344.5	2,138
11/13/1929	198.69	04/17/1930	294.07	48.0	155
07/08/1932	41.22	09/07/1932	79.93	93.9	61
02/27/1933	50.16	02/05/1934	110.74	120.8	343
07/26/1934	85.51	03/10/1937	194.40	127.3	958
03/31/1938	98.95	11/12/1938	158.41	60.1	226
04/08/1939	121.44	09/12/1939	155.92	28.4	157
04/28/1942	92.92	05/29/1946	212.50	128.7	1,492
05/17/1947	163.21	06/15/1948	193.16	18.4	395
06/13/1949	161.60	01/05/1953	293.79	81.8	1,302
09/14/1953	255.49	04/06/1956	521.05	103.9	935
10/22/1957	419.79	01/05/1960	685.47	63.3	805
10/25/1960	566.05	12/13/1961	734.91	29.8	414
06/26/1962	535.76	02/09/1966	995.15	85.7	1,324
10/07/1966	744.32	12/03/1968	985.21	32.4	788
05/26/1970	631.16	04/28/1971	950.82	50.6	337
11/23/1971	797.97	01/11/1973	1,051.70	31.8	415
12/06/1974	577.60	09/21/1976	1,014.79	75.7	655
02/28/1978	742.12	09/08/1978	907.74	22.3	192
04/21/1980	759.13	04/27/1981	1,024.05	34.9	371
08/12/1982	776.92	11/29/1983	1,287.20	65.7	474
07/24/1984	1,086.57	08/25/1987	2,722.42	150.6	1,127
10/19/1987	1,738.74	07/16/1990	2,999.75	72.5	1,001
10/11/1990	2,365.10	07/17/1998	9,337.97	294.8	2,836
08/31/1998	7,539.07	03/24/2000	11,112.72	47.4	571
Mean				86.8	738
Median				69.1	614

Notes: A bull market requires a 30 percent rise in the Dow Jones Industrial Average after 50 calendar days or a 13 percent rise after 155 calendar days. Reversals of 30 percent in the Value Line Composite since 1965 also qualify. The NYSE was closed from 7/31/1914 to 12/11/1914 because of World War I. The DJIA was then adjusted to reflect the composition change from 12 to 20 stocks.

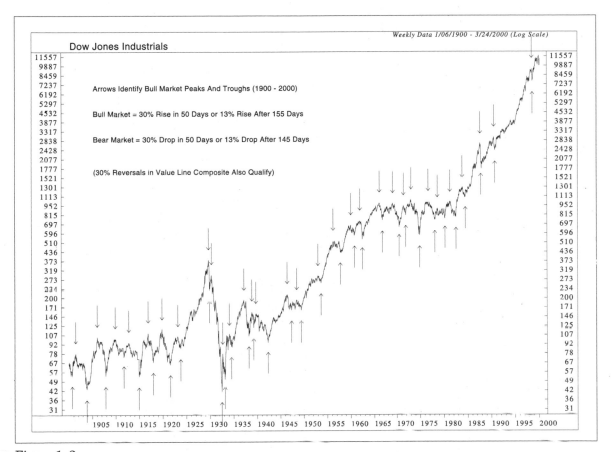

Figure 1–2

moving average is still rising, the short-term decline could be classified as a correction within a longer-term advance. If the short-term moving average is rising but the long-term moving average is falling, the short-term advance could be classified as a rally within a long-term downtrend.

In smoothing out the data to reveal the direction of the current short-term and longer-term trends, moving averages lend themselves to the development of market indicators. An indicator might call for buying when a short-term moving average crosses above the long-term average and selling when it crosses below the long-term moving average. I will discuss moving average indicators in more detail in Chapters 4 and 5.

A key point to keep in mind is that your preferred time horizon will determine whether you will strive to identify turning points that mark the start of moves that are short-term, intermediate-term, long-term, or very long term. In this book, *short-term*

T A B L E   1–6

Largest Correction in Each Bull Market (09/24/1900–3/24/2000)

Bull Market	Largest Correction	DJIA % Decline	Days
09/24/1900–06/17/1901	05/01/1901–05/09/1901	−11.3	8
11/09/1903–01/19/1906	04/14/1905–05/22/1905	−14.8	38
11/15/1907–11/19/1909	01/14/1908–02/13/1908	−11.0	30
09/25/1911–09/30/1912	10/14/1911–10/27/1911	−4.9	13
12/24/1914–11/21/1916	04/30/1915–05/14/1915	−15.9	14
12/19/1917–11/03/1919	07/14/1919–08/20/1919	−12.3	37
08/24/1921–03/20/1923	10/14/1922–11/27/1922	−11.0	44
10/27/1923–09/03/1929	02/11/1926–03/30/1926	−16.7	47
11/13/1929–04/17/1930	12/07/1929–12/20/1929	−12.4	13
07/08/1932–09/07/1932	08/10/1932–08/12/1932	−9.1	2
02/27/1933–02/05/1934	07/18/1933–10/21/1933	−23.0	95
07/26/1934–03/10/1937	04/06/1936–04/29/1936	−11.3	23
03/31/1938–11/12/1938	04/16/1938–05/31/1938	−11.0	45
04/08/1939–09/12/1939	07/22/1939–08/24/1939	−9.2	33
04/28/1942–05/29/1946	07/14/1943–11/30/1943	−11.1	139
05/17/1947–06/15/1948	07/24/1947–03/16/1948	−11.5	236
06/13/1949–01/05/1953	06/12/1950–07/13/1950	−13.5	31
09/14/1953–04/06/1956	09/23/1955–10/11/1955	−10.0	18
10/22/1957–01/05/1960	08/03/1959–09/22/1959	−9.1	50
10/25/1960–12/13/1961	09/07/1961–09/25/1961	−4.8	18
06/26/1962–02/09/1966	05/14/1965–06/28/1965	−10.5	45
10/07/1966–12/03/1968	09/25/1967–03/21/1968	−12.5	178
05/26/1970–04/28/1971	06/19/1970–07/07/1970	−7.1	18
11/23/1971–01/11/1973	05/26/1972–07/20/1972	−6.3	55
12/06/1974–09/21/1976	07/15/1975–10/01/1975	−11.1	78
02/28/1978–09/08/1978	06/06/1978–07/05/1978	−7.0	29
04/21/1980–04/27/1981	11/20/1980–12/11/1980	−9.2	21
08/12/1982–11/29/1983	11/03/1982–12/16/1982	−7.1	43
07/24/1984–08/25/1987	09/04/1986–09/29/1986	−8.6	25
10/19/1987–07/16/1990	10/21/1987–12/04/1987	−12.9	44
10/11/1990–07/17/1998	08/06/1997–10/27/1997	−13.3	82
Median		**−11.0**	**37**

Notes: Study uses NDR-defined bull and bear markets. (The table uses corresponding high and low dates and values for the DJIA.)
Days = calendar days.

T A B L E 1–7

Largest Rally in Each Bear Market (06/17/01–12/30/98)

Bear Market	Largest Rally	DJIA % Gain	Days
06/17/1901–11/09/1903	08/08/1903–08/17/1903	13.7	9
01/19/1906–11/15/1907	07/13/1906–10/09/1906	13.6	88
11/19/1909–09/25/1911	07/26/1910–06/19/1911	18.3	328
09/30/1912–07/30/1914	06/11/1913–03/20/1914	15.7	282
11/21/1916–12/19/1917	02/02/1917–06/09/1917	13.9	127
11/03/1919–08/24/1921	12/21/1920–05/05/1921	19.9	135
03/20/1923–10/27/1923	07/31/1923–08/29/1923	7.8	29
09/03/1929–11/13/1929	10/29/1929–10/31/1929	18.9	2
04/17/1930–07/08/1932	10/05/1931–11/09/1931	35.0	35
09/07/1932–02/27/1933	11/03/1932–11/11/1932	16.7	8
02/05/1934–07/26/1934	05/19/1934–06/18/1934	10.2	30
03/10/1937–03/31/1938	11/24/1937–01/11/1938	18.2	48
11/12/1938–04/08/1939	01/26/1939–03/10/1939	11.6	43
09/12/1939–04/28/1942	06/10/1940–11/09/1940	23.5	152
05/29/1946–05/17/1947	10/09/1946–02/08/1947	13.1	122
06/15/1948–06/13/1949	09/27/1948–10/23/1948	8.1	26
01/05/1953–09/14/1953	06/16/1953–08/13/1953	5.3	58
04/06/1956–10/22/1957	02/12/1957–07/12/1957	14.5	150
01/05/1960–10/25/1960	03/08/1960–06/09/1960	9.6	93
12/13/1961–06/26/1962	05/28/1962–05/31/1962	6.3	3
02/09/1966–10/07/1966	08/29/1966–09/16/1966	6.2	18
12/03/1968–05/26/1970	02/25/1969–05/14/1969	7.7	78
04/28/1971–11/23/1971	08/10/1971–09/08/1971	9.7	29
01/11/1973–12/06/1974	08/22/1973–10/26/1973	15.9	65
09/21/1976–02/28/1978	11/10/1976–12/31/1976	8.7	51
09/08/1978–04/21/1980	11/14/1978–02/13/1980	15.1	456
04/27/1981–08/12/1982	03/08/1982–05/07/1982	9.3	60
11/29/1983–07/24/1984	04/05/1984–05/02/1984	5.0	27
08/25/1987–10/19/1987	09/21/1987–10/02/1987	5.9	11
07/16/1990–10/11/1990	08/23/1990–08/29/1990	6.0	6
07/17/1998–08/31/1998	08/14/1998–08/18/1998	3.4	4
Median		**11.6**	**48**

Notes: Although the rally of 11/14/78–02/13/80 met the NDR bull market criteria, it is classified as a rally, since the 09/08/78 high was never exceeded before the bear market criteria were achieved. Study uses NDR-defined bear markets. (The table uses corresponding high and low dates and values for the DJIA.) Days = calendar days.

generally refers to five or more reversals per year, *intermediate-term* is five to two reversals per year, *long-term* is two per year to one every two years, and *very long term* is anything less frequent.

Generally, your time horizon focus will reflect your risk tolerance and reward requirements. A short-term focus will tolerate greater risk for greater reward. A very long term focus will be risk-averse, tolerating limited reward. But many investors will structure their portfolios with several time horizons, ranging from a speculative short-term portion to a very long term portion intended for preserving capital. For the sake of consistency, this book is most oriented toward the intermediate-term and long-term, the general duration of the bull and bear markets listed in Tables 1–4 and 1–5.

At the broad market level, the top-down analysis should emphasize the analysis of trends and tape conditions in general, the assessment of sentiment conditions (relative optimism and pessimism), valuation conditions (the market's price relative to its normal valuation), monetary conditions (primarily the analysis of interest rate trends), and the related areas that exert an influence on the broad market. All of these will be discussed in later chapters.

The end result of the broad market analysis will be a view of the market's current direction as well as a determination of risk and reward. When the market is in an uptrend, risk is gauged as the probability that the advance will end and turn into a decline, while reward is measured as the expected upside potential. Risk and reward can also be viewed as the market's position in the bull-bear market cycle. Early in the advancing stage of the cycle, risk is low and reward is high; in the mature stage, risk is high and reward is low.

THE ALLOCATION QUESTION

The risk/reward determination and the identification of the market's location in the cycle are important considerations in continuing with the top-down approach, descending to the levels that deal with stock selection. These include questions of how to allocate assets and what to buy and sell. The broadest of the considerations relates to size, the relative emphasis to place on small-cap and large-cap stocks.

A common argument for buying small-cap stocks is that they outperform large-cap stocks over time. But this largely depends upon which data series you are using and what "time" is being measured. From 1925 through 1999, the small caps as measured by the Ibbotson Small Companies Total Return Index have in fact outperformed large caps as measured by the comparable Ibbotson large company index, doing so by 1.3 percentage points per annum. From 1979 through 1999, however, data from the Frank Russell Co.[2] show that small caps as measured by the Russell 2000 Index underperformed large caps as measured by the Russell 1000, doing so by 1.8 percentage points per annum. And they have underperformed by 2.0 percentage points per annum over the 10 years since 1989.

The more significant point is that the small caps tend to outperform during certain periods, gaining impressively when conditions are right. The Russell 2000 outperformed the Russell 1000 in 123 (49 percent) of the 251 months over the 20-year span, yet the median amount of outperformance in those months was 1.85 percentage points. When the Russell 1000 outperformed, it did so by a median of 1.67 percentage points. Small-cap outperformance tends to be most dramatic in the early stages of bull markets, typically in conjunction with broad market strength.

When the top-down analysis determines that the market is in the early stages of a new bull market, the time is usually right to increase allocation to small caps, and the small-cap strength itself is confirmation that a new bull market is under way. Accordingly, many of the same tape indicators that can be used to identify a new bull market can also be used to indicate a developing period of small-cap outperformance. Small caps tend to benefit from falling interest rates and from expectations of improved economic performance, among other factors.

With the economic expansion mature and interest rates rising, the market is often in the late stages of a bull market or the early stages of a bear market. As will be shown in Chapter 9, bear markets are usually accompanied by small-cap underperformance, and the small caps have underperformed large caps in 21 of the last 24 bear markets. A big reason for their relative weakness is their greater volatility, which is also a major reason for their relative strength at the beginning of new bull markets.

The next selection question is whether to focus on growth stocks or value stocks. Again, the top-down analysis will help answer this question. Growth stocks are driven by expectations for improving earnings momentum, while value stocks benefit from their low prices, their perceived value. But as Richard Bernstein (1995) has explained, the performance of growth stocks and value stocks is, like so much else, affected by supply and demand. Growth stocks tend to perform better when the supply of growth stocks is small, the supply of value stocks is large, the economy is weak, and corporate earnings momentum is slow. During such periods, growth stocks are relatively scarce, and the demand for them is great. With supply low and demand high, the prices of those stocks tend to rise.

Value stocks are affected in a similar way, but respond to the opposite set of circumstances. They tend to perform better when the supply of value stocks is small, the supply of growth stocks is large, the economy is strong, and earnings momentum is high. Growth stocks are easy to find during such periods, whereas value stocks are relatively scarce and in greater demand.

Most of the time, the question of growth versus value is one of relative exposure, not an all-or-nothing concern. Portfolio managers, for instance, may "tilt" portfolios toward growth or value, depending upon their preferences. But whether the intent is to determine what to emphasize or to make an absolute call, indicators of economic growth, earnings momentum, and other factors can be applied to the growth/value question. I will show examples of those indicators in Chapter 9.

Through this level of the top-down approach, small caps have been compared to large caps and growth has been compared to value, making it possible to combine the two assessments in gauging the relative appeal of small-cap growth, small-cap value, large-cap growth, and large-cap value. This can be achieved via asset allocation models, or more simply with relative strength rankings.

For a momentum-based approach, a relative strength ranking would be based on a formula applied to each style category. For example, the average of a 4-week rate of change, an 8-week rate of change, and a 12-week rate of change would be calculated for the Russell 2000 Growth Index, a small-cap growth stock proxy. The same calculation would be made for the Russell 2000 Value Index (small-cap value), the Russell 2000 Growth Index (small-cap growth), the Russell 1000 Value Index (large-cap value), and the Russell 1000 Growth Index (large-cap growth). The average rates of change would then be ranked, and changes in the ranking could be used to identify relative strength and relative weakness, as shown in Table 1–8.

SECTORS AND GROUPS

The determination of style strength and weakness provides a broad framework as you descend into the sectors, groups, and individual stocks. Among the 19 broad industry groupings classified as sectors by NDR, several are dominated by stocks of specific

T A B L E 1–8

Relative Strength Ranking for Growth and Value Indices

Index	% Change	March				February				January	
		24	17	10	3	25	18	11	4	28	21
Russell 1000 Growth	13.86	1	2	3	3	2	3	2	2	2	2
Russell 2000 Growth	13.49	2	1	1	1	1	1	1	1	1	1
Russell 1000 Value	6.85	3	4	4	4	4	4	4	4	4	4
Russell 2000 Value	5.29	4	3	2	2	3	2	3	3	3	3

Notes: Ranking based on average of 4, 8, and 12 week rates of change of Russell growth and value indices through March 2000. Percent Change is current average.

styles. The technology sector, for example, is dominated by growth stocks, and several of the technology groups are heavy with small-cap growth stocks in particular. The foods sector is also heavy with growth stocks, but those groups are dominated by the more defensive growth stocks that tend to have large capitalizations.

The extent to which consumer stocks are growth stocks can be seen in the composition of the large-cap Morgan Stanley Consumer Index. Of its 30 component stocks in early 2000, 10 could be considered growth stocks based on the Russell index criteria, while only 6 could be considered value stocks and 14 could not be classified in a specific style category. Even more pervasive is the value dominance of the Morgan Stanley Cyclical Index, as 25 of its 30 component stocks could be classified as value stocks in early 2000. Accordingly, Figure 1–3 shows that when the Russell 1000 Growth Index has been outperforming the Russell 1000 Value Index, the Morgan Stanley Consumer Index has typically been

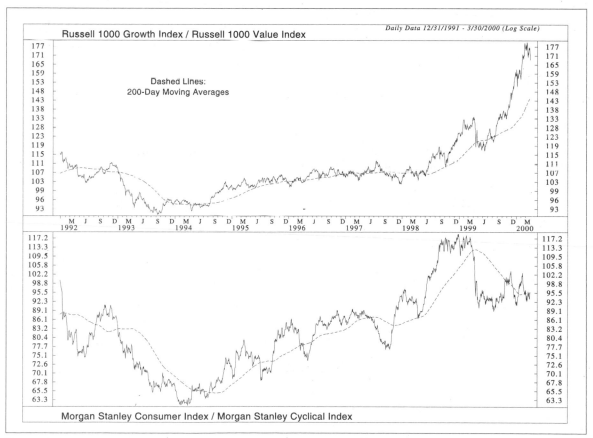

Figure 1–3

outperforming the Morgan Stanley Cyclical Index, and the two ratios have tended to decline in sync as well. The chart illustrates that with the exception of a divergence starting in 1999, when technology stocks sent the growth index skyward, the 200-day moving averages of the two ratios have almost always been moving in the same direction.

As I will show in Chapter 9, groups from the automotive, industrial materials, and capital goods sectors are high on the list of groups with the heaviest percentages of value stocks. Those sectors are considered "cyclical" because they are sensitive to changes in the economic outlook, performing well when the economy is expected to strengthen and poorly when the economy is expected to weaken. This is consistent with the tendency for the value indices to show relative strength when the economy is strong and relative weakness when the economy is weak. Consumer sectors, such as the growth-dominated foods sector, tend to hold up better when the economy is weak. Food stocks are considered defensive since the firm's products are viewed as necessities that will still be in demand during periods of economic weakness.

In the small-cap universe, the distinction between growth and value applies along similar lines, with value represented by cyclical groups such as the machine tools group and growth represented by technology groups such as the semiconductor group. But also in the world of value, two types of stocks are even more dominant than cyclical stocks—financials and utilities. In fact, the utility sector is the king of value stocks. Of about 1900 stocks in the NDR stock universe in late February 2000, 123 (6 percent) were utility stocks, and of those 123 utility stocks, 104 (85 percent) were value stocks.

Financials and utilities both respond favorably to falling interest rates, consistent with the general tendency for the Russell value indices to perform well when interest rates are falling. But utilities, as the purest value play, share the additional value-stock characteristic of holding up well in bear markets. Chapter 9 will include a table identifying the groups that have tended to hold up best after market peaks, showing that utility groups have dominated the list of top performers. The chapter will also include a chart illustrating the tendency for value to perform better than growth in bear markets and a table quantifying the tendency for large caps to hold up better than small caps. Chapter 5 will include a discussion of the value-dominated utilities, including an illustration of how the Dow Jones Utility Average has tended to exhibit relative strength in bear markets by holding up better than the Dow Jones Transportation Average and the Dow Industrials.

DESCENDING TO THE STOCK LEVEL

An excellent way to identify dominant and emerging market themes is to examine the common characteristics of the most attractive individual stocks, which are identified as the top-down process descends to its lowest level. Chapter 10 will explain how a technically based ranking system can be used to identify the most attractive securities as well as the least attractive. It will also illustrate how valuable perspective can be gained by identifying the top stocks in the most attractive industry groups. If two stocks have similar rankings, but one is part of a high-ranked industry group while the other is part of a low-ranked group, the stock in the high-ranked group is more attractive. Over time, strategies based on selecting the top stocks in top groups have tended to outperform strategies based on stock selection that does not recognize the group effect.

Once the top stocks in top groups have been identified and organized into a "Focus List," the groups can be compared by the number of Focus List stocks they include. But such comparisons can lack significance since some groups contain only a few stocks, and thus only a few potential Focus List members, while others contain many. More useful comparisons can be made by grouping the stocks by their broader sectors. Chapter 10 will include a table that ranks the sectors by the number of the sector's stocks appearing on the NDR Focus List. The table will include not only the number of Focus List stocks in each sector, but also the percentage of each sector represented by its Focus List components and each sector's percentage of representation within the broad stock universe. When the sector's representation on the Focus List is greater than its share of the stock universe, the sector has a relatively heavy weighting in the Focus List.

The relative Focus List weightings and the changes in those weightings lend themselves to the identification of major themes, emerging themes, and those that are dissipating. And the same analysis can be done with the Focus List's composition of large caps, small caps, growth stocks, and value stocks. When technology is dominant and gaining Focus List representation, you might also expect to see a relatively high presence of small caps, and small-cap growth stocks in particular. When the utility sector is dominant and gaining ground, you might expect to see a relatively heavy weighting of value stocks, and large-cap value in particular. You might also expect to see a heavy weighting of value when the industrial materials and capital goods sectors are well represented, and their presence could reflect late-cycle economic conditions. When the foods sector is dominant, boosting the large-cap growth percentage, you might expect to see the economic outlook worsening and the stock market trending lower in anticipation of future economic weakness.

Unfortunately, the market never behaves quite like you think it should. And the picture can become very fuzzy during periods of rapid rotation, indecisive leadership, or trendless broad market activity. But generally, over the span of many cycles, different styles and sectors tend to exhibit relative strength at different times.

A TYPICAL CYCLE

To illustrate, let's walk through an ideal stock market cycle, starting with the late stages of a typical bull market. At this point, the data will typically indicate strong economic growth, interest rates will be rising, market optimism and consumer confidence will be high, and cyclicals will be moving higher in relative strength. The strong performers will be manufacturing cyclicals or consumer cyclicals, not the home building stocks and other interest-rate-sensitive cyclicals most likely held back by the inhibiting influence of rising interest rates. In addition to the cyclical segment of the value universe, the more aggressive segments of the growth universe, such as technology, will be performing well.

But as the market starts to view the interest rate uptrend as a threat to economic growth, the market's momentum will start to slow, and breadth and volume divergences will start to appear. Among growth stocks, foods and other consumer staples will start to look more appealing than technology stocks. And among value stocks, utilities will start to hold more promise than the cyclicals, and value in general will start to hold more appeal than growth. As will be illustrated in Chapter 9, value tends to outperform growth during the mature stages of an economic expansion, and that's also when the market starts to decline in anticipation of the next economic downturn.

As the breadth and momentum turn from divergent to decisively negative, and mounting pessimism replaces excessive optimism as the market driver, the highfliers of the previous bull market will start to fall fast, with small caps, especially small-cap growth stocks, generally faring the worst. Large caps will be holding up better, with large-cap utilities most likely the top performer. And the likely relative strength in utilities and relative weakness in technology will boost value indices relative to growth indices. As the market decline continues, interest rates will start to fall, and eventually the economic numbers will start confirming an economic contraction.

By the time the contraction is broadly recognized, the market will be fairly valued again, pessimism will be extremely high, confidence will be low, the market will be oversold, and the atmosphere will be conducive to a selling climax that will leave the market washed out and ready for a new bull market, fueled by renewed optimism that the economy will recover in response to the falling interest rates. Growth stocks, which typically outperform value stocks while the economy is still weak, will then lead the charge higher. And the setting will be ideal for small-cap growth stocks in particular. The new bull market would receive reassuring confirmation with a breadth thrust, as discussed in Chapter 5. And by the time the economic data start to confirm that a recovery has started, the market advance will be broad, with consumer durables, technology, and retail stocks all performing well.

THE RESEARCH CHALLENGE

To conclude this illustration with a neat ending, I could say that the market advance would then mature and that the cycle would then repeat itself. But as I noted earlier, the stock market has led 17 of the past 9 recessions. The market could enter a bear market without a subsequent economic downturn, as occurred in 1987, or the market could experience several bull and bear market cycles in the midst of a longer-term economic contraction as occurred during the 1930s. The relative strength implications will be affected accordingly.

But while history rarely if ever repeats itself in exactly the same way, human nature is constant from generation to generation. And human nature, including fear and greed, pessimism and optimism, is what makes markets rise and fall, and economies expand and contract. From cycle to cycle, the differences will relate to size, scope, and degree—the degree to which the market is influenced by the numerous factors that affect the behavior of the market's participants, its buyers and sellers. The challenge over time is to identify those factors and then gauge their current influences. For example, program trading was not a factor in the 1930s, but it was a factor, and a major influence, in 1987. Perhaps it won't be a factor in 2020. On the other hand, commodity prices have been a factor throughout, though with differing levels of influence.

Later chapters will zero in on the major factors that have been present over time, often called "the fundamentals." And I will illustrate that the major benefit of the "technicals" is that they have nothing to do with the fundamentals, or the reasons why the market is rising or falling. Pure technical analysis is concerned only with what the market's current activity says about where the market is headed. The beauty of technical analysis is that it focuses on the repetitive and cyclical tendencies of human nature, recognizing that the repeated behavior is represented in chart patterns and data characteristics evident around market reversals and during market advances and declines.

Ultimately, when it comes to making money, a thorough knowledge of what the stock market is doing is more essential to investment success than is the knowledge of why the market is doing what it is doing. The market is constantly discounting future news, hence the expression "buy on the rumor and sell on the news." The reasons for the market activity may become apparent only in hindsight, well after the market has already responded to the rumor of the news to come.

This point would be emphasized by proponents of a theory known as the Efficient Market Hypothesis, which holds that the market's discounting process makes analysis a futile endeavor. Supporters of the theory would say that it's simply impossible to beat the market. But even the most hardened cynic would have a hard time refuting the wealth of evidence demonstrating how investment success can be improved through the use of technical approaches with leading tendencies and through an understanding of the broader environment affecting interest rate trends and other factors that influence the investor's responsiveness to buy on "the rumor" and the subsequent motivation to sell on "the news."

Moreover, a successful top-down strategy can ensure healthy asset growth on an ongoing basis. As mentioned earlier in the context of the mountain analogy, it is usually easier to descend from the top down than to climb from the bottom up. And it is usually more effective. Using another analogy, the investor using a top-down approach is akin to a doctor assessing the entire health of the patient before examining specific areas. If the patient's overall health is good, wounds should heal quickly. When the market's health is good, corrections should be short-lived. But when the environment is an unhealthy influence and the market is sick, wounds will fester and recovery will be slow. The investor using the bottom-up approach is like a doctor who examines the patient's affliction without first assessing the patient's overall health. The top-down approach is safer and more reliable. It is conducive to profitable investing.

E N D N O T E S

1. National Bureau of Economic Research, 1050 Massachusetts Avenue, Cambridge, MA 02138, 617-868-3900.
2. Frank Russell Company, 909 A Street, Tacoma, WA 98402, 253-572-9500.

REFERENCES

Bernstein, Richard. 1995. *Style Investing: Unique Insight into Equity Management*. New York: John Wiley & Sons.

Davis, Nathan E. (Ned). 1991. *Being Right or Making Money*. Venice, FL: Ned Davis Research.

Dent, Harry S., Jr. 1999. *The Roaring 2000s: Building the Wealth and Lifestyle You Desire in the Greatest Boom in History*. New York: Simon and Schuster

Graham, Benjamin, and David Dodd. 1934. *Security Analysis*, 1997 rpt.ed., New York: McGraw-Hill.

Graham, Benjamin, and Warren Buffett (preface). 1985. *The Intelligent Investor: A Book of Practical Counsel*, 4th ed. New York: HarperCollins.

Lynch, Peter, and John Rothchild. 1994. *Beating the Street*. New York: Simon and Schuster.

CHAPTER 2

Gathering the Information and Getting Started

The process of top-down analysis cannot be effective without a crucial raw material, accurate information. This includes information on current market news, which is readily available and usually accurate, via CNBC television, CNN Financial News, Bloomberg television, and others. It includes the Web sites affiliated with those networks, plus other sites devoted to financial news and commentary, such as TheStreet and CBSMarketWatch. It includes financial newspapers such as *The Wall Street Journal*, *Investors Business Daily*, *Financial Times*, and *Barron's*. And it includes their Web sites.

Staying up on current events is an obvious prerequisite to profitable investing. But as discussed in Chapter 1, a key to staying ahead of the crowd, to getting aligned with a new uptrend or downtrend in its early stages, is to "buy on the rumor and sell on the news" when the news is good, and to "sell on the rumor and buy on the news" when the news is bad. An example of the latter occurred in the summer of 1999. In June, the rumor began to circulate that the Fed would raise interest rates for the first time since October of 1998, when the last in a series of rate cuts helped launch a new bull market. As the media reported economic numbers, comments from Fed Chairman Greenspan, and analyst interpretations of the data and the chairman's comments, the rumor of a rate hike became the consensus, bond yields rose, and the stock market sold off. When the Fed in fact raised the Fed funds rate by 25 basis points at its June meeting, yields fell and the market took off. The bad news had been fully discounted.

But investing this way can be hazardous, since it requires accurate subjective assessments of the nature of the rumor, the extent to which the news has been discounted, and the probability that the rumor is true. If the news had turned out worse than expected, with the Fed raising the rate by 50 basis points, the news might have only perpetuated a bigger sell-off.

Moreover, this game of second-guessing is a short-term timing strategy. In the long run, it's the ability to identify trends in the underlying data that's most essential to profitable investment decisions. Again, 1999 included an example. When the market rallied on the news, short-term contrarians were rewarded. But the rate increase was confirmation that the six-month bond yield uptrend was for real and that a new interest rate uptrend was in fact under way, with negative longer-term implications for the stock market. Whatever the rumors and short-term reactions, the bottom line is that the market will tend to perform poorly when rates are rising, and it will tend to perform well when rates are falling. The challenge, as discussed later, is to define *rising* and *falling* and to determine when the definition applies.

So above and beyond market news, the information that simply must be accurate is the essential raw material, the financial data. With clean and accurate data at the core of your analysis, decisions can be made independently of what, at times, are psychotic ups and downs of market opinion. There is no shortage of subjective interpretation and blind guessing reported in the media. When a few facts spawn an abundance of opinion that develops into a consensus, the best approach is to use the consensus as an indicator of market opinion, as discussed in Chapters 6 and 7. The consensus can then be used as a sentiment indicator to be weighed against your own analysis, based on the messages provided by the data.

WHERE TO GO FOR CLEAN DATA

Where, then, do you go for clean data? Fortunately for the investor, financial news isn't all that has become widespread and accessible via the Internet. Data that at one time could be obtained only in printed form, and later on diskette with the advent of computers, can now be downloaded from numerous Web sites. And at this writing, much of the data can be downloaded for free, including recent data as well as historical data.

Economic Data

A good starting point for economic data as well as financial market data is Economagic (www.economagic.com), a site that claims to carry more than 100,000 data series, with charts and Microsoft Excel files for each. The site includes extensive histories on numerous economic series updated by the U.S. Treasury, the Federal Reserve, the Bureau of Labor Statistics, the Commerce Department, the Census Bureau, and even the Internal Revenue Service. It also includes data series from the central banks of Japan and Canada, data by state, and numerous commodity price indexes and subindexes from Bridge Commodity Research Bureau. All of this data appears to be updated on a timely basis, and when the source agency revises historical data, the revisions are reflected on the site.

This raises an important point. The initial reports on economic series such as GDP, nonfarm payrolls, retail sales, and banking reserves are often subject to revision; and in some cases an entire history will be revised. At the end of 1999, for example, the U.S. Commerce Department revised the historical data for the U.S. GDP, at which point any charts and indicators using the GDP data needed revision as well. Accurate historical data is essential for effective analysis. Otherwise, if current reported data is compared to historical data that does not reflect historical revisions, the comparisons will be skewed. And if the historical revisions are major, then the adage of "comparing apples to oranges" will apply. Inaccurate data can lead not only to inaccurate conclusions, but to misleading conclusions, causing the analyst to see a bullish influence when in fact the influence is bearish.

Beyond economic and commodity price data, Economagic's offerings thin out. For the stock market, the data is limited to the major Dow Jones indices. But the site does include daily closing data for the Dow Jones Industrial Average since 1896, the average's daily high and low since 1928, and the high, low, and closing data for the Dow Jones Transportation Average since 1928 and the Dow Jones Utility Average since 1930. All of the data series can be viewed in chart form and easily downloaded by simply clicking on an option to download an Excel file. At this writing, there is no charge for any of the data, charting, and download offerings, although Economagic does charge for more customized services such as forecasting.

Economagic includes links to various government sites; and a comprehensive list of U.S. government agencies has been compiled by Louisiana State University (www.lib.lsu.edu). For money rates, money flow data, and foreign exchange data, try the New York Federal Reserve Bank (www.ny.frb.org) or the St. Louis Federal Reserve Bank (www.stls.frb.org). Demographic and trade data can be obtained from the U.S. Census Bureau (www.census.gov); and the Bureau of Economic Analysis (www.bea.doc.gov) is a good source for GDP data and other economic series.

Stock Market Data

For data on the stock market, a good starting point is Yahoo! (www.yahoo.com), the popular site initially known for its Internet search capabilities. The site's financial section, called Yahoo! Finance, is an excellent source for current information on individual stocks, recent financial statement data, and company profiles from Market Guide. It includes information on analyst recommendations, via a link to the Zacks data source, SEC filings, via a link to the EDGAR Online data source; insider activity, via a link to the CDA/Investnet data source; and recent news reports, via links to news services such as Reuters, Standard & Poor's, and the Associated Press. The site includes global market coverage, via Yahoo! Finance sites for more than a dozen countries.

But perhaps most important for analytical purposes, the site updates open, high, low, close, and volume data series for numerous market indices and thousands of individual stocks. Any stock or index can be charted on a daily, weekly, or monthly basis, with substantial historical data in most cases. Provided by Commodity Systems Inc. (CSI), the data can be downloaded at no cost, and updates can be downloaded daily to a spreadsheet or personal database.

Among the other features of Yahoo! Finance is a screening capability that enables the user to screen the database for stocks by industry category, by average analyst recommendation, and by factors such as price-earnings ratio, earnings growth, and historical performance. The user can also screen for mutual funds by fund category and by such factors as turnover and performance.

A good screening program is also available at the CBS MarketWatch site (cbs.marketwatch.com), which includes the Hoover's Stock Screener. The user can screen for stocks based on 20 different criteria. The tickers resulting from the screen can then be used on the Technical Charting page, a nice complement to the screening program. The charts are provided by BigCharts (www.bigcharts.com), a CBS MarketWatch subsidiary that also generates the charts for the Fidelity Investments Web site (www.fidelity.com).

The site's charting page enables the user to view stock and market index charts customized to include specified moving averages and other technical analysis applications such as stochastics and trading bands. The only drawback of these charts is that unlike the charts to be discussed later, they do not include signals or hypothetical performance statistics to help the user gauge the value added by specific techniques. The site also lacks a direct approach to downloading historical data, in contrast to Yahoo!

Nevertheless, the CBS MarketWatch site is an excellent source for financial market information, and it includes a far greater emphasis on commentary and analysis than does Yahoo! and other sites. In fact, it's nearly on a par with TheStreet (www.thestreet.com) in that regard, and TheStreet's major emphasis is timely on-line news and commentary.

For find free data, a better alternative to Yahoo! is Wall Street City (www.wallstreetcity.com), which carries historical stock and index data that can be downloaded in seven different file formats. The data can then be easily imported into a technical analysis package or spreadsheet. The site includes a broad array of stock market news, information, and commentary. And the charting page not only includes customization features similar to those of CBS MarketWatch, but it also indicates buy and sell signals and summarizes an indicator's historical record based on those signals. Additional features include "breakout alerts" that indicate when, for example, a stock breaks above or below its 200-day moving average, and comparison charts that enable the user to view several different stocks or indices on the same chart.

Data from Exchanges

Another way to obtain data at no charge is to go directly to the exchanges via their Web sites. For currency, futures, and bond files, the site for the Chicago Mercantile Exchange (www.cme.com) is worth a visit. For stock market data, check in on the New York Stock Exchange and Nasdaq/AMEX sites. At the NYSE site (www.nyse.com), the Data Library includes historical data on price-earnings ratios, volume, NYSE indices, margin debt, and other trading statistics. All of the data is available for download, as is the data offered at the Nasdaq/AMEX Web site (www.nasdaq.com). Data can be downloaded on index values, market value, and volume of the composite index, and the site also carries data on sector indices such as the Nasdaq Utility Index and the Nasdaq Bank Index. The market statistics start in 1971, and the site also offers a wealth of short interest data starting in 1995. In addition, the site offers daily and intraday charting as well as stock screening, enabling the user to screen stocks by market capitalization, fundamental factors, and risk factors.

Data from Vendors

If you're willing to pay, you can simplify the process of data acquisition by downloading from a vendor that provides a comprehensive range of data series as well as timely updates. For example, Pinnacle Data (www.pinnacledata.com) offers three distinct databases, covering stocks, bonds, commodities, and economic data, with several series starting in the early 1900s. The service bills itself as the keeper of data that's "the cleanest in the industry," and it offers an update service for as low as $12 per month.

Another comprehensive site is Global Financial Data (www.globalfindata.com), which carries a unique set of series that spans several centuries, such as English consumer prices since 1264 and England's bull and bear markets since 1693. In fact, the service claims to carry more than 5000 series, including current and historical data for the United States, plus more than 150 other countries. In addition to stock market and inflation data, the database includes exchange rates dating back to 1590, interest rates since 1700, and commodities since 1500.

For data spanning several centuries, it makes the most sense to look for the very long term perspective that annual data can provide, and the annual data is in fact available free from this Web site. For a greater density of data with less history, the service charges $25 for individual monthly and weekly files, $50 for daily files prior to 1975, and $25 for daily files starting in 1975. Global Financial Data also offers "annual mini-databases" at $300 each. The only apparent drawback of this service is that to update a file, either you must do so yourself with data from another source, or you must pay again to download the entire file.

In contrast to Global Financial Data, which emphasizes the breadth of its historical data base, NexTrend (www.nextrend.com) is a service whose biggest selling point is its trading tools. Neil Leeson, Director of Quantitative Research for Spyglass Trading L.P., says the site is "truly the blue collar man's institutional financial software service." Leeson, who helped review Web sites and software programs for this chapter, points out that for a base of $39.95 per month, "investors can get virtually everything a New York trader can with a $1000 to $5000 a month service such as ADP, Bridge, CQG, Bloomberg, or Instinet."

Covering stocks, mutual funds, market statistics, bonds, commodities, and currencies, NexTrend offers daily data since 1988 and intraday history for 18 months in many cases. Like many of the other services, NexTrend also provides quotes, news, portfolio management tools, and charting capabilities. Obviously, this site is best used for a short-term perspective, and it is therefore a good complement to a site emphasizing longer-term perspectives, such as Global Financial Data.

Another site that's strong for its timeliness is Commodity Systems Inc. (www.csidata.com). A well-known service with a good reputation among Wall Street professionals, CSI takes pride in the accuracy of its data. It offers customized diskettes with any combinations of data series on commodities, options, stocks, indexes, and mutual funds. The historical data is priced based on frequency, extent of history, and type of data, ranging from 20 cents to 80 cents per file with a $100 minimum. And for an additional charge, CSI provides daily updates, a convenient feature.

You may note that the Yahoo! Finance site includes a statement that CSI is the source for its data updates. This is almost always a good sign when considering a data vendor, as it lends to the credibility of the service. The same can be said for the Zacks service (www.zacks.com), a leader in fundamental data. The service provides the earnings-related data used by Yahoo! Finance and other Web-based services.

EDUCATION

Each of the aforementioned sites emphasizes a different area. Some sites are strongest for the extent of their historical data. Others can claim to have an impressive breadth of data. Others can emphasize the data density and the timeliness and ease of updates. And others can point to features that supplement the data, such as news updates and commentary, quoting features, and charting capabilities. But very few emphasize education. One such site is run by highly regarded technical analyst Martin Pring (www.pring.com), author of *Technical Analysis Explained* and other books. Upon visiting the home page, the visitor is informed that the site is "the only site dedicated to the art of technical analysis and charting." A Trader's Den membership gives the visitor free access to a Tech Campus, chart packs, and a featured weekly chart.

Another site offering a thorough dose of education is the Decision Point site (www.decisionpoint.com). The site includes a short course on technical analysis, in which technical analyst Carl Swenlin discusses how to calculate and use various indicators and how to interpret chart patterns. At the site's Live Charts page, the user can customize indicators and apply them to stocks and indices for a daily perspective, and the site also enables the user to view indicators from a long-term historical perspective. The NYSE Advance/Decline line, for example, can be viewed over various incremental time frames starting as long ago as 1927. And the charts of each indicator are accompanied by an explanation not only of how the indicator is constructed, but also of how to use it.

Full access to the Decision Point site requires a subscription of $10 a month, or you can gain free access by subscribing to one of its six newsletters. The site offers major stock market data series starting in 1980, but it does not emphasize data downloads. For extensive historical data, the user is directed to a link to the Pinnacle Data site described earlier.

NEWS AND TRADING SERVICES

In addition to the numerous sites that you can consider as sources for historical data, you should also find it useful to bookmark other sites for general financial information. Those include CNBC (www.cnbc.com), CNNfn (www.cnnfn.com), Bloomberg (www.bloomberg.com), Smart Money (www.smartmoney.com), the Wall Street Journal Interactive Edition (www.wsj.com), and Barron's Online (www.barrons.com). The Dow Jones pages of the latter two sites are also good for updating data when updates are not available via your historical data provider.

Also, be sure to bookmark InvestorLinks, which includes commentary and charting capabilities in addition to its primary feature, links to other Web sites devoted to the financial markets. The site includes links to the sites for the various discount brokers, organized into four commission categories ranging from $7 to $35 per trade. Those lists include links to the sites for lesser-known brokerages as well as well-known firms such as Fidelity (www.fidelity.com), Charles Schwab (www.eschwab.com), and E*TRADE (www.etrade.com). In addition to their electronic trading services, the sites of these and other brokerage firms typically offer financial planning tips, stock research, and other features.

It's not an easy task to stay up to date on the evolving Web site spectrum as sites are enhanced and as new sites of merit appear on the scene. But when it comes to data sources, it's important to remember that new and bigger isn't necessarily better, and it can be worse if the latest enhancements have compromised data integrity. Again, the major considerations when obtaining data are that it is accurate, that you will be made aware of data revisions that can be applied efficiently to your historical data, and that the data can be updated easily. One advantage of downloading data from a major exchange, for instance, is that you can be confident that the data will be clean, with timely updates available.

DATA MANAGEMENT AND ANALYSIS PROGRAMS

Also, when it comes to ease and efficiency, a major factor will be your familiarity with the software program that you will rely upon when putting your data to use. Before deciding on a data source, you need assurance that the downloads will occur smoothly with minimal glitches when making future data revisions and updates. And when you choose a program, the most important consideration should be its ability to deal with different file formats. If a program is set up with its own file format, make sure that it will be able to easily convert, for instance, a Microsoft Excel file. Also make sure that once the historical data has been downloaded and converted, the program will be able to handle downloads of future updates, efficiently appending the updates to the existing database.

On top of the data management issues, your program selection should take into account the program's speed, capacity to iterate, and suitability for developing a wide range of indicators. Whereas one program might allow you to conduct a moving average crossover test from 5 days to 50 days in increments of 5 days for a total of 10 iterations, another might enable you to test from 5 days to 50 days in 1-day increments for a total of 50 iterations. And while one program might limit you to moving average or momentum analysis, another might be suitable for analyzing everything from moving averages to Japanese candlestick formations.

As I will discuss in Chapter 3, there are substantial risks to using a powerful program to conduct iteration after iteration on a broad array of data series and with a wide range of possible indicators to test. But as long as the analysis is conducted properly, the rewards can be substantial. You certainly don't want a slow or limited software program to hinder your efforts.

For identifying the programs to consider and then narrowing down your list, a good starting point is *Technical Analysis of Stocks and Commodities*. The magazine devotes an annual special issue to reviewing software programs, and it's available on their Web site (www.traders.com). Neil Leeson suggests that before choosing a program and making the purchase, you take advantage of trial offers. He explains that "although it may be a hassle sending software back and making sure you get a credit card refund, the time spent during the trial period will help in your selection in the long run. I suggest that you list your needs first and then try one package at a time—usually for a 30-day trial—and make notes about the pros and cons of the package and how well it meets your needs."

Along with the considerations of data management and analytical capacity, it is important that you are comfortable working with the program. Your comfort level may relate to your computing experience and background with similar programs.

As an example of what you will need to look at when reviewing a program, let's take a closer look at the well-known Metastock Professional package developed by the Equis Group (www.equis.com). Priced at $1500 with a 30-day trial period, Metastock is enhanced on an ongoing basis and includes very good documentation and support, although Equis charges for answering programming questions. A Windows-based package, it features point-and-click analysis, more than 50 indicators that can be charted and analyzed easily, several samples of historical data series, and its own downloading software, which is available for free from the Web site. According to Leeson, "the ease of use and documentation is a big positive for this analysis package. Although all data must be in 'metastock format' the downloading and conversion package that is attached to the software makes the task relatively easy." Metastock's conversion package handles several well-known file types, including Microsoft Excel and Lotus.

Another popular package is Tradestation 2000, one of the various analytical packages developed by Omega Research (www.omegaresearch.com). With a high-end price of $2400, Tradestation is well suited for experienced traders, as it includes extensive analysis and charting capabilities. However, a good degree of programming knowledge can be needed at times to decipher some of the language within the program. Leeson explains that "both Metastock and Tradestation are excellent packages with all the bells and whistles. However, the drawback of both packages is the lack of flexibility that comes with buying software. In both cases you must use their converted file format and data-updating software. If you do not have data in their format and do not intend to get it that way in the future, updating and downloading the data for charts and indicators can become tedious."

Leeson also points out that the ability to customize data with these programs is limited, as neither allows the user to screen or filter results based on a specific statistical factor, such as gain per annum. Also, in the process of developing an indicator, the user is unable to specify the number of signals generated over a time frame studied, and there is no easy way to combine indicators into models, a needed ability to be discussed in later chapters. Leeson recommends using Microsoft's Excel spreadsheet program with the Microsoft Access database software, which enables you to develop models using spreadsheet templates and to build database-updating macros using additional macro software or the included VBA tools. Spreadsheet templates, he says, "are capable of doing everything that Metastock or Tradestation can do and more. Your time commitment to develop templates that equal those of the prepackaged software may be extreme. But the added flexibility will enhance your analysis."

T A B L E 2–1

Referenced Web Sites in Chapter 2

Market Information
TheStreet	www.thestreet.com
CBSMarketWatch	www.cbs.marketwatch.com
CNBC	www.cnbc.com
CNNfn	www.cnnfn.com
Smart Money	www.smartmoney.com
Wall Street Journal	www.wsj.com
Barron's	www.barrons.com
Stocks and Commodities	www.traders.com

Economic/Monetary Data
Economagic	www.economagic.com
New York Federal Reserve Bank	www.ny.frb.org
St. Louis Federal Reserve Bank	www.stls.frb.org
U.S. Census Bureau	www.census.gov
Bureau of Economic Analysis	www.bea.doc.gov

Market Data and Charting
Yahoo!	www.yahoo.com
Big Charts	www.bigcharts.com
Wall Street City	www.wallstreetcity.com
Chicago Mercantile Exchange	www.cme.com
New York Stock Exchange	www.nyse.com
Nasdaq/AMEX	www.nasdaq.com
Pinnacle Data	www.pinnacledata.com
Global Financial Data	www.globalfindata.com
Commodity Systems Inc.	www.csidata.com
Zacks	www.zacks.com
Bloomberg	www.bloomberg.com

Trading Services
Fidelity	www.fidelity.com
NexTrend	www.nextrend.com
Charles Schwab	www.eschwab.com
E*TRADE	www.etrade.com

Education
Pring's IIER	www.pring.com
Decision Point	www.decisionpoint.com

Links
Louisana State University	www.lib.lsu.edu
InvestorLinks	www.investorlinks.com

Trading Software
Metastock Professional	www.equis.com
Tradestation 2000	www.omegaresearch.com

Once you've identified the software program that will work best for you, and once you've explored the Web sites discussed in this chapter (see Table 2–1), you should be able to determine which data sources will best provide the historical data you need, you should have a clear picture of how to update the data efficiently, and you will be able to get started building a database that will become the key to effective analysis and profitable decision making. And with the most informative Web sites bookmarked on your computer, you should also have a good idea of where to go for timely financial information.

The next step is to make optimal use of the information, data, and your program's capabilities, creating and tracking indicators that will help you develop a market view. In Chapter 3, I will discuss indicator development and the issues to be kept in mind when selecting indicators and putting them to use.

REFERENCES

Pring, Martin J. 1991 *Technical Analysis Explained: The Successful Investor's Guide to Spotting Investment Trends and Turning Points,* 3d ed. New York: McGraw-Hill.

PART TWO

Developing a View of Where the Market Is Heading

How Stock Market Indicators Can Help You

Once you have established a database, having selected your sources for historical data and future updates, you can begin the task of putting the data to use. But as basic as that may sound, making use of data can be hazardous if approached incorrectly. The potential to misuse data has never been greater.

UNDERSTANDING THE DATA

Thanks to the plethora of free and low-cost data on the Internet combined with the explosion of Internet use in recent years, never before has so much data been so accessible to so many people. Not only has this underscored the need to distinguish between data that's clean and data that's corrupt, but it has also made it especially important to understand the data—understanding not only how it can help you, but also how it can lead you astray.

To illustrate, let's start with an example. The European Central Bank (ECB) raises interest rates, and you want to determine what kind of impact that will have on U.S. stocks. So you surf the Internet, finding a German-based Web site with history back to 1970. You download the data, and then run regression analysis using regression software. The results reveal a relationship that leads you to conclude that a quarter-point increase in the European interest rate will produce a 1 percent decrease in the S&P 500.

But unbeknownst to you, the data series changed dramatically over its history, including an average of vastly different European rates in the earlier years followed by German-only data until 1999, when the ECB replaced the Bundesbank as the central bank establishing interest rate policies. Also unknown to you, the ECB had made major revisions to a year's worth of recent data, but the data source had failed to incorporate the changes in its history. Yet the software tells you that a relationship exists between the corrupt and inconsistent interest rate data and the U.S. stock data. The correlation, however, is pure chance, or "spurious,"[1] to use statistical parlance. Had the rate data been consistent and clean in this example, the software might have indicated that the relationship between the two series was insignificant.

As this hypothetical case would suggest, it's important to check and double check the accuracy of your data before you do anything with it. If possible, verify every data point with a second source. If there are differences, check with a third source. If you are left uncomfortable with the accuracy of the data, don't use it, and use one of the alternative sources instead if its accuracy can be verified.

Also be aware of adjustments that may be made by one data source but not by another. An example is the early history of the Dow Industrials, which is adjusted by some sources but not by others. You may recall that Chapter 1 included tables of NDR-defined bull and bear markets, tables that reflect the adjustment. As noted at the bottom of Tables 1–3 and 1–4, the New York Stock Exchange closed from July 1914 to December 1914 because of World War I, after which the level of the Dow Industrials was revised to reflect the change from 12 to 20 stocks. The earlier data is adjusted for better comparison with postrevision data values.

It's also important to recognize the differences in the frequency of updates over the historical course of a data series. When working with daily data for the Dow Industrials, for example, you need to keep in mind that up until 1952, the stock market was open for Saturday trading, which means that the same span of time included more trading days prior to 1952 than it has since then. This has implications for various indicators, studies, and historical comparisons, such as those that compare the length of bull or bear markets. As shown in Table 1–5, the bull market of 1990 to 1998 was the longest in terms of calendar days, lasting 2836 days. But it was the second longest in terms of trading days since the 1923 to 1929 advance lasted 1750 days, surpassing the 1990 to 1998 advance by 212 trading days.

Also, when working with data series from different countries, be sure to note the impact of holidays on market trading schedules. The Japanese market, for instance, closes for several consecutive days during its "golden week" of holidays every spring. Meanwhile, trading in the United States and elsewhere continues as usual. This affects comparisons based on moving averages of daily data, daily rates of change, daily volatility, and more. If you expect to use data series from different countries, a program's approach to handling different trading schedules will be a key consideration when selecting a program for use with your database. Microsoft Access, for instance, can handle all data on the basis of calendar days, enabling you to distinguish trading days from days when a market is closed.

DEFINING YOUR OBJECTIVES

If you are comfortable with the accuracy of your data and understand any possible idiosyncrasies, you must then address the question of what you hope to accomplish with the data. And that will depend upon your financial goals, risk tolerance, and time horizon. By laying out a framework and establishing a plan, you will be more productive at getting the data to tell you what you need to help you make money. You won't waste time with needless number crunching that will only confuse the picture and make it more difficult to derive the information that will add value to your decision-making process.

For example, if your goals are risk-averse and conservative, with an aim of meeting the stock market's long-term per annum return, it will make little sense to work on a short-term indicator designed to catch 3 percent reversals in the S&P 500. You will be wasting time and effort, as any resulting indicators will only add distracting noise to your indicator messages. It's likely that instead of timing market reversals, your primary concern will be identifying the right index funds and blue chip stocks, and your data would thus serve you better by giving you historical perspective and enabling you to screen for big-name large-cap stocks. For some investors, data downloads may not even be needed, as on-line charting programs and screening tools may sufficiently address what you are hoping to accomplish.

If, on the other hand, you are an investor who is willing to accept a dose of risk in return for potential returns exceeding the buy-and-hold per annum gain, and if you plan to time the market and trade with regularity, then you will have a greater need for a database that will enable you to view charts and create indicators that are customized to your needs, goals, and ability to execute trades efficiently.

MINING PROHIBITED

With the data in place and your objectives identified, you can start digging into the data. But this doesn't mean that you should "data mine." In fact, the prohibition on data mining will remain a key consideration in all that follows in this book. *Data mining* is the process of digging so deeply into the data, and manipulating the data to such an extent, that you will be able to find whatever result you would like to see. With extensive data, a fast computer, and efficient software, you can achieve results supporting just about any preconceived conclusion.

Let's say, for example, that you have just taken a big bullish position in the stock market, increasing your equity exposure to 95 percent. Perhaps you would like to assure yourself, or convince someone else, that this was the right thing to do. You might go to your computer, access your database, and start working on an indicator that generates buy signals when a moving average turns up by a certain percentage and sell signals when a moving average turns down by a certain percentage. You would simply need to keep changing the moving average until the indicator would generate a buy signal. And to make your case more convincing, you could keep extending the moving averages until settling on an indicator that would have produced very good hypothetical returns with very few signals, making the most recent signal appear more impressive.

Of course, anyone looking over your shoulder would catch on very quickly to this basic form of data mining, known as "curve fitting." And that person wouldn't waste time scoffing at any argument based on the indicator's latest hypothetical signal. The data miner in this example is interested in selling a viewpoint, primarily to himself. He is determined to tell himself that he was right to take the big position. He is convincing himself that the *Titanic* can't sink, and he will continue to state his case even as his ship is rapidly taking on water.

I summarized this problem in "The Quantification Predicament,"[2] which explained that "the process of developing a market outlook must be based entirely on research, not sales. The goal of research is to determine if something works. The goal of sales is to show that it does work. Yet in market analysis, the lines can blur if the analyst decides how the market is supposed to perform, then sells himself on this view by focusing only on the evidence that supports it." In Chapter 4 I will show how easy it is to deceive yourself through data manipulation and to use this self-deception to create your personal reality.

Stepping back in time, it wasn't long ago when the primary reasons for a good historical database were for studying repetitive chart patterns, drawing trendlines to identify uptrends and downtrends, and establishing support and resistance levels. These remain excellent uses of data. It was all that the original Dow Theory theorists needed, as I will explain in Chapter 5. And it should remain an integral aspect of your market analysis. What is often called the "subjective" approach to analysis, otherwise known as chart reading, is in the many ways the most pure form of analysis. Not a single data point is manipulated in any way—no averages, no ratios, no rates of change.

The alternative to the "objective" computer-based approach is, as I described in "The Quantification Predicament," "the purely subjective approach that uses trendlines and chart patterns alone, making no attempt to quantify historical activity. But when the quantification process fails to deliver, instead producing misleading messages, the subjective approach is no worse an alternative—a misguided quantification effort can be worse than none at all."

When objective research turns into a data mining endeavor with excessive curve fitting, the objectivity is lost. And the research effort can also be spoiled by other forms of data mining. Selective reporting, for instance, can be just as deceptive as excessive curve fitting. In this case, the miner conducts a study but acknowledges only those results that support the preconceived conclusion.

If, for example, you had convinced yourself that a bout of dollar weakness would be bearish for the market, you would study the relationship, but with mixed results. To support your case, you would simply emphasize those results that supported your bearish case, while ignoring the equally valid evidence that disagreed with your contention.

In academia, an ongoing topic of debate centers around the existence of "anomalies," described as recurrent market conditions that continue to drive stock prices in certain ways. One argument is that with enough data or the right kind of data at your disposal, you can identify an anomaly. But as time passes and more data is observed, the anomaly fades away.

An example is the performance of small-cap stocks relative to large-cap stocks, as explained in Chapter 1. After generally outperforming large caps over the course of many years, small caps have generally underperformed during the past 20 years. Renowned quantitative analyst Fischer Black wrote in 1993 that "it's a curious fact that just after the small-firm effect was announced, it seems to have vanished. What this sounds like is that people searched over thousands of rules until they found one that worked in the past. Then they reported it, as if past performance were indicative of future performance. As we might expect, in real-life, out-of-sample-data, the rule didn't work any more." Also, he noted, "most so-called 'anomalies' don't seem anomalous to me at all. They seem like nuggets from a gold mine, found by one of the thousands of miners all over the world."

Also well known in academic circles, finance professor Josef Lakonishok voiced a more optimistic view of historical analysis in a 1999 *Dow Jones Asset Management* interview. He explained that data-based approaches can beat the market, a premise of this book. But he also noted that "'data sloping' and 'data torturing' are big problems with empirical work in finance. You can always find some patterns that can produce higher returns on any given set of data. Then people start to use those models to manage money and you see that those wonderful returns are not there anymore."

Moreover, as I explained in "The Quantification Predicament," once an indicator, model, or trading system has been developed, the actual performance in real time is bound to deteriorate: "Whatever the approach, real-time results are likely to be less impressive than they were during an optimization period. The reality of any indicator developed through optimization is that, as history never repeats itself exactly, it is unlikely that any optimized indicator will do as well in the real-time future."

But this doesn't mean that, as Black would suggest, there's no point to using historical data as a guide to the market's future. And there's no reason to admit defeat at the hands of the proponents of the Efficient Market Hypothesis. As explained by Reilly and Brown (1997), the hypothesis holds that current stock prices reflect all public and private information, and that past rates of return and any other historical data can be of little value when making trading decisions. While numerous academic studies of anomalies and time-series tests have been designed to assess the validity of the hypothesis, the results of those studies have varied, with mixed conclusions. And the debate is bound to continue.

GUIDANCE VERSUS AUTOMATION

Keep in mind that the process of developing an indicator or a set of indicators should not be an attempt to discover the Holy Grail. Since the early 1990s, in particular, there have been numerous attempts to develop automated trading systems that use the computer-based techniques *du jour*, such as neural networks or expert systems, to replicate the mind of the human trader, but freed of the emotional influences that affect trading decisions. If these systems have been used successfully for real-time trading, we aren't hearing much about them. And even if they can be applied successfully, they are far too complicated for you or me to even attempt to develop, unless you are a highly skilled computer programmer.

What you can do is to create and follow good market indicators that provide valuable information, combine them into models that provide an aggregate assessment, and use the indicators in developing a market view. At the same time, rankings and other screening systems can be devised for the purpose of assisting, but not dictating, stock selection decisions. This is a key distinction. The various tools should be treated as guides that will help you make more accurate and profitable decisions. They should not be viewed as automated alternatives that will actually make the decisions for you.

Even in the broad universe of professional money managers, very few rely *exclusively* on automated screening." The automated approaches to top-down market timing and stock selection can be excellent input for decision making, as I will demonstrate in Chapter 10. But it can be risky to use any such system exclusively, without regard to the broader market environment.

I like to think of the analogy of a jet flying on autopilot. No matter how good the automated system, the pilot will need to stay near the controls in the event of unexpected turbulence, such as a period of high volatility never experienced during the back-tested period. And the pilot will want to be at the controls during take-off, which is like the beginning of a new bull market when breadth is accelerating and stock prices are moving quickly, and during landing, which is like the early stage of a developing bear market, when proper asset allocation is crucial.

Prior to 1987, nothing like that year's October crash had ever been experienced, at least not since 1929. And in 1929, program trading did not exist. A back-tested model would not be able to factor in the magnitude of the program-trading influence. At the time, NDR's long-term model was updated monthly, and it was slow to recognize the potential severity of the approaching crash. Yet by focusing on program trading, shorter-term models, and other influences that the long-term model could not detect, Ned Davis was able to seize the controls and avoid crashing with the market, warning clients of the risky conditions.

As I will demonstrate, a model can be developed by combining indicators for a composite message. For the vast majority of time, those models will enhance your decision making. But models should still be viewed as indicators, albeit comprehensive indicators. And when it comes to indicator development, it's important to remember that flawed or misleading data in the hands of an ambitious miner can be an explosive combination. Even when clean data is used and the indicator is developed through a sound methodology, no resulting indicator or model should be considered to be a nugget of gold that's guaranteed to bring riches.

Indicators are also analogous to chunks of coal that will keep you warm, or even hot, when assessing the market outlook. And at times, an indicator's warning will be like the proverbial canary in the coal mine, alerting you to potential trouble. If developed correctly and handled with care, indicators can provide excellent input as you develop a market view.

E N D N O T E S

1. A spurious correlation occurs when two data series are shown to have a statistical correlation (i.e., the movements in one series are statistically related to movements in the other), but there is no real underlying causal relationship between the two series. This is often due to the presence of a third variable that is correlated with both of the two original (unrelated) variables, causing them to appear to be correlated.

2. Written for 1997 Charles H. Dow Award. Published in *Market Technicians Journal* (see reference).

REFERENCES

Black, Fischer. 1993. Estimating Expected Return. *Financial Analysts Journal*, September–October, 37.

Burton, Jonathan. 1999. Leaders in Finance. *Dow Jones Asset Management*, March–April, 28.

Hayes, Timothy. 1996. The Quantification Predicament. *Market Technicians Association Journal*, Spring–Summer, 9.

Reilly, Frank K., and Keith C. Brown. 1997. *Investment Analysis and Portfolio Management*, 5th Ed., Orlando, FL: Dryden Press.

CHAPTER 4

Developing Indicators

Using the Past to Gain Insights into the Future

The indicator possibilities are, of course, virtually unlimited. One might argue that the temperature in New York City is an indicator. Another might argue that the phase of the moon is an indicator. Another might argue that the current trend of interest rates is an indicator. An argument could be made on behalf of each. But the most convincing argument will be the one with the most substantial backing in historical data, and the most convincing evidence drawn from that data.

STATISTICS TO CONSIDER

The most common approach to assessing the value of an indicator is to test for buy and sell signals. When the data reflect the condition deemed to be bullish for the market, the indicator flashes a buy signal and assumes that a long position is taken. That position remains in effect until the data meet the bearish condition, at which point a sell signal is generated and the indicator assumes that a short position is established.

Since such an indicator works like a trading system, it lends itself to a variety of statistics on hypothetical performance. The statistic that's especially appealing for its simplicity is the accuracy rate—an indicator that had generated hypothetical profits on 30 of 40 trades would be more appealing than an indicator that had generated hypothetical gains on 15 of 40 trades. On top of that statistic, the gain per trade and the gain per annum can be determined. And the gain per annum can then be compared to the buy-and-hold return, or the gain that would have been produced by simply buying the asset at the start of the test period and holding it for the entire time.

TABLE 4–1

The Impact of Transaction Costs

	% Profit on Current Trade	Accuracy Rate (%)	% Gain per Annum	Buy/Hold % Gain per Annum	Value of 10,000 Investment
No transaction costs	—0.56	49	19.3	3.9	$5,599,032
Transaction cost of 0.25% per trade	—1.06	46	14.6	3.9	$1,360,173

Note: Summary results for Value Line reversal indicator in Figure 5-29, 04/30/1964–03/29/2000.

But when this type of analysis is conducted, two important statistics are easy to overlook. The first is the maximum drawdown, or the maximum loss between any consecutive signals. Let's say that a buy signal is flashed on a stock trading at $100 per share. The stock price rises to $110, drops to $50, and then rises back to $110, at which point a sell signal is generated. Your results would indicate a $10 profit on the trade and the indicator's accuracy rate, gain per trade, and per annum gain would all increase. But in the interim you would have had a paper loss of 50 percent, which would be unsuitable to a volatility-averse investor or a trader who buys on margin and is thus vulnerable to margin calls when a stock drops in price.

The second key statistic is the transaction cost, which can quickly turn profits into losses. Table 4–1 demonstrates how a quarter-percent commission per trade erodes performance statistics and eats away the profit on a $10,000 investment. The greater the number of trades, the bigger the impact, which is a big reason why so many day traders end up losing money. If you decide to emphasize the historical results of an indicator that you plan to use as input for your real-time trading decisions, make sure that the trade frequency is in line with your trading tendencies, and then factor in the transaction costs.

An even bigger issue is the application of historical results to future decisions. As I discussed in Chapter 3, it's almost a foregone conclusion that any back-tested indicator will perform worse in real time than it did over the test period. The more rigorous the optimization and the more impressive the hypothetical results, the greater the inevitable performance gap between the hypothetical and the real.

OPTIMIZING WITH CARE

But this doesn't mean that you should forget about optimizing altogether. Several simple approaches can be taken to lessen the real-time deterioration and make you less inclined to scrap the indicator soon after its development.

First, avoid focusing your energy on mining for the most impressive of statistics such as gain per annum. Instead, emphasize an indicator's robustness, its ability to generate effective signals even when the formula is altered within a substantial range. The selected indicator should be an example of the rule, not the exception to the rule.

A hypothetical example is shown in Table 4–2. The results in the top half of the table show that you could make minor changes to the moving average, buy level, or sell level with very little impact on the number of trades, accuracy rate, or gain per annum. Any indicator could be expected to perform as well as any other in real time. The results in the bottom half of the table show a different hypothetical set of results in which, when making small changes to the variables, a specific combination stands out as superior to the others. One would be tempted to select the stand-out formula, but there would be no reason to expect it to produce real-time results that would be any better than the results produced by the similar formulas.

The stand-out indicator could, for example, be the result of a chance combination of variables producing an unusually timely signal at an important market bottom or top, followed by an unusually large profit for that trade and, in turn, impressive results overall. But when an indicator so lacking in robustness is used, it would be wishful thinking to expect the indicator to generate such accurate signals in real time.

T A B L E 4–2

An Exception to the Rule

Consistent Results

No. of Trades	Moving Average (Periods)	Buy Level	Sell Level	Accuracy Rate	% Gain per Annum
50	20	15.6	8.6	55	11.8
49	21	15.8	8.4	56	12.0
48	22	16.0	8.2	56	12.1
47	23	16.2	8.0	57	12.1
46	24	16.4	7.8	56	12.0
*Inconsistent Results**					
40	70	100	110	50	11.2
39	71	99	111	50	11.3
37	**72**	**98**	**112**	**55**	**15.1**
37	73	97	113	52	10.1
36	74	96	114	50	9.8

*See middle row.

The possibility of a rogue signal skewing your results should be recognized when back-testing over a period that includes the 1987 peak and subsequent crash, especially when the test period includes only a few years. An optimization program will be certain to catch the crash, showing a huge hypothetical gain by flashing a sell signal around that year's August top and a buy signal after the October bottom. But among bear markets since the 1930s, the 1987 drop in the Dow Industrials was the second shortest yet the second most severe, with only the prolonged bear of 1973–1974 greater in severity. It would be very hard to argue that a repetition of the 1987 catastrophe would be more than a remote possibility. Yet, by selecting the indicator that performed so well during the crash, and by expecting that indicator to produce equally impressive results in real time, you would be counting on another exceptional decline, despite its improbability.

Again, overoptimization can be kept in check by looking for a robust indicator that may not have the greatest hypothetical record, but should be less prone to deteriorate in real time. You can also have more confidence if your data history is great enough to enable you to test over numerous bull and bear market cycles. If an indicator signaled the 1987 top, would it also signal the tops of, for instance, 1983 or 1973?

THE MORE CASES THE BETTER

For historical testing, more is better when it comes to data. And the same statement applies to the number of signals generated by the indicator. All else being equal, you would have more confidence in an indicator if the 1987 crash signal was one of 50 sell signals than if the crash signal was one of just 8 signals. While the latter indicator's statistics would be more skewed by the 1987 gains, it would also be questionable because of the small sample size. You can generally have more confidence in an indicator based on 50 cases than an indicator based on 8, and 30 cases is generally a good benchmark to keep in mind.

Unfortunately, there will be many times when it's simply impossible to consider many cases. An attempt could be made, for example, to develop an indicator that would confirm new bull markets by signaling the end of economic recessions, but such analysis would be limited to only nine recessions since 1945 and none since 1991. It's especially tempting to develop indicators based on extremes, such as an oil price spike or a volume surge. But the greater the extreme used to generate the signals, the fewer the cases.

A limited number of cases doesn't mean that the analysis should ignore the indicator possibility. And you definitely should not ignore it if, for example, the market's performance was consistent after all 10 cases. But the lack of cases should be factored in as a possible detriment to the indicator's future reliability.

REGRESSION

The matter of cases is an important consideration in regression analysis, which discusses the number of observations in terms of "degrees of freedom." In regression analysis, the effect of the "X" independent variable (an external influence such as interest rates) on the "Y" dependent variable (such as the rate of change of a stock market index) is illustrated by a regression line that shows the best fit of the relationship between the two data series. For any given level of interest rates, an expected level of market performance could be determined. And the precision of that predicted value would be gauged using the "standard error of the estimate," which measures the dispersion around the regression line using the size of the deviations around the line as well as the degrees of freedom. The greater the deviations and the fewer the degrees of freedom, the greater the standard error. A regression line with a low standard error is similar to a robust indicator with a high accuracy rate—you can have higher confidence in its real-time ability to provide accurate market assessments.

Figure 4-1 illustrates how regression analysis can be applied to a time series, with the Dow Industrials total return (price appreciation plus reinvested dividends) regressed against its history since 1903. In this case, the regression line is the best fit between the total return and time. As indicated, the line represents a gain of 9.7 percent per annum, a rate of change that could be used as a historical benchmark to indicate the total return that you could expect, all else being equal.

In Figure 4-1, the actual total return is compared to the historical growth rate represented by the line, considering the market long-term overbought with the total return far above the line and long-term oversold with the total return far below the line. As indicated in the chart's box, the market has tended to perform far better than normal during oversold periods, when major bottoms form and new bull markets get started. And despite the gains amassed during the overbought periods of the late 1920s and late 1990s, the results show that over the course of history, the market has performed worse than normal during the overbought periods, reflecting the impact of the bear markets spawned under the overbought conditions. Thus in this case, the regression is used not to forecast a level, but instead to identify a historical relationship that can be used to place the current market action in a long-term context of risk and reward.

A great deal of research has been done in the field of regression analysis, with the major consideration boiling down to how much confidence you can have in the value predicted by the regression formula. The greater the statistical significance of the predicted value, the more confidence you can have in its accuracy. Making the correct assessment of significance is therefore an objective of regression analysis, requiring the use of "T" statistics, degrees of freedom, and "levels of confidence." Without going into all the de-

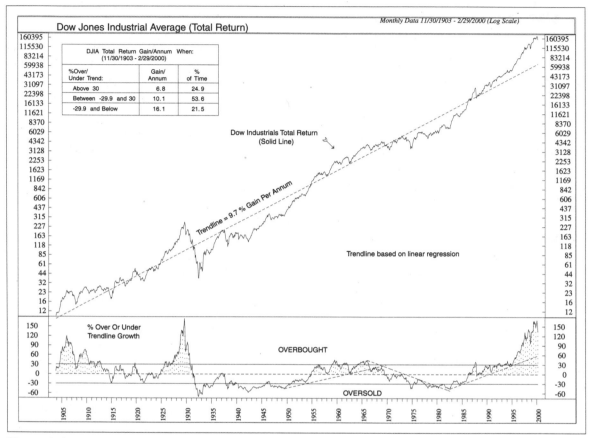

Figure 4–1

tails on formulas and calculations, which can be found in books that focus on regression analysis, I'll simply say that the end result of the regression effort is to make statements like "we can have 95 percent confidence in the predicted value" or "95 percent of the time, the predicted value will be correct."

Regression analysis is therefore designed to use historical relationships to predict the future with an expected margin of error. So like any other approach, the analysis depends upon historical data. And the predictive ability of the data series may begin to erode if a new and unexpected factor changes the volatility of the data and its relationship with the market. In such cases, a quantitative analyst would cite a tongue-twisting condition called *heteroskedasticity*, perhaps determining that the altered relationship had rendered the regression analysis less reliable, if not useless.

REAL-TIME TESTING

In time series analysis, several other methods can be used to simulate real-time performance and thereby determine whether the indicator will continue to add value to future decision making. These methods are far less precise in statistical terms than regression analysis. And they require a large dose of subjectivity related to the degree of indicator deterioration that you can live with and the bearing that you expect the indicator to have on your decisions. But they are relatively straightforward and user-friendly.

If you have time on your hands, one approach is to build an indicator that you consider robust and likely to suffer limited deterioration. You would put the indicator away and forget about it for an amount of time that would equal a substantial percentage of the indicator's historical test period, also called its *in sample* period. If you built an indicator that generated 15 signals a year over a 5-year test period, you could put the indicator aside for 2 years, expecting it to flash about 30 signals during that period. If you built an indicator that produced six signals a year over a 10-year test period, you might feel comfortable with a longer period for your real-time evaluation.

In either case, at the end of the real-time test period, you would dust off the indicator and assess the real-time signals. You might decide to start using the indicator if, for example, the accuracy rate dropped from 80 percent during the in-sample period to 70 percent during the real-time period, with a similar degree of deterioration indicated by other statistics. But if the accuracy rate dropped to 45 percent along with a consistent downfall in other statistics, you might decide to send the indicator to the scrap heap.

The benefit of this approach is that you may end up with an indicator that, like a fine wine that has been left to age, you will savor, one that you will feel comfortable about using. Other indicators will end up like wine that's turned into vinegar, and you will toss them out. The obvious drawback of the real-time testing process is the time required to complete it. If you discover what you believe to be an excellent tool, you will have to postpone using it until your belief has been confirmed by the real-time test.

OUT-OF-SAMPLE TESTING

To speed up the testing process, an alternative is to simulate the real-time test by assessing "out-of-sample" performance. There are many variations to this type of test, but in its most basic form, you would back-test over the first half of the historical data and then simulate the real-time test over the more recent half of the data. You would then compare the two performance records. If the indicator experienced limited deterioration from the in-sample period to the out-of-sample period, you would go ahead and start using the indicator.

A potential problem with this approach is the urge to continually reoptimize the in-sample period until you find an out-of-sample result that you would consider acceptable, in effect defeating the purpose of your simulation by turning the out-of-sample period into an in-sample period. To use the approach correctly, you must do all of your optimizing in the earlier in-sample period and then consider the testing completed. If the indicator would fail to hold up in the out-of-sample period, you would scrap the indicator and try something else.

Resisting the temptation to optimize the out-of-sample period is not easy. But it can be averted by complicating the process, perhaps shortening the in-sample period and then comparing the results over several different out-of-sample periods. This can be done when your data history is extensive. Another approach is known as *blind simulation,* in which you would randomly select different portions of your out-of-sample period. You might, for instance, see how the indicator would hold up over a random two-month period as well as a random one-year period.

Yet another variation is to optimize over the middle third of the data and then use the first third and the final third for out-of-sample comparisons. This technique is appealing for its comparison of periods that may be in very different stages of the stock market and economic cycles. If an indicator can hold up relatively well during various cycle stages and despite differing external influences, the indicator can be considered robust and likely to hold up in real time. A key objective of out-of-sample testing is to determine whether the indicator will survive a variety of market circumstances.

The greater the data history, then, the more options you will have for out-of-sample testing and the more comprehensive your testing process will be. A premise of this book is that markets move in cycles, as do the various environmental influences that affect them, such as interest rates and economic growth. These cycles occur over a variety of time frames and can be barely recognizable when they repeat, yet several underlying conditions will be similar at similar stages of different cycles.

Excessive optimism, for example, invariably is present at market tops, although it often takes different forms. At the peak of 1976 it was evident in the proliferation of bullish advisory services. In early 2000 it was evident in the number of investment clubs, household ownership of equities, and other signs of extremely high public exposure. While this illustrates why it's a good idea to use multiple indicators to confirm a market condition, it's also an indication of why you should include as many cycles as possible in your analysis. You will increase your chances of detecting repetitive tendencies that may be pervasive in most cycles but at other times lie relatively dormant. If your out-of-sample window is too narrow, perhaps including a cycle in which the indicator's behavior is aberrant, you may end up rejecting an indicator that could actually prove to be useful in real time.

When your data history is limited, a good approach is to optimize over an in-sample period, select the indicator if it holds up during an out-of-sample period, and then let it run in real time over a time frame similar to that of the out-of-sample period. At the end of the real-time period, you would decide whether or not to keep the indicator. In this case, you would be less demanding of impressive results in the out-of-sample period, but you would expect equal or even better results during the real-time test.

Whether your test period is out-of-sample, real-time, or a combination of the two, it needs to be long enough to enable you to distinguish an indicator that has gotten off to a bad start from an indicator that's simply a bad indicator. If an indicator had a record of profits on 80 percent of its in-sample signals and 70 percent of its out-of-sample signals, you wouldn't want to reject it just because its first real-time signal turned out to be ill-timed. After all, you might say, since 3 of 10 signals had been losers in the out-of-sample period, an initial losing signal would not be out of line with the out-of-sample record. But if the next 3 of 4 signals were also losers, you probably wouldn't be comfortable using the indicator.

MODE ANALYSIS

Up to this point, I've discussed indicators and analytical approaches as they relate to buy and sell signals. But the approaches also apply to zone analysis, alternatively known as *mode analysis*. When an indicator uses signal analysis, it is always either long or short, bullish or bearish. Its recommendation is to take a long position on a buy signal and hold that position until a sell signal is generated, at which point the long position is closed out and a short position is assumed. The problem with such a recommendation is that, except for professional traders and day traders, few investors actually manage their money that way. The more common approach, and in fact the more manageable approach for the investor with at least an intermediate-term investment horizon, is to scale into the market and scale out, in order to systematically increase or decrease exposure.

Zone analysis is more suitable for that approach, since instead of a black or white assessment, a zone indicator recognizes one or more shades of gray between. Such an indicator would typically be bullish in the upper zone, bearish in the lower zone, and neutral in the middle zone, thus recognizing the periods when the indicator has no strong opinion on the market outlook. Viewed another way, such an indicator recognizes that indicators operate with degrees of decisiveness. The indicator would be decisively bullish at high levels, decisively bearish at low levels, and indecisive between.

Zone indicators are especially useful when the relationship between the analyzed data and the market is such that the indicator's message becomes increasingly bullish as its reading increases and increasingly bearish as its reading falls. The higher the indicator reading, the more bullish its message; the lower the indicator reading, the more bearish its message. By indicating how the market has performed with the indicator in the various zones, the indicator can help you determine whether you should increase or decrease exposure.

Signals versus Modes

To illustrate the differences between signal indicators and zone indicators, let's look at how each is applied to Big Mo, one of the major models used by Ned Davis Research. Figure 4–2 shows the model as it's used on a signal basis, with the signals applied to the Value Line Composite. When the model rises above 50 percent, it generates a buy signal, and it remains on that signal until the model drops to 47 percent, at which point a short position is recommended and maintained until the model returns to a buy signal.

Note that after the model's timely sell signal in advance of the 1998 bear market, it never returned to a high enough reading to advise returning to the subsequent bull market, primarily because of the market's unfavorable valuation and unimpressive breadth on the advance. But as shown in Figure 4–3, the zone version of the same model indi-

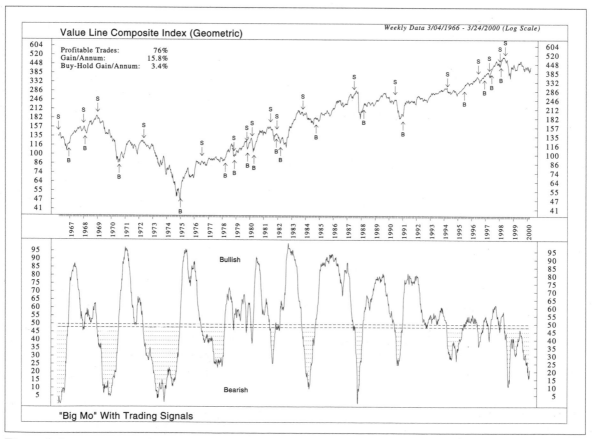

Figure 4–2

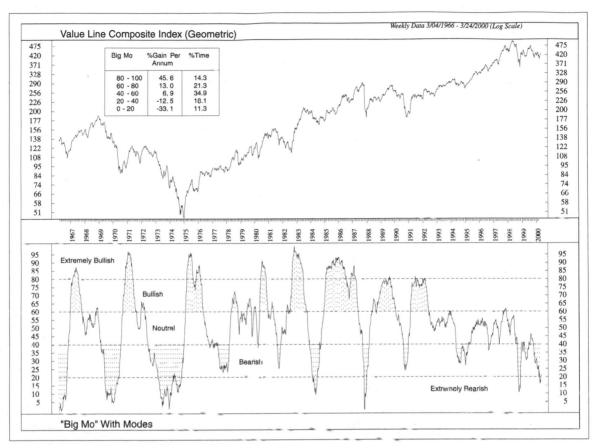

Figure 4–3

cated that once the model exceeded 40 percent, it had entered a zone in which the Value Line Composite has risen about 7 percent per annum. Although that's less than the S&P 500's historical return of about 9 percent since March 1966, the 7 percent return is more than double the Value Line Composite's 3 percent per annum gain during that period. But regardless of the market index used for the historical perspective, you could have used the mode message as a reason to increase your equity exposure from a low level to a moderate level during the periods in which the model stayed above 40 percent. The model's black-and-white signal message would have kept you out of the market altogether.

The mode returns listed in Figure 4–3 show that Big Mo is an example of an indicator that tiers very well, an indicator for which the higher reading the better. Whereas the Value Line Composite has declined at a substantial per annum rate when the model has been 20 percent or lower, the gains have been higher in each successive higher mode, with a substantial per annum gain of about 46 percent with the model higher than 80 percent.

Time and Frequency

When looking at the box summarizing the returns, note the percentage of time listed next to the return for each mode. This is a key statistic, as it tells you not only how often the indicator has been in the mode, but also how much confidence you can have that the result is representative of future performance with the indicator in that zone. Holding all else constant, a per annum return for a mode visited for 30 percent of the time would usually be considered more representative than a mode visited for 15 percent of the time. As stated earlier, the more observations the better, and 30 percent of the time will include more data than 15 percent of the time.

Similarly, you should consider the number of times that the indicator has visited a particular zone. A move into a zone can be thought of as a signal, and the more signals the better, covering as many cycles as possible. Even if an indicator is in a mode for 30 percent of the time, the reliability will be in question if the 30 percent of the time was based on just two or three blocks of time in that zone. If you wouldn't use a signal-based indicator with just three signals, you probably would not want to use a mode-based indicator that visited its modes on only two or three occasions.

Also recognize that the gain per annum statistic itself can mislead. Even if your zone indicator made 30 trips to its highest mode, with those visits accounting for 30 percent of the time, the per annum gain will be weighted toward the performance in a particular cycle if, for instance, a particular visit accounted for 15 percent of the total time, or half of the time spent in that mode. When developing an indicator with multiple modes, when the number of modes makes it a challenge to get even 20 percent of the time in a single mode, make sure that all modes have at least a year's worth of data in total. When the per annum gain calculation is based on less than a year, it will present an exaggerated picture of performance. With less than a year in a mode, the indicator's per annum gain statistic could show a gain of 20 percent, when in fact the market gained no more than 3 percent during each of the four visits to the mode.

Considering the potential for a misleading gain per annum statistic, the ideal approach would be to set up your computer program to give you not only the per annum gains in the various modes, but also the number of visits to each mode, the average return per visit, and the average amount of time per visit. If you determined that, for instance, the market gained 3 percent per visit, with the visits lasting an average of one month, you could then compare that to the market's average one-month gain of, say,

2 percent per month. You would then be comparing the average performance with the historical benchmark. And you could do the same for the per annum gain statistics, comparing them to the per annum gain statistic for the entire period.

As with signal analysis, the indicator's robustness is an important consideration. You should be able to make minor changes to your parameter levels without dramatic changes to the performance-in-mode statistics. When looking at the per annum gain statistics, make sure that your results show a smooth transition from level to level and from mode to mode. You wouldn't have much use for an indicator that, for instance, produced alternating positive and negative results in successively higher modes. And again, as with signal analysis, the best approach is to compare your in-sample results with out-of-sample and real-time results.

A desirable aspect of mode analysis is that once the modes have been determined, they can be presented in chart form with a select set of statistics such as per annum gain and percentage of time in each mode. As shown in Figure 4–3, such charts do not require buy and sell arrows implying that the indicator has a black-and-white relationship with the market. Instead, these charts present the indicators as they should best be used, as a gauge of the relative market impact of a particular condition or set of conditions.

But when looking at these charts, it should be kept in mind that for any mode, the calculations used for the statistics begin with the first observation within the mode and end with the first observation outside of the mode. In 1982, for example, Big Mo rose from 74 to 82 percent, thus entering its "extremely bullish" mode. It stayed in the mode until June 1983, when it dropped to 73 percent. From the 82 percent reading to the 73 percent reading, the Value Line Composite gained 72 percent, consistent with the per annum gain for that mode.

Upon an initial glance at the chart, it would not be obvious that the calculations for the statistics were based on some data that were not actually inside the zone, and some data that was actually outside of it. And in the case of an indicator with extremes that are visited for a small amount of time, the statistics may actually be telling you how the market has performed with the indicator reversing down from an extremely high level or reversing up from an extremely low level.

Directional Modes

For all modes, in fact, the indicator's direction within the mode will be responsible for the bulk of the percentage points of the per annum gain statistics. After an indicator's rise into its "bullish" mode, the market might actually have a tendency to drift downward, only amassing the positive gains after the indicator starts falling within the mode. One approach to getting a better handle on the differing impact of movement within the zones is to use what NDR describes as "directional modes." In Figure 4–4, directional

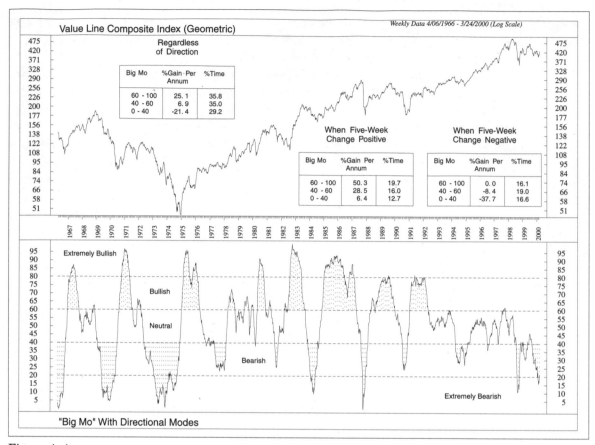

Figure 4–4

mode analysis is applied to Big Mo by determining whether it is higher or lower than its level of five weeks earlier. If the model is higher than its level five weeks ago, it is "rising" in the mode. If the model is lower than its level five weeks ago, it is "falling" in the mode.

The boxes in the chart's top clip demonstrate the impact of direction. The box at upper left indicates that for about a third of the time since March 1966, Big Mo has ranged between 40 and 60 percent, with the Value Line Composite rising, gaining 7 percent per annum with the model in that "neutral" mode. But when the model has been "rising" in the mode, as shown in the middle box, the performance has been far better than "neutral," with the Value Line Composite gaining about 29 percent per annum. When the model has been "falling," as shown in the right box, the performance has been far worse than neutral, with the S&P 500 falling at a rate of 8 percent per annum.

The cost of this increased precision, however, is increased complexity, since a thorough analysis would require an assessment of accuracy rates, gain per trade, data quantity, and number of cases for each of the various directional modes. While the process is still manageable with a three-mode indicator, requiring the analysis of six different directional modes, the process would start to become unwieldy with a five-mode indicator, requiring an examination of 10 directional modes. Keep in mind that as the number of directional modes increases, the time spent in the various modes decreases, throwing into greater question the reliability of the various per annum gain statistics. Again, if the time spent in the mode is less than a year, the per annum gain statistics will present a misleading picture of performance.

SUBSEQUENT PERFORMANCE

In addition to the black-and-white signal approach and the multihued mode approaches, the value of an indicator can be assessed using subsequent-performance analysis, in which an indicator flashes a green light that may fade over time and eventually turn off altogether. This approach zeros in on a specific bullish level and/or a specific bearish level and then determines how well the market has performed over various time periods following the signals generated at those levels. Once the longest of the periods has passed, the indicator no longer carries a message, at least not until it flashes another bullish or bearish signal. Thus in contrast to the other approaches, which are always active in calculating the market's performance based on the indicator's latest signal or current mode, the subsequent-performance method can go through long periods of inactivity. But when such an indicator does flash a signal, it's especially worthy of note.

This approach is therefore most applicable to indicators that have strong leading tendencies at extreme levels. An extremely high reading from such an indicator would typically be followed by impressive market strength, while an extremely low reading would be followed by dramatic market weakness. Those tendencies would become evident in analyzing how the market has performed over subsequent incremental periods following the signals. In Table 4–3, for example, the percent change of the NASDAQ Composite is listed for periods of 10, 22, 63, and 126 days following an extreme initial reading of at least 1.87 by the ratio of the 10-day total of advancing volume to the 10-day total of declining volume. This indicator would be considered a "thrust" indicator, marking the onset of NASDAQ strength or weakness.

After you have identified the signal dates and returns over the periods following those dates, you can determine the arithmetic mean and the median for each period. When the mean differs substantially from the median, it's likely that one or a few extreme observations are skewing the averages. Since this is often the case (and especially evident for the 63-day period in Table 4–3), it's usually a good idea to emphasize the me-

T A B L E 4–3

NASDAQ Volume Thrust Buy Signals

Percent Gains of NASDAQ Composite Index

Signal Date	Days Later			
	10	22	63	126
10/08/1981	0.7	4.7	0.5	−5.2
03/26/1982	3.2	5.5	−2.7	7.7
08/23/1982	6.5	10.8	35.0	53.8
11/22/1983	−0.8	−2.8	−13.2	−15.8
08/03/1984	1.7	1.8	0.7	13.1
01/16/1985	7.0	10.6	8.9	18.3
07/05/1985	3.1	0.5	−6.1	9.2
11/11/1985	2.5	6.0	14.1	27.9
01/08/1987	4.1	7.5	15.2	12.7
12/18/1987	5.2	2.2	15.8	18.1
06/07/1988	2.2	4.0	−0.5	−1.0
12/06/1988	−0.3	2.2	7.8	20.2
03/08/1990	−0.5	−1.4	6.3	−13.2
12/05/1990	0.1	−3.2	28.3	35.6
01/06/1992	3.6	6.5	−1.3	−5.8
09/14/1992	−3.2	−3.0	10.4	17.0
06/20/1995	1.3	3.4	14.0	7.8
08/07/1996	−1.3	0.7	7.7	18.2
05/05/1997	0.1	3.8	19.9	19.0
10/22/1998	7.9	16.1	39.2	55.8
11/10/1999	8.4	15.9	42.1	38.4
Median	**2.2**	**3.8**	**8.9**	**17.0**
Mean	**2.5**	**4.4**	**11.5**	**15.8**
All Periods	**0.8**	**1.6**	**3.9**	**8.4**
% of Cases >				
Return > Benchmark	**62%**	**71%**	**67%**	**67%**

dian, the midpoint of the values. In Table 4–3, the median performance is consistently positive following the NASDAQ indicator's bullish signals and consistently negative following the indicator's bearish signals.

But that is not enough to deem the indicator useful. You must compare the returns to the benchmark for each period. For example, the NASDAQ's median gain for the

10-day period following bullish signals has been 2.2 percent while the median gain for any given 10-day period has been 0.8 percent, indicating that the NASDAQ has tended to perform relatively well following the signals. If the median return has been positive but lower than the benchmark, you could conclude that the indicator's signals have had no impact, or even a negative impact, on the subsequent 10-day period.

In addition to the average returns, Table 4–3 includes the percentage of cases in which the index has been higher than the benchmark return for each period. That statistic can help you gauge the risk that the market's performance following a signal will be an exception to the historical tendency.

Also to gauge the risk following a signal, you might determine the average maximum drawdown for each signal over each period. For the 63-day period following bullish signals, for example, you would determine the market index's low point prior to the end of the 63-day period. For bearish signals, you would determine the index's maximum gain prior to the end of the period.

As with the approaches discussed earlier, your confidence in the indicator will have a lot to do with the number of cases. All else being equal, you can trust an indicator based on 20 cases more than an indicator based on 10 cases. You should also recognize the potential for double-counting and its impact on your results.

Let's say that you are gauging an indicator's subsequent performance over 63 days based on 30 cases, but 5 of the cases occur within 10 days of each other. It's likely that your 63-day returns will be very similar for those 5 cases, as they would occur in the same market trend and the same market cycle. Your results would thus be weighted by the market's performance during that period, giving you a misleading assessment of the indicator's impact on the market. It should also be kept in mind that for an indicator that leads the market and hasn't flashed a signal for a long time, its initial signal will have the most influence on your decision making.

To minimize the repeat signals, you can use time screens that prevent the indicator from generating another signal within a specified period following the first signal. For example, a 65-day screen eliminates repeat signals from the NASDAQ indicator in Table 4–3, shown graphically in Figure 4–5. If the indicator flashes a bullish signal by rising to 1.87, falls back, and then climbs back to 1.87 before 65 days have passed, the second signal will not be generated. Without the screen, numerous repeat signals would be evident after the NASDAQ bottoms of 1982 and 1990, among others.

Subsequent performance indicators can be excellent tools for indicating significant changes in the market outlook. And while they are well suited for measures of market breadth, like the NASDAQ thrust indicator, the approach is also useful for assessing the impact of a market event, such as an increase in the prime rate. If the rate were increased for the second time, for example, you could refer to Table 8–2 in Chapter 8 to help you determine the event's likely influence, in this case a bearish influence, on the

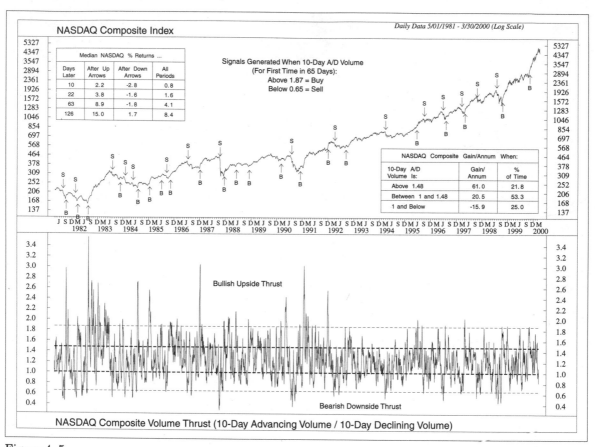

Figure 4–5

market's subsequent performance, again while recognizing the caveat that the historical cases have been limited.

METHODS OVERLAID FOR CONFIRMATION

You could then overlay the subsequent performance message with the reading of a mode indicator, a signal indicator, or both. In the case of the prime rate, you could refer to the signal indicator in Figure 8–6 in Chapter 8. If a market uptrend was intact and the prime rate increase moved the indicator to a sell signal, it would only heighten the warning of the subsequent performance analysis. But if the indicator remained on a buy signal, you might conclude that the rate hike's impact would be enough to slow the market's advance, but not enough to stop it altogether.

In Figure 4–5, the subsequent performance approach is shown along with the mode approach, with the historical results of each method quantified in a separate box. By viewing the differing approaches together in this way, you could say that when the indicator has been above 1.48, the NASDAQ has performed impressively, and after it has reached 1.87, it has continued to perform better than normal over the subsequent six months.

To further illustrate how the various approaches can be used together, let's return to Big Mo, shown earlier with signals, modes, and directional modes. In Figure 4–6, the model is presented on a subsequent performance basis, with a Big Mo rise to 70 percent followed by strong outperformance and a Big Mo drop to 28 percent followed by significant underperformance. The four approaches could then be used to confirm or lend a degree of caution to their respective messages.

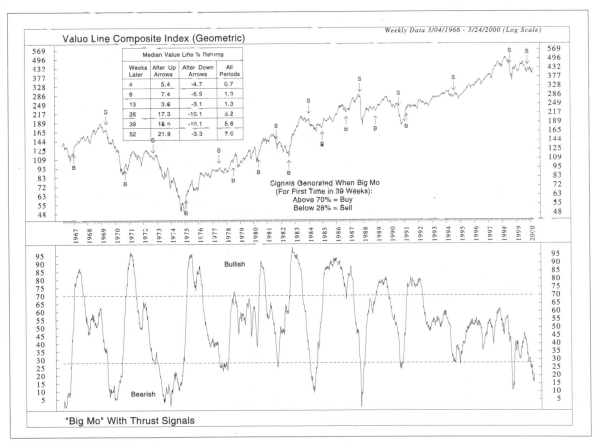

Figure 4–6

This is how, for example, the four methods could be used together to simulate a sequence that would lead to an increasingly bullish outlook following a market bottom: (1) the model rises from 30 to 39 percent over six weeks, still in its lower mode (Figure 4–3) but rising within the mode (Figure 4–4); (2) the model reaches its middle mode above 40 percent and continues rising in that mode; (3) the model rises above 50 percent and flashes a buy signal (Figure 4–2); (4) the model reaches its upper mode above 60 percent and continues rising in that mode; (5) the model reaches 70 percent, flashing a bullish subsequent performance signal (Figure 4–6).

REVERSAL PROBABILITY

On top of all these approaches to evaluating the indicator's assessment of the market outlook, you might also want to get more specific and assess the chances and timing of a market peak or trough. In that case, you could superimpose the NDR-defined bull and bear market dates on the indicator's history. By comparing those dates with the dates of signals or changes in mode, you could determine whether the indicator has any consistencies in leading or confirming market peaks and troughs.

In examining Big Mo, for example, you would find that the model's directional version has started falling in its neutral or bearish mode prior to, or within a month of, 8 of the past 10 NDR-defined bull market peaks. Conversely, the model has been rising in those modes prior to, or within a month of, 8 of the past 11 bear market troughs. The signals are shown in Figure 4–7 with their corresponding market peaks and market troughs. So if a bear market has been in progress and Big Mo starts to rise, surpassing its level of five weeks earlier, that bullish indication of a market bottom could be inserted at the very beginning of the sequence of indications leading to an increasingly bullish outlook based on the model's reading.

The chances of a market peak or trough, what I call *reversal-probability* analysis, are also considered in conjunction with other approaches in Figure 4–8. In this case, the results of using a mode approach, a subsequent performance approach, and a reversal probability approach are all listed in rows corresponding to a series of parameters determined by the year-to-year change of the Dow Industrials at year end. The chart's upper box shows that the twentieth century included 21 years in which the Dow Industrials rose more than 25 percent for the year (first two columns). A mode analysis (third column) shows that during those years, the DJIA rose about 34 percent on average, and a subsequent performance analysis (fourth column) shows that in the year after those years, the DJIA has risen about 16 percent on average. Finally, the reversal-probability statistics show a 45 percent chance of a market peak in that subsequent year (fifth column) and an 80 percent chance of a peak within either the first or second subsequent year (sixth column).

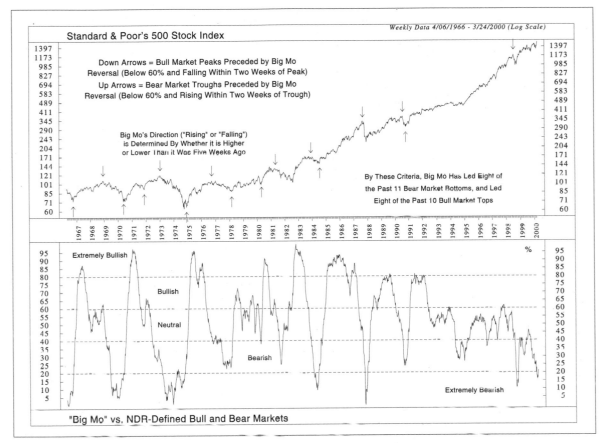

Figure 4–7

As with the other approaches, the reversal-probability percentages should be compared to benchmarks for relevance. And in the case of the market-peak probability for the first subsequent year, the benchmark is about 32 percent, since there were 32 bull market peaks during the 99-year span. Following a strong year in which the DJIA gains more than 25 percent, you should thus be aware that the chances of a market peak are greater than normal: at 45 percent historically, the chances have been greater than the 32 percent chance of a market peak during any given year.

The chart's lower box shows similar relationships between down years and market bottoms. And it shows how the greater the market strength, the greater the chances of a peak; and the greater the market weakness, the greater the chances of a trough. Thus illustrating the market's tendency to cycle between extremes of strength and weakness, the chart demonstrates why effective market timing and asset allocation can be so valuable.

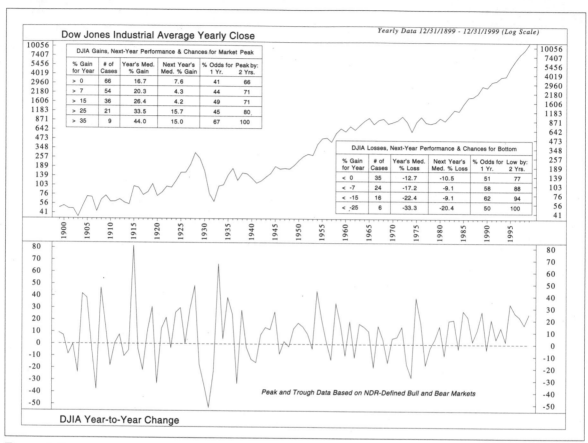

Figure 4–8

REVERSE BRACKETS

Using the various approaches to quantifying an indicator's historical performance and the implications of its past signals, you can determine an indicator's reliability and gauge the relative significance of its signals. I have shown how these approaches can quantify historical tendencies based on an indicator reaching specified levels or reversing by specified amounts. But indicators can also be developed based on reversals in which the data moves through a fixed band from one direction, reverses, and moves back through the level in the other direction, producing the signal.

Called *reverse bracket* indicators by NDR, such indicators are often used to identify reversals from overbought and oversold conditions, with sell signals generated when the indicator rises above the upper band and drops back below that level and buy signals generated when the indicator drops below the lower band and rises back above that level. Figure 4–9, for example, signals a reversal from an overbought condition when the

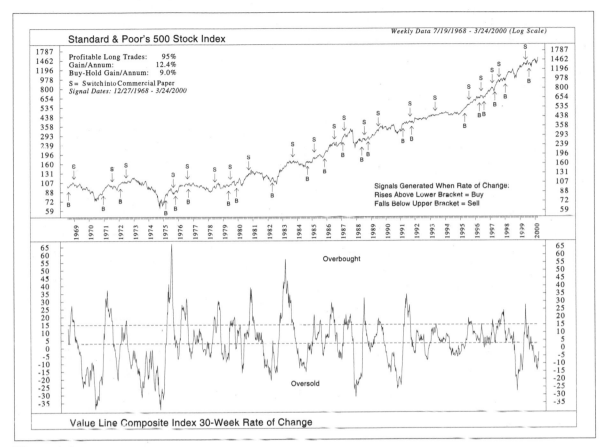

Figure 4–9

30-week rate of change of the Value Line Composite rises above 15 percent and then drops below that level, and it signals a reversal from an oversold condition when the rate of change drops below 3 percent and rises back above that level. I will take a closer look at overbought/oversold indicators in Chapter 7.

MOVING AVERAGES AND BANDS

The various methods of generating signals and modes, and of quantifying performance, can also be applied to moving targets, such as indicators derived from moving averages and moving bands. When indicators are based on moving averages, they are based on the running average of the data derived from a specified number of data points. A 10-day moving average indicator, for example, would be based on the average value for the latest 10 days. To give more weight to more recent data, you can use an exponential moving average (EMA) or a front-weighted moving average (FMA).[1]

While mode indicators can be developed based on whether the data is above or below the moving average, signal indicators can be created based on reversals in the moving average. An indicator might, for example, generate a buy signal when the data reverses upward by 3 percent and a sell signal when it reverses downward by 2 percent. Signals can also be generated by the data crossing above and below the smoothing by specified percentages.

Indicators based on trading bands take the moving averages and place them above and below the data by specified percentages. Such an indicator can be used in the same way as a fixed bracket indicator, including the reverse bracket application. The difference is that the brackets move in line with trends in the data. This is desirable when the range of the indicator's data changes over time, from a low range to a high range and vice versa. The bands enable you to determine whether the current data is high or low relative to the specified historical period. When bands are placed 10 percent around a 200-day moving average, for example, a rise above the upper band will indicate that the data has reached levels that are high from the perspective of the past 200 days.

As with indicators based on fixed levels, the historical performance of such indicators can be quantified with signals and modes. And the same can be said of Bollinger bands,[2] also known as *volatility bands.* Shown in comparison to a moving average and trading bands in Figure 4–10, volatility bands are fine-tuned variations of trading bands that detect shifts in the indicator's volatility. Instead of using a fixed percentage around a moving average, volatility bands are based on the standard deviation, a widely used volatility measure based on the deviations from the data's average value over the specified period.[3]

Whereas trading bands move in lock step with a moving average, volatility bands widen during periods of high volatility and narrow when volatility is low. The longer the specified period and the higher the standard deviation, the harder it becomes for the data to move beyond the upper or lower band, and the opposite applies to shorter periods and smaller standard deviations. Depending upon the formula, the bands can almost appear to be fixed, with movement that's barely detectable, or they can move so much that they appear to hug the data.

With so much flexibility for indicator development, the optimization possibilities are immense, which means that the analyst needs to be very careful not to overoptimize with excessive curve fitting. To keep the data mining in check, one approach is to hold something constant, either the periods or the standard deviation, when developing a volatility band indicator. If a useful indicator cannot be developed by doing so, then you will need to question your approach.

The same warning applies to the percentages used to generate signals based on data reversals and moving average crossovers. If you developed a signal indicator that, for example, produced buy signals with 10 percent increases in the data and sell signals with 1 percent declines in the data, you would doubt the robustness of the indicator if it

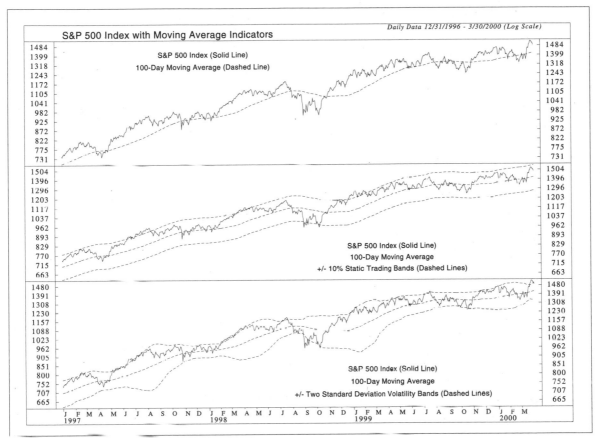

Figure 4–10

broke down when respective percentages of 9 and 2 percent were applied. For a moving average crossover indicator generating buy signals with a 2 percent rise above the moving average and a 1.5 percent drop below the moving average, you would question the indicator if the results deteriorated when the percentages were reversed.

You should recognize, however, that in many cases, you will be comfortable with an indicator's ability to generate buy signals but less confident in its ability to produce profitable signals for shorting. In that case, instead of shorting, you could have the indicator respond to sell signals by switching into cash or another alternative asset, the approach taken in Figure 4–9. You would then focus solely on the indicator's buy signal record. Again, whatever method you use for generating signals or identifying modes, out-of-sample testing and, ideally, real-time testing are essential for assessing the indicator's reliability.

This chapter has introduced techniques for developing indicators and for quantifying their ability to add value. But even if you develop what appears to be a great indicator, it is important to understand the rationale behind the indicator and why the data series and the market relate as they do. You will then have a better understanding of the indicator's nuances, and you will be more effective in applying the indicator to real-time decisions. The next four chapters focus on various types of indicators and the relationships between data series, including examples of numerous indicators and how they can be used most effectively. Chapter 5 begins the process with a look at indicators based on the action of the market itself.

E N D N O T E S

1. An exponential moving average gives more weight to the most recent data points compared to a simple moving average. Calculation:

$$X_i = C(D_i - X_{i-1}) + X_{i-1}$$

where
   X_i = current EMA
   C = 2/(periods + 1)
   D = current price
   X_{i-1} = previous EMA

A front-weighted moving average is similar in that it gives more weight to the most recent observations.

Calculation:
   N = number of periods in moving average
   C = sum of integers from 1 to N (e.g., for a 5-day FMA,
       $C = 1 + 2 + 3 + 4 + 5 = 15$)
   F_i = current price times N
   F_{i-1} = previous period price times $(N - 1)$
   F_{i-2} = price of two periods ago times $(N - 2)$
   etc.

For an n-day FMA:

$$FMA = (F_i + F_{i-1} + \cdots F_{i-n})/C$$

2. Bollinger bands are named for John Bollinger, the technical analyst credited with developing the technique. The bands are lines plotted two (or some other number) standard deviations above and below the moving average of a price. The standard

deviation is calculated using the same number of periods as in the moving average. For example, you could find the standard deviation of the last 20 periods' prices, multiply by 2, and plot lines that distance above and below a 20-day moving average of prices. For more information, contact: John A. Bollinger, Bollinger Capital Management, Inc., P.O. Box 3358, Manhattan Beach, CA 90266.

3. Standard deviation is a statistical measure of dispersion or variation from an average value. It is calculated by (1) finding the difference between each data point in the sample and the mean (average) of the entire sample; (2) squaring each of those differences; (3) adding all of the squared differences together; (4) dividing that sum by the number of data points minus 1; (5) taking the square root of the result.

CHAPTER 5

Trend-Sensitive Indicators

Taking the Pulse of the Market

When you set out to furnish a medicine bag of indicators, the starting point should be the market itself. As obvious as that might sound, it's easy to get distracted by the market-moving news of the day, be it a rising oil price, a tax debate, a conflict overseas, or an earnings announcement season. Such influences may lend themselves to indicators. But none will have the day-to-day reliability, and include the depth of information, of indicators based on the market's "tape."

A holdover from the days when stock quotes could be found on the ticker tape, the *tape* continues to encompass not only the movement of the market averages, but also the fluctuations of the stocks that make up those averages, known in the aggregate as *market breadth.* The tape tells us about the supply and demand balance that explains the current prices of individual stocks, and the resulting levels of the market averages. When demand exceeds supply, stock prices rise and the market averages move higher; when supply exceeds demand, stock prices fall and the market averages move lower.

The purpose of tape indicators is to assess the direction of the supply/demand balance, regardless of the reasons, which can be gauged via other types of indicators. In its purest form, technical analysis is conducted without any concern for the factors influencing the supply and demand. In their perpetually relevant *Technical Analysis of Stock Trends* (1991), a book originally published in 1948, Edwards and Magee explain that "it doesn't in the least matter what creates the supply and the demand. The fact of their existence and the balance between them are all that count. No man . . . can hope to know and accurately to appraise the infinity of factual data, mass moods, individual necessities, hopes, fears, estimates and guesses which, with the subtle alterations ever proceeding in the general economic framework, combine to generate supply and demand. But the summation of all these factors is reflected virtually instantaneously in the market. The technical analyst's task is to interpret the action of the market itself."

This interpretive process can be considered using the medical analogy applied earlier. When your tape indicators enable you to diagnose the market as healthy, you can expect it to remain strong. When your tape indicators lead you to a diagnosis that the market is unhealthy, the market is at risk. And when you determine that the market is terminal, a bear market can be expected.

DOW THEORY

The market diagnostics should begin with the tenets of what is known as Dow Theory, the term that describes the principles discussed in a series of *Wall Street Journal* editorials by Dow Jones cofounder Charles H. Dow starting in the late nineteenth century. Dow emphasized the discounting process described above by Edwards and Magee, as well as the market's tendencies to move in trends—"primary" trends otherwise known as *bull and bear markets,* "secondary" trends that we commonly describe as *bull market corrections* or *bear market rallies,* and the more numerous "minor" trends found within the secondary trends. Further, the Dow Theory cornerstones include the concepts that the Dow Industrials and Dow Transports must confirm, that volume precedes price, and that a trend should be assumed to continue until a reversal has been confirmed.

As with anything that's considered a "theory," the practical application of the Dow Theory tenets can involve a great deal of subjectivity, and can therefore evoke debate. The varying interpretations of the primary trend, for example, are as great as the differing criterion for bull and bear markets. The NDR definition, for instance, includes magnitude and duration requirements that differ from other definitions, such as the common definition that a 20 percent move is a bull or bear market.

But the most debatable topic is the one used most often in conjunction with Dow Theory—the application of the tenet that the Dow Industrials and Dow Transports must confirm. According to Dow Theory, the confirmation of a new bull market occurs when, following new lows in the Industrials and Transports, both indices experience secondary rallies, drop back to higher lows, and then break out above the secondary highs, usually with one index following the other. If only one of the two indices broke out, the signal would be delayed until the other index followed suit. In Figure 5–1, for which NDR used a consensus of published material to identify the confirmed breakouts in new bull markets and confirmed breakdowns in new bear markets, you can see that while the Dow Theory signals have tended to be late, they have rarely been wrong about the presence of a bull or bear market.

What makes the confirmation analysis so subjective is that one person's secondary high may to another be nothing more than a minor high. Where the first person would

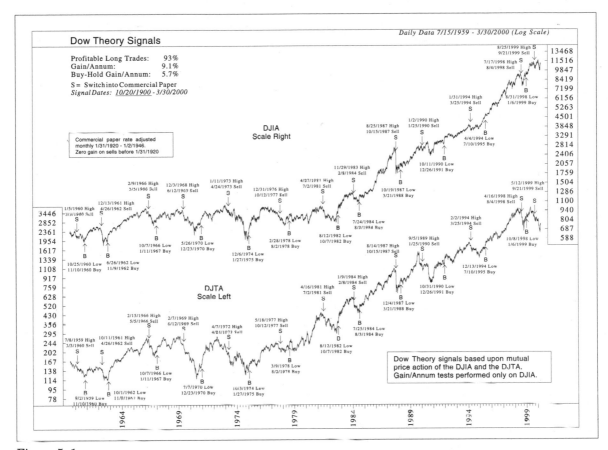

Figure 5–1

see a breakout, the next person would see an advance that had yet to reach a secondary high. And the subjectivity is compounded by the need to identify breakouts by two different averages. When you are bullish for other reasons, or simply would like to be bullish due to your market exposure, you might see a breakout; when you are bearish for other reasons, or have a vested interest in being so, you might see the downtrend remaining intact.

Yet, the subjectivity problem does not detract from the crucial concept that confirmation is bullish in a developing uptrend and bearish in a developing downtrend. And the subjectivity can be removed by developing indicators that, while venturing away from the Dow Theory rules, are nevertheless useful for identifying confirmation. Figure 5–2, for example, shows moving average indicators for the Dow Jones indices. When the 42-week moving average of the Dow Industrials turns upward, the indicator turns bull-

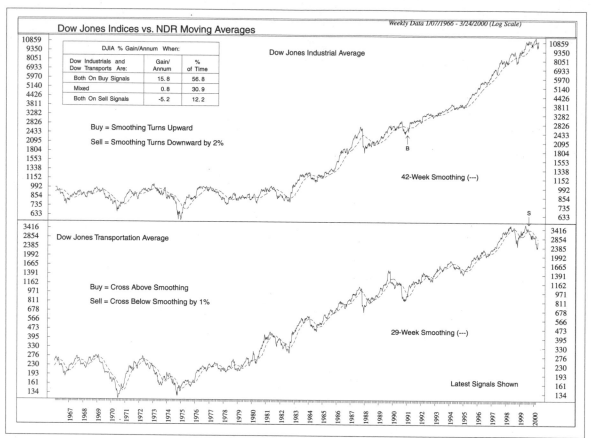

Figure 5–2

ish, and when the smoothing turns down by 2 percent, the indicator turns bearish, with the sell signal filter a reflection of the market's historical upward bias. In a similar manner, the trend of the Dow Transports is bullish when it rises above its 29-week moving average and bearish when the index falls below the smoothing by 1 percent. When both indicators are on the same signal, the confirmation is evident.

THE BENEFIT OF BROAD CONFIRMATION

But there's no reason to limit the analysis to just the Industrials and Transports. Whereas the two averages may have represented the market sufficiently in the days of Charles Dow, it has since become necessary to gauge confirmation with additional market indices like the capitalization-weighted NASDAQ Composite and S&P 500, and with equal-weighted breadth indices like the weekly advance/decline line.

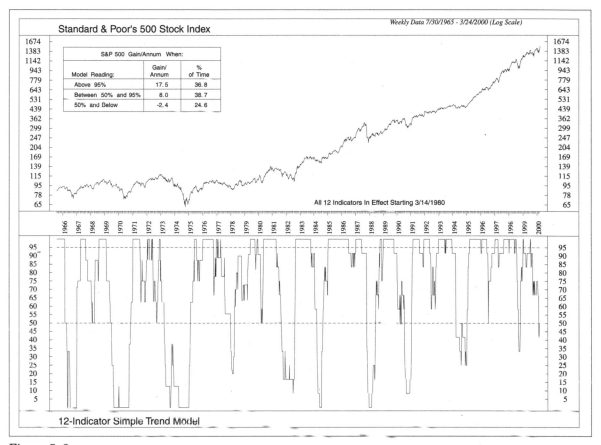

Figure 5–3

The strength of the confirmation message is, in fact, proportional to the number of confirming indices. This can be seen in Figure 5–3, which adds the bullish (+1) or bearish (–1) readings of the Dow Industrials and Transports indicators to the readings of similar trend indicators based on 10 other market indices. The total is then expressed on a percentage basis, from 0 percent bullish to 100 percent bullish, and plotted in the chart. As indicated in the chart's mode box, the S&P 500 has tended to perform far better during periods of widespread confirmation than it has during other periods, especially when index downtrends have kept the model reading below 50 percent.

Confirmation can be thought of as a shot of insulin for an afflicted market or a dose of Viagra for a market that's long-lived, but still healthy. In either case, the confirmation indicates that market conditions have yet to deteriorate. In contrast, when a period of confirmation is followed by a lack of confirmation, and conditions begin to deteriorate, a "code blue" is issued when the market breaks down.

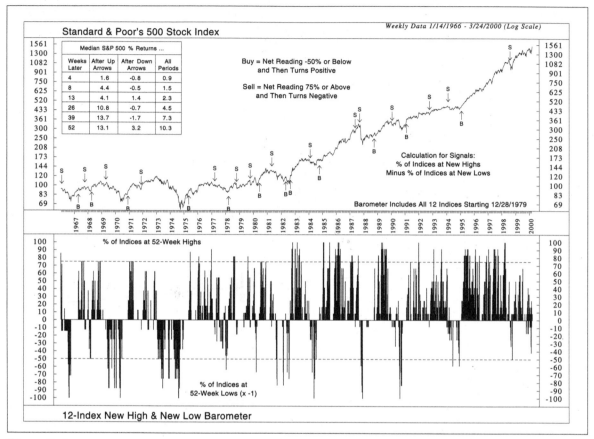

Figure 5–4

Using the same indices as those used in the trend model, the NDR New High & New Low Barometer in Figure 5–4 generates a sell signal when, after a bullish period including confirmed 52-week highs by at least 75 percent of the indices, none of the indices are able to continue to the higher levels, and one of them drops to a 52-week low. That development would indicate that the confirmed bullish period had been replaced by a period of divergence, or even worse, a period of bearish downside confirmation. Once bearish downside confirmation has been indicated by at least half of the indices at 52-week lows, a buy signal is generated when the indices stop reaching new lows and at least one of them moves back to a 52-week high. As indicated by the medians in the chart's subsequent-performance box, the S&P 500 has tended to perform better than normal after buy signals and worse than normal after sell signals.

A similar approach is taken in Figure 5–5, which shows an indicator that recognizes the global scope of major market trends. When the major developed markets con-

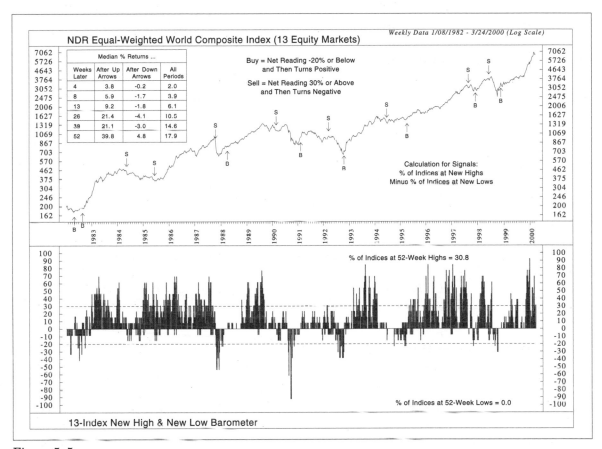

Figure 5–5

firm with 52-week highs, the global trend is healthy; when they confirm with 52-week lows, a confirmed downtrend is present. A sell signal can be generated when, after at least 30 percent of the indices have confirmed with new highs, the confirmation ends and at least one of the markets breaks to a new low. A buy signal can be generated when, after at least 20 percent of the indices have confirmed with new lows, downside confirmation ends and at least one market rises back to a new high. Again, the subsequent performance box quantifies the indicator's record.

When these indicators show an abundance of new highs or new lows, they illustrate the Dow Theory tenet that the averages must confirm. But their approach to generating signals is essentially an application of the tenet that a trend can be assumed to continue until a reversal has been signaled. The signal methodology also demonstrates that divergence can be as significant as confirmation, if not more so. The warning from divergence is especially pertinent in a bull or bear market that has reached its mature stages, having reached the age at which bull and bear markets tend to meet their demise—as shown in Chapter 1, the median bull market has lasted about a year and two-thirds (Table 1–5) while the median bear market has lasted about a year (Table 1–4). The more dramatic and widespread the divergence, the stronger its implication, a statement that applies to divergences among major developed markets around the globe, among major market indices in the domestic U.S. market, and among individual stocks, as will be evident later, when I discuss market breadth.

But your confirmation and divergence analysis should not be limited to an assessment of quantity. In a bull market, for instance, you shouldn't stop with a count of the number of indices confirming, with bullish implications, or the number of indices diverging, with bearish implications. You should also assess the quality of the confirmation or divergence, doing so by examining what it is that's confirming or diverging. The implications will be greater if those indices have a proven record of leading the rest of the market.

Among market indices, the most reliable leading indicators are those that are most sensitive to interest rates. When interest rates pressures begin to build, those indices will be the first to detect that negative market influence. By the time the rest of the market follows suit, the rate-sensitive leaders are likely to be far past their peaks.

THE LEADING UTILITIES

The leading index with the longest track record is the Dow Utilities, an index sometimes used in conjunction with Dow Theory analysis. Since the index's component stocks generally pay high dividends, they are often viewed as vehicles for income rather than capital gains, and are thus considered bond equivalents. Their dividend yields (dividend/price) compete with income-generating fixed-income vehicles, and their stock prices are quick to react when the competition starts gaining ground.

Of course, other factors can affect the utility stocks at various times, such as deregulation, new regulation, or merger activity. In recent years, as states have deregulated and allowed for competition among utility concerns, many have joined through merger or have diversified by merging with firms outside of the industry, such as energy firms. Nevertheless, the interest rate sensitivity has remained an overriding characteristic of utilities.

In fact, rate sensitivity is one of the reasons why utilities have been the classic defensive play in bear markets. Once a bear market has become widely recognized, with consumer confidence waning and expectations of economic weakness on the rise, interest rates tend to stabilize, and they may fall if a flight to quality sends investors into the bond market. In either case, utilities will tend to withstand the bear market far better than other stock sectors, not only because of their rate sensitivity, but also because of their ability to produce steady dividend income when less income-oriented sectors are leaving their stockholders with diminishing capital gains, or capital losses. Utilities also tend to be less volatile than most other sectors, and thus less at risk during a downtrend.

Typically, then, the utilities become relative strength leaders at some point after a bear market has been confirmed. And they tend to maintain relative strength during the bottoming process and the early phases of the next bull market, which is usually fueled by falling interest rates. Once a bull market is confirmed, the advance reaches its mature stages, and interest rates start rising again, the utilities tend to begin losing relative strength. And by the time the interest rate rise starts to become a threat to the bull market, the utilities will often peak out and become relative strength laggards.

This leading tendency is evident in Table 5–1, which compares bull market peak dates with the peak dates for various indices with leading tendencies. For their part, the Dow Utilities have led 19, or 83 percent, of the past 23 bull market peaks. Although the table includes the median number of weeks between the index peaks and the market peaks, I wouldn't put much weight on that statistic for indices with lead times that have varied greatly.

Rather than dwell on the amount of the lead time, the key analytical consideration is whether the Dow Utilities are in fact diverging from the major market indices, potentially leading a peak and thus raising the level of market risk, or whether they are confirming, with bullish implications. Whereas it's usually a good omen for the market's future performance when the Dow Utilities confirm the Dow Industrials by reaching a new high, the risk of a market peak increases the longer the utilities diverge from the industrials and remain unable to rise past a previous high, as illustrated in Figure 5–6.

The utilities can also be watched for their relative strength versus indices representative of specific sectors, including the Dow Transports. The leading and defensive nature of the Dow Utilities can be seen in Figure 5–7, which shows the average pattern of the Dow indices around market peaks since 1959. Whereas the utilities are shown turning downward before the bull market peak, the transports and industrials are shown peaking together and then falling faster than the utilities.

In fact, the contrasting tendencies of the transports and utilities lend themselves to an indicator to call the industrials, as shown in Figure 5–8. Since the 1960s, the ratio of the transports to the utilities has trended upward. But with a "deviation from trend" indicator, in which the ratio's 16-week moving average is divided by its 72-week moving average, significant variations in the trend can be detected.

As shown in the chart's bottom clip, the ratio of the shorter smoothing to the longer smoothing produces an oscillator. When the oscillator rises into its upper mode, the market implications are bearish since the transports are gaining at too fast a pace relative to the utilities, the sign of the utility divergence often evident in advance of market peaks. By the time the oscillator peaks and turns down, the industrials are usually falling as well. When the oscillator reaches the lower mode, the implications are bullish, as

T A B L E 5-1

Leading Indices for Bull Market Peaks (05/14/1928–03/31/2000)

DJIA Bull Market Peak	Weekly Volume	Weekly New Highs	Daily A/D Line	Weekly DJUA	Weekly Long-Term Government Bonds
09/03/1929			05/14/1928 -68		
04/17/1930			04/01/1930 -2	04/12/1930 -1	
09/07/1932			09/07/1932 0	09/03/1932 -1	
02/05/1934			04/21/1934 11	07/15/1933 -30	
03/10/1937			01/21/1937 -7	01/16/1937 -8	
11/12/1938			11/12/1938 0	11/12/1938 0	
09/12/1939			09/18/1941 105	08/05/1939 -6	
05/29/1946			05/29/1946 0	04/20/1946 -6	
06/15/1948			05/22/1948 -3	06/12/1948 -1	
01/05/1953			03/18/1953 10	03/13/1953 9	
04/06/1956			03/15/1956 -3	08/03/1956 17	
01/05/1960			03/13/1959 -43	03/20/1959 -42	
12/13/1961			05/17/1961 -30	11/17/1961 -4	
02/09/1966			05/06/1965 -40	02/05/1965 -53	
12/03/1968	06/07/1968 -26	06/07/1968 -26	08/02/1967 -70	11/22/1968 -2	01/20/1967 -98
04/28/1971	02/12/1971 -11	01/22/1971 -14	04/28/1971 0	01/22/1971 -14	03/26/1971 -5
01/11/1973	03/10/1972 -44	04/14/1972 -39	03/09/1972 -44	11/24/1972 -7	12/01/1972 -6
09/21/1976	01/30/1976 -34	01/30/1976 -34	07/22/1977 43	07/22/1977 43	01/07/1977 15
09/08/1978	08/04/1978 -5	08/04/1978 -5	09/11/1978 1	08/04/1978 -5	03/23/1978 -24
04/27/1981	01/09/1981 -16	09/19/1980 -32	09/19/1980 -31	11/28/1980 -22	06/20/1980 -45
11/29/1983	10/15/1982 -59	10/15/1982 -59	06/16/1983 -24	10/28/1983 -5	11/05/1982 -56
08/25/1987	08/14/1987 -2	03/14/1986 -76	03/23/1987 -22	02/06/1987 -29	04/18/1986 -71
07/16/1990	10/20/1989 -39	08/04/1989 -50	08/08/1989 -49	12/15/1989 -31	08/04/1989 -50
07/17/1998	10/31/1997 -38	07/11/1997 -54	04/03/1998 -16	07/02/1998 -2	07/10/1998 -1
01/14/2000	03/17/2000 9	07/02/1999 -28	01/06/1999 -53	06/04/1999 -32	10/09/1998 -66
Median	**-30**	**-37**	**-5**	**-5**	**-35**
#Leads	**10**	**10**	**15**	**19**	**9**
#Coinc	**0**	**0**	**4**	**1**	**0**
#Lags	**0**	**0**	**5**	**3**	**1**
#Lds/Total	**100%**	**100%**	**63%**	**83%**	**90%**
Range	**57**	**71**	**175**	**96**	**113**

DJIA Bull Market Peak	Insider Selling (5-Week Avg.)	Daily NDR S&L Group	Weekly NDR Home Building Group	NDR Brokers Group
06/15/1948				
01/05/1953				
04/06/1956				
01/05/1960				
12/13/1961				
02/09/1966				
12/03/1968				
04/28/1971		04/16/1971 −2		
01/11/1973		11/24/1972 −7	04/14/1972 −39	
09/21/1976	03/05/1976 −29	04/15/1977 29	04/09/1976 −24	
09/08/1978	09/15/1978 1	08/11/1978 −4	04/27/1979 33	09/15/1978 1
04/27/1981	09/05/1980 −34	06/13/1980 −46	04/03/1981 −4	11/28/1980 −22
11/29/1983	06/17/1983 −24	05/11/1983 −29	06/17/1983 −24	07/01/1983 −22
08/25/1987	03/21/1986 −75	03/04/1987 −25	03/13/1987 −24	04/18/1976 −71
07/16/1990	09/08/1989 −45	10/05/1989 −41	09/01/1989 −46	09/01/1989 −46
07/17/1998	01/08/1993 −289	04/17/1998 −13	07/10/1998 −1	07/17/1998 0
01/14/2000	12/11/1998 −57	11/25/1998 −59	12/31/1998 −54	03/24/2000 10
Median	**−34**	**−13**	**−24**	**−22**
#Leads	**6**	**8**	**7**	**4**
#Coinc	**0**	**0**	**0**	**1**
#Lags	**1**	**1**	**1**	**1**
#Lds/Total	**86%**	**89%**	**88%**	**67%**
Range	**290**	**75**	**79**	**72**

Notes: Leads (−) and lags (+) are expressed as weeks between week of index peak and week of bull market peak, which is peak following rise of 30 percent in DJIA or Value Line Composite after 50 days, or 13 percent rise after 155 days. Bear market is a decline of 30 percent after 50 days or 13 percent decline after 145 days. Index peak is the maximum index level between a bear market bottom date and the halfway date of the bear market following the bull market peak. Range is the number of weeks from longest lead date to the longest lag date or the shortest lead date if there were no lags. The range does not include current (1/14/2000) peak data. All of the index peaks met this criteria with the following exceptions: (1) the bull market peak of 1/11/1973 was followed by a volume spike near the midpoint of the subsequent bear market, and the high was marginal, so we used the leading high instead. The volume high of 10/23/1987, which was posted just after the market bottom, was excluded as a lead since it was directly related to the crash. (2) The bull market peaks of 9/12/1939 and 9/21/1976 are shown with lagging A/D line peaks that occurred after the bear market midpoint but were included since they were higher than the previous lagging peaks. (3) The same exception was made for the DJIA's lag of the 9/21/1976 market peak. (4) Our study of the S&L Group is based on weekly data prior to 1979 and daily data thereafter. (5) Current peak is based on current high for week ending 1/14/2000, which is not included in summary data for indices. All statistics relative to current peak are through 3/28/2000.

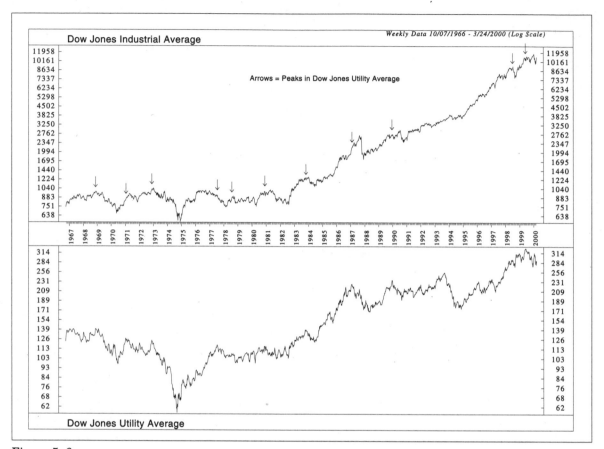

Figure 5–6

the outperformance has become so pronounced that a change is trend is imminent. When the new advance is well under way, the transports start gaining relative strength versus the utilities, and the oscillator moves upward and out of the lower mode.

COMPARING THE FINANCIALS

The utilities can also be compared to the financials, a market sector that has leading tendencies of its own owing to the interest rate sensitivity of financial stocks. But the financials differ from the utilities in that they lack the defensive characteristics that enable the utilities to exhibit relative strength during bear markets. As shown in the top clip of Figure 5–9, the New York Stock Exchange Utilities Index has outperformed the New York Stock Exchange Financials Index over the course of each of the past five bear markets, starting with the dashed lines and ending with the solid lines.

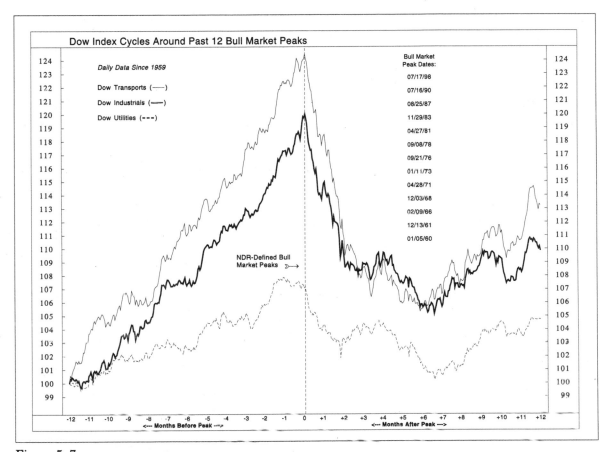

Figure 5–7

Also note that soon after market troughs, the ratio of the Utilities to the Financials has reversed downward, often quite decisively. After the bear market has weakened the financials to the point at which, like the transports in Figure 5–8, they are oversold relative to the defensive utilities, the financials tend to respond more dramatically to the favorable interest rate conditions that are typically prevalent at the start of bull markets.

In the process of assessing the quality of leadership and confirmation, it's thus a good idea to keep an eye on the utilities, watching for them to diverge in a mature bull market, show relative strength in a bear market, and pass the leadership baton to more oversold and volatile sectors at the start of a new bull market. I will take a close look at those tendencies in Chapter 9, which includes tables of the group performance after peaks and after troughs.

But the financials should also be monitored closely, especially in mature bull markets and at the beginning of new ones. The sector is, however, so broad that it can be more

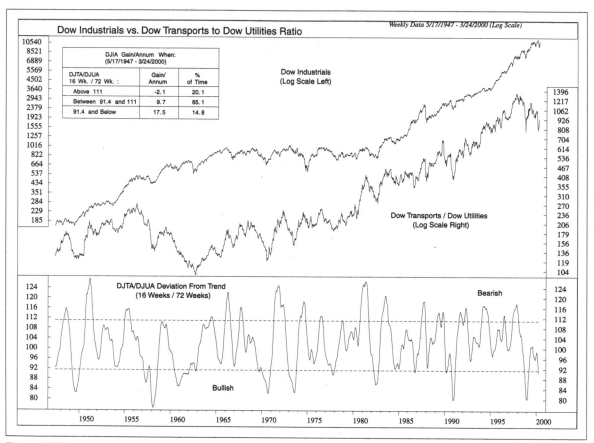

Dow Industrials vs. Dow Transports to Dow Utilities Ratio

Weekly Data 5/17/1947 - 3/24/2000 (Log Scale)

DJIA Gain/Annum When: (5/17/1947 - 3/24/2000)		
DJTA/DJUA 16 Wk. / 72 Wk. :	Gain/ Annum	% of Time
Above 111	-2.1	20.1
Between 91.4 and 111	9.7	65.1
91.4 and Below	17.5	14.8

Dow Industrials (Log Scale Left)

Dow Transports / Dow Utilities (Log Scale Right)

DJTA/DJUA Deviation From Trend (16 Weeks / 72 Weeks)

Bearish

Bullish

Figure 5–8

useful to focus on the financial groups with the most reliable leading tendencies. Two of those groups are the brokerage firms group and the savings and loans group, which have tended to lead bull market peaks. Those groups are included in the leading indicator table (Table 5–1) along with the home building group, considered a housing group rather than a financial group, but nonetheless sensitive to interest rates. As shown in Figure 5–10, the relative strength of all three sectors versus the S&P 500 has tended to weaken in advance of market peaks and strengthen soon after market bottoms.

THE BREADTH INDICATORS

Once you have completed your assessment of the confirmation and divergence among major indices and various industry groups, you can move to the assessment of broad market confirmation and divergence, as reflected by indicators of market breadth. These are the indicators based on the number of advancing stocks and declining stocks

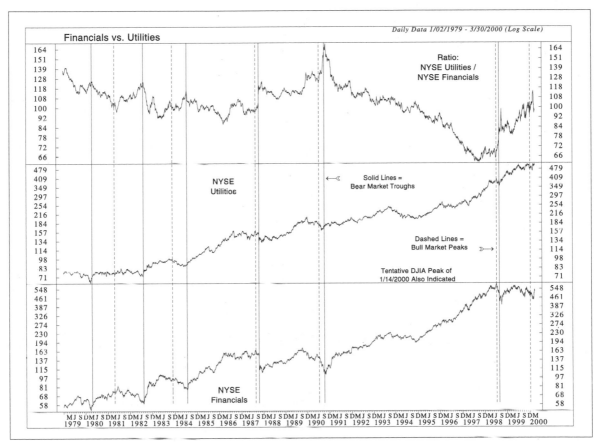

Figure 5–9

and the number of stocks reaching new highs and new lows. When the major indices are in uptrends with confirmation from a relatively large number of advancing stocks, many of which are reaching new highs, the market is healthy. When the major averages are driven higher by just a handful of large-cap stocks, as indicated by a relatively small number of advancing stocks and a lack of new highs, the market's health is suspect and the outlook is more risky.

Advance/Decline Lines

The breadth measure most familiar to most people is the advance/decline line (A/D line), which is the running total of advancing stocks minus declining stocks. But the A/D line is often misunderstood and misinterpreted. Since the line has the appearance of a market index, it's tempting to compare its rate of change and level with those of an index. But such comparisons neglect to recognize that while an index is the composite of stock

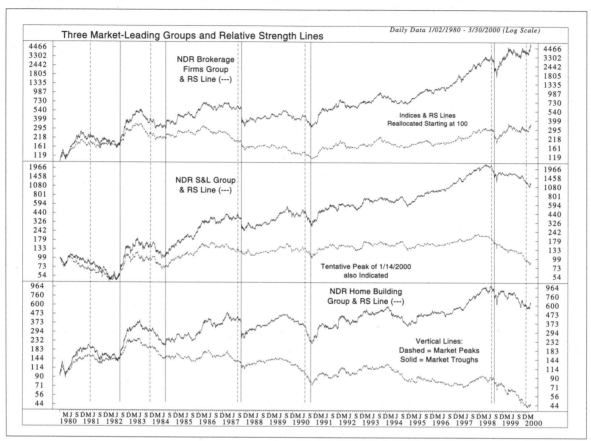

Figure 5–10

prices, an A/D line is the composite of stock movement, giving the daily A/D line a downward bias relative to the weekly A/D line and the price-based indices. The bias of recent years can be seen in Figure 5–11.

The reason for the downward bias is that the average stock tends to experience about as many up days as down days, but the gains tend to accumulate much faster than the losses. If a $100 stock is up on two straight days for a gain of 30 percent, but then loses 5 percent of the $130 total over the next two days, it contributes nothing to the A/D line despite a net gain of 23.5 percent.

The tendency for gains to outpace losses is quantified in Table 5–2. The table demonstrates that from 1994 through late March 2000, the average stock's gain on up days has exceeded its loss on down days, with the ratio 1.108 for the large-cap S&P 500 stocks and 1.123 for the stocks in NDR's broader Techno-Fundamental Ranks (TFR) universe. Yet in both cases, the number of up days was about equal to the number of down days, as

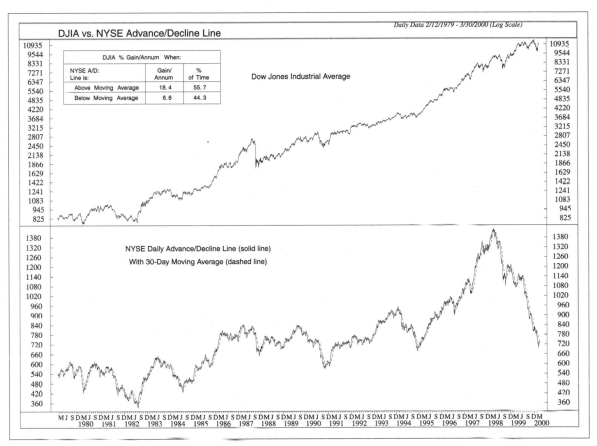

Figure 5–11

shown by ratios of 1.006 and 0.994. In addition, the table shows that when weekly data is used, the contrast is less striking, which explains why the weekly A/D line is less downwardly biased than the daily measure. But the weekly A/D line is still understated versus the price-based indices.

You will therefore run into problems if you attempt to make historical comparisons based on A/D lines. But the downward bias has a benefit. It lends greater significance to new highs in the index, since they are harder to come by. Moreover, new highs in the daily A/D line have tended to lead peaks in the market, especially in recent years, as shown in Table 5–1. When the A/D line is breaking out to the upside, you can usually breathe easily about the market's prospects over at least the next few months.

A/D lines can also add value to the analytical process when used in conjunction with moving averages, which keeps the A/D line comparisons in the context of recent history. Figure 5–12 shows that since the start of 1965, when the weekly NYSE A/D line has

T A B L E 5-2

Advance/Decline Study

Current S&P 500 Components: Daily

Period	Avg. No. of Days Up	Avg. No. of Days Down	Ratio	Avg. % Gain	Avg. % Loss	Ratio	Gain/ Annum	No. of Stocks
12/30/1994–3/23/2000	615.79	612.42	**1.006**	1.786	−1.612	**1.108**	17.34	469

Current S&P 500 Components: Weekly

Period	Avg. No. of Weeks Up	Avg. No. of Weeks Down	Ratio	Avg. % Gain	Avg. % Loss	Ratio	Gain/ Annum	No. of Stocks
12/30/1994–3/23/2000	139.08	124.98	**1.113**	3.791	−3.369	**1.125**	16.93	469

Current NDR Stock Universe: Daily

Period	Avg. No. of Days Up	Avg. No. of Days Down	Ratio	Avg. % Gain	Avg. % Loss	Ratio	Gain/ Annum	No. of Stocks
12/30/1994–3/23/2000	591.10	594.66	**0.994**	2.052	−1.827	**1.123**	17.39	1496

Current NDR Stock Universe: Weekly

Period	Avg. No. of Weeks Up	Avg. No. of Weeks Down	Ratio	Avg. % Gain	Avg. % Loss	Ratio	Gain/ Annum	No. of Stocks
12/30/1994–3/23/2000	134.47	125.19	**1.074**	4.351	−3.743	**1.162**	17.09	1496

been 4 percent above its 32-week moving average, the Dow Industrials have gained 20 percent per annum. When the A/D line has been 3 percent below its smoothing, the Dow Industrials have returned −15 percent per annum over the same period.

For additional information, the A/D line can be compared with its smoothing at the same time that the price-based index is compared to its smoothing. In those cases, the implications are most bullish when both the price and the A/D line are above their smoothings and most bearish when both are below their smoothings. This approach is used widely at NDR, which monitors the A/D lines for a wide range of indices, including mega-cap indices like the NDX Index (Figure 5–13), broader composites like the NASDAQ Composite (Figure 5–14), style and capitalization groupings like the NDR Small-Cap Index (Figure 5–15), and industry groups like the NDR Electronic Semiconductors Group (Figure 5–16). As long as you can track the movement of the component

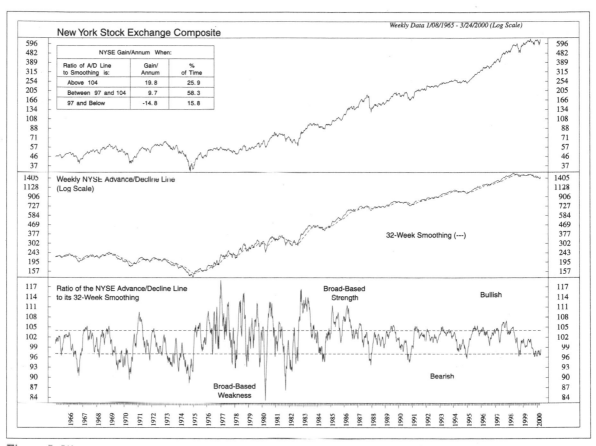

Figure 5-12

stocks, you can create an A/D line indicator for any group of stocks, giving you a valuable breadth perspective to complement your assessment of the price-based index.

A/D Ratios

But the A/D line is not the only vehicle for illustrating breadth with advances and declines. A simple alternative is to determine the ratio of the advances to the declines using totals for a period that suits your time frame. Figure 5–17, for example, uses data on the composite tape (the NYSE plus regional exchanges) to plot the ratio of the 90-day total of advances to the 90-day total of declines, providing perspective that can be used for long-term comparisons. In mature bull markets, the ratio will tend to reach lower highs as

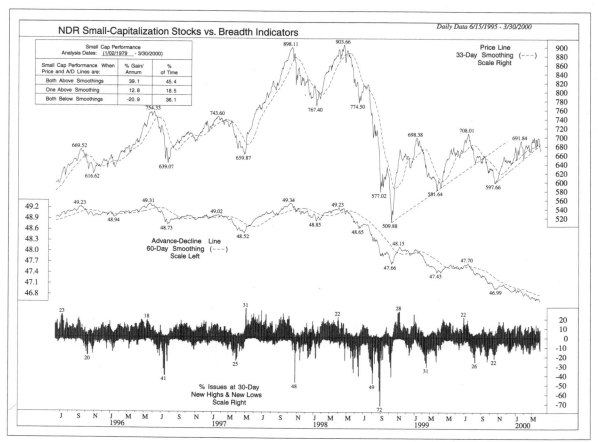

Figure 5–15

The effect is quantified in Table 5–3, which uses the 10-day A/D ratio, which is faster than the 90-day ratio in detecting thrust conditions. Following up on analyst Dan Sullivan's[1] work in using the 10-day ratio as a thrust indicator, NDR identified 1.91 as the key threshold. The record following signals shows that the Dow Industrials have had a strong tendency to perform well over subsequent periods, with the relative outperformance diminishing over time. Whereas the median gain 10 days later has beaten the benchmark gain by a factor of nearly 5, that ratio has diminished to about 3 after half a year and to about 2.5 after a year. Yet throughout, the median gain has beaten the benchmark median in about 75 percent of the cases.

The indicator's drawback is that it can be affected by the changing size and composition of its universe. From January 1990 to January 1999, for example, the number of NYSE issues nearly doubled, and it should be recognized that the listings include pre-

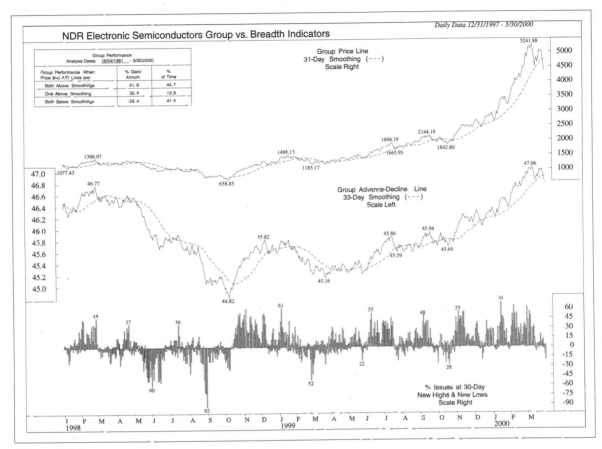

Figure 5–16

ferred issues, closed-end funds, and foreign stocks trading as American Depository Receipts. As shown in Figure 5–18, this expansion of the NYSE universe dampened the volatility of the A/D ratio, as reflected by the greater frequency of signals in the earlier, more volatile periods.

One way to reduce the influence of the number of issues traded is to express your breadth statistics as a percentage of issues traded. Figure 5–19, for example, uses a 10-week exponential moving average of NYSE weekly advances as a percentage of the total, a calculation that gives the indicator a fixed range (from 0 to 100 percent) and consistent volatility over its history. Breadth is considered weak when the percentage is less than 46 percent and strong when it is more than 46 percent. And when the percentage exceeds 52 percent, a breadth thrust is indicated, with the bullish implications summarized by the results in the chart's upper-left-hand corner. Because of the stable vola-

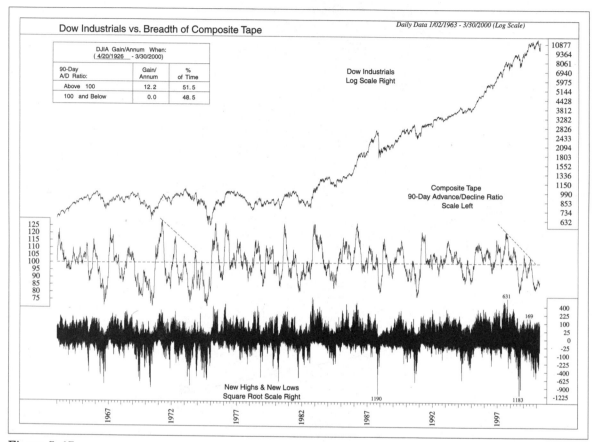

Figure 5–17

tility and a thrust signal requirement that's less stringent than that of the 10-day A/D ratio indicator, this indicator generates signals with more consistent frequency.

Figure 5–20 takes another approach, likewise using the percentage of advancing issues but subtracting out the percentage of declining issues. The result is then smoothed with a 39-day exponential moving average, which is then subtracted from a 19-day exponential moving average. This is a variation of the widely followed McClellan Oscillator, developed by Sherm McClellan.[2] Traditionally used as an overbought/oversold indicator, the indicator in Figure 5–20 identifies upside breadth thrusts when the oscillator reaches an extremely high reading of 5.7, and it identifies a downside thrust when the oscillator falls below –7.5.

A similar but less volatile indicator is shown in Figure 5–21, based not on moving averages, but on a running five-week total of the spread. When the five-week total

T A B L E 5–3

Breadth Thrusts 06/23/1947–03/14/2000
(10-Day Advances / 10-Day Declines)

Date	A/D Ratio	10-Day Dow Industrials % Change (Trading Days Later)					
		5	10	22	63	126	252
06/23/1947	1.96	−0.1	2.9	5.3	0.3	0.1	3.7
03/29/1948	2.05	2.2	3.2	5.8	11.2	4.0	0.6
07/13/1949	2.06	1.4	1.9	3.5	7.0	15.2	28.4
11/20/1950	2.01	1.5	−1.7	−1.4	10.0	9.8	18.8
01/25/1954	2.00	0.5	1.1	0.3	8.3	18.2	36.4
01/24/1958	2.00	−0.1	−0.4	−3.1	0.6	10.3	31.4
07/10/1962	1.98	−1.4	−2.0	0.9	0.0	14.0	21.5
11/07/1962	1.91	2.4	3.5	4.8	10.3	17.3	21.1
01/13/1967	1.94	1.4	1.1	2.6	2.9	5.6	6.9
08/31/1970	1.91	1.1	−1.8	−0.5	3.9	15.5	17.9
12/03/1970	1.95	1.5	1.7	3.6	11.1	14.1	5.0
12/08/1971	1.98	1.0	3.5	6.2	10.6	10.4	20.2
01/08/1975	1.98	2.8	2.7	12.0	20.9	37.2	41.4
01/06/1976	2.05	2.5	6.6	8.3	12.7	11.3	10.9
08/23/1982	2.02	0.2	2.6	3.9	14.6	22.6	34.0
10/13/1982	2.03	1.9	−0.9	2.4	6.7	13.9	24.6
01/21/1985	1.93	1.3	2.3	1.4	0.4	7.6	20.1
01/14/1987	2.19	2.9	6.3	7.3	10.7	22.1	−5.4
02/04/1991	1.94	4.7	5.8	6.9	6.1	7.8	16.7
01/06/1992	1.97	−0.5	1.7	1.8	1.5	4.3	3.4
Median		**1.4**	**2.1**	**3.6**	**7.7**	**12.6**	**19.4**

Notes: Breadth thrusts occur when the 10-day total of advances on the NYSE is at least 1.91 times the 10-day total of declines on the NYSE and a minimum of 50 calendar days apart.

reaches 1.65 percent, breadth thrust signals are generated. The signal frequency is less than that of the McClellan Oscillator and similar to that of the 10-day A/D ratio. But in contrast to the 10-day A/D ratio, the indicator's recent extremes occurred at levels comparable to its earlier extremes, with the indicator generating a 1997 thrust signal not produced by the 10-day A/D ratio.

But more is going on in this chart. Along with the breadth thrust signals, the chart includes bullish, neutral, and bearish modes. And to round out this breadth perspective, the chart includes the Friday close of the daily A/D line with short-term, intermediate-term, and long-term trendlines. In the best case, new highs in the Dow Industrials

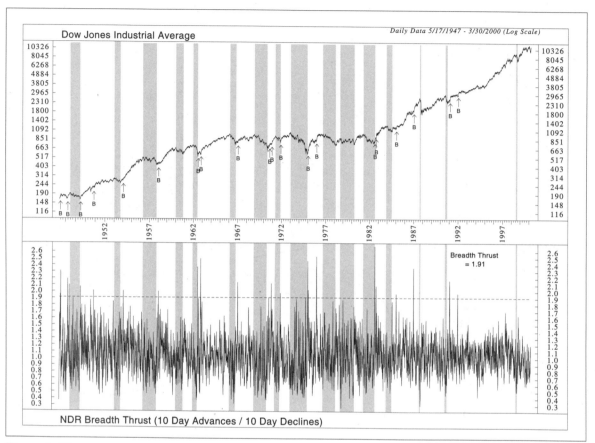

Figure 5–18

are confirmed by an A/D line breakout and a breadth thrust signal. In the worst case, the indicator and A/D line both diverge, with the indicator dropping to weak breadth readings. But if the indicator drops to a very oversold level, the breadth weakness becomes a hopeful sign, indicating that the decline has reached its final, climactic stages.

New Highs and New Lows

For monitoring breadth for the type of extreme oversold conditions found at market bottoms, indicators based on new highs and new lows are preferable. Whereas A/D data indicate how many stocks have risen or fallen by any amount, new high and new low indicators are based on the number of stocks that have risen impressively or fallen severely. While useful for identifying market bottoms, indicators based on these data are excel-

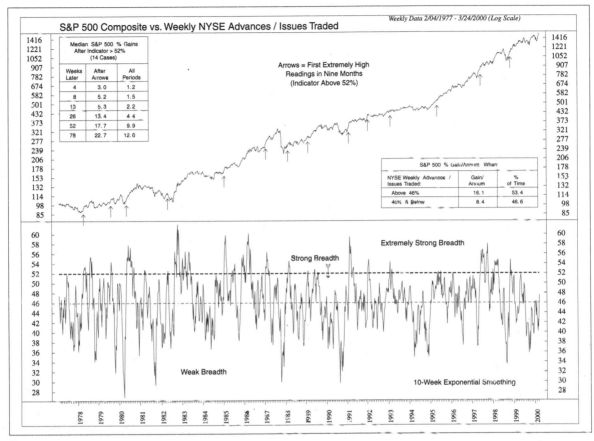

Figure 5–19

lent for indicating breadth thrusts in new bull markets, breadth divergences in mature bull markets, and general market strength and weakness.

Figure 5–22 illustrates NYSE weekly new highs in the middle clip and weekly new lows in the bottom clip, both divided by issues traded. When new lows have been scarce, as indicated by less than about 2 percent of the issues at weekly new lows, the market has tended to perform well, as reflected by the per annum returns in the box in the right half of the chart. When more than about 7 percent of the issues are reaching weekly new lows, the market tends to decline. And by the time about 40 percent of the issues are at weekly new lows, the market is generally very oversold. But that alone doesn't guarantee that a bottom is at hand. In 1973, for example, new lows reached oversold levels, but they returned to those levels several times before the market finally bottomed at the end of 1974.

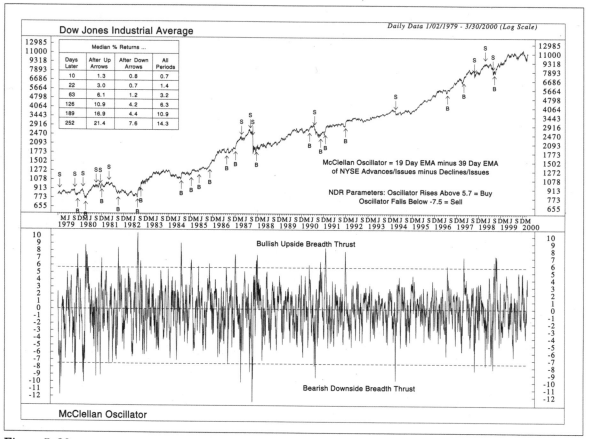

Figure 5–20

The development missing in 1973 was a breadth thrust to stop the bleeding and get the market pointed in the right direction. But the thrust conditions did become evident after the 1974 bottom, as indicated in the middle clip, by more than 30 percent of the issues at weekly new highs. When new lows reach the extremely high levels normal for market bottoms, diminish, and are followed by new highs reaching extremely high levels, the implications are quite bullish, as summarized in the box in the upper left of Figure 5–22.

You should keep in mind that new highs and new lows usually are not necessarily mirror images in the market cycle. While new lows tend to reach their extreme in conjunction with, or not long before, the bear market bottom, new highs tend to reach their extremes long before the bull market peak. The difference is consistent with the tendency for market bottoms to occur rapidly amid highly vocal market panic and wide-

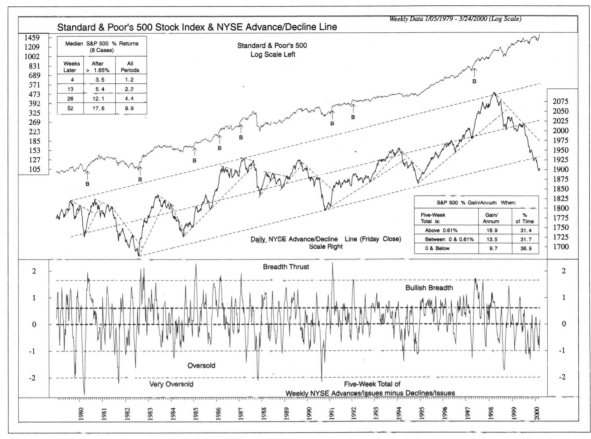

Figure 5–21

spread fear that the world is coming to an end. Tops, on the other hand, are typically reached after extended periods of divergence and distribution, with hardly a whisper of concern to be heard in the midst of all the quiet complacency. Tops tend to form so slowly that they become widely apparent only after the downtrend is well under way, if not nearly over.

An extreme in new highs is not, then, an indication of a market peak, as a new low extreme would be the sign of a market bottom. Rather, as illustrated in Figure 5–23, an extreme in new highs can occur in conjunction with a breadth thrust, the case when weekly new highs exceeded 1000 in 1982, or they can occur later in an advance, indicating that a topping process lies ahead. Examples include the extreme in 1989 and the extreme in 1997, a high that represented a peak in momentum and sentiment, to be discussed in the next two chapters.

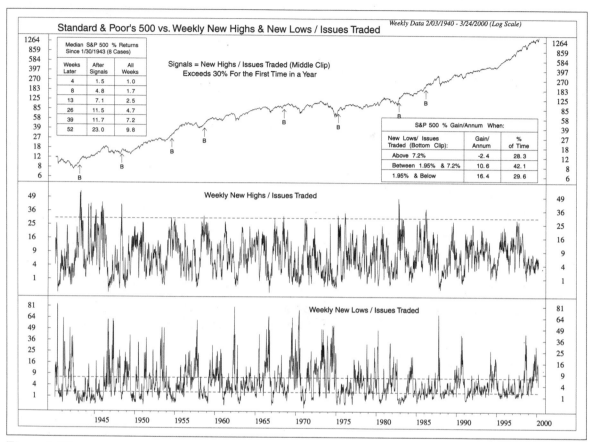

Figure 5–22

The time between peaks in new highs and peaks in the market can therefore vary widely from cycle to cycle, as listed in Table 5–1 and shown in Figure 5–23. But the one consistency to remember is that, invariably, new highs lead, having peaked in advance of each of the past 11 bull markets. When a bull market is under way and new highs reach their highest level yet for that bull, you can be confident that the bull market will continue for many more weeks. The median lead time has been 37 weeks, although I wouldn't place too much weight on that average, owing to the wide range of lead times and limited number of cases.

A good way to consolidate the messages provided by new highs and new lows is to subtract new lows from new highs and then divide by issues traded. The indicator in Figure 5–24 applies the calculation to daily new highs and lows, and then smooths the resulting percentage over five days. The S&P 500 has tended to perform well when the

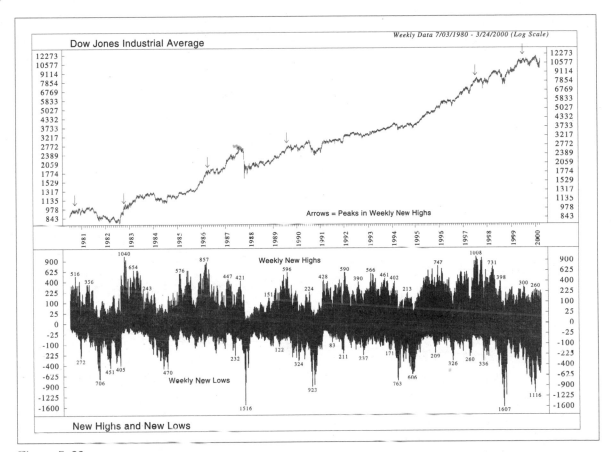

Figure 5-23

smoothed percentage has been above 1.6 percent and the S&P 500 has tended to decline when the smoothed percentage has been below –2.6 percent. Similarly, Figure 5–25 shows the percentage produced by the weekly data, illustrating that the market has tended to perform well when the percentage has been higher than about 9 percent and poorly when the percentage has been lower than about –4 percent.

With both indicators, extremely low percentages have reflected the deeply oversold conditions normally present at market bottoms. In fact, Figure 5–24 indicates that when extremely low levels are reached by the indicator based on the daily data, the breadth is so bad that the weakness is actually an encouraging sign, as it could be evidence of a high-panic selling climax. Table 5–4 looks at the past 11 bear market bottoms, showing that during the three months prior to and including the market lows, the percentage has troughed at a median level of –19 percent, with six of the indicator lows oc-

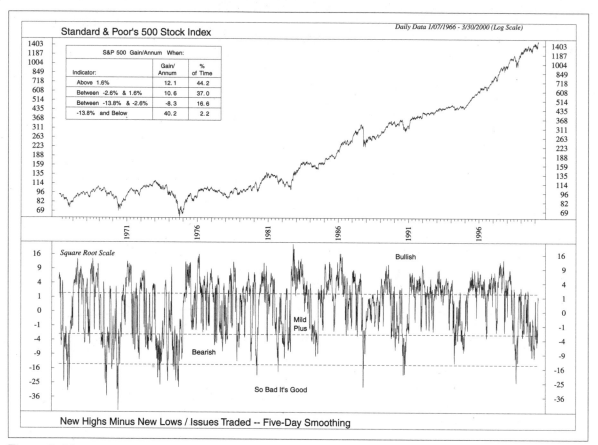

Figure 5–24

curring before the market bottoms and five occurring at the same time. For the indicator that uses weekly data in Figure 5–25, Table 5–4 indicates that the median level at the past seven bottoms has been –41 percent, with three of the indicator lows leading the market troughs, three coincident, and one lagging.

Of course, as discussed earlier, bottoms can be known only in hindsight. And the difficulty with trying to identify a bottom based on an extremely oversold condition is that a deeply oversold market can become even more deeply oversold before the major market averages reach their low points. Again, the oversold levels of 1973 are a case in point. To be confident that a bottom is in place, you need to see confirmed evidence that the lows have been reached, and that requires renewed bullish breadth. Although breadth thrusts have generally been less apparent on these two breadth charts than they have been on others discussed, indicator readings of about 12 percent have usually been enough to confirm that the bear has in fact turned into a bull.

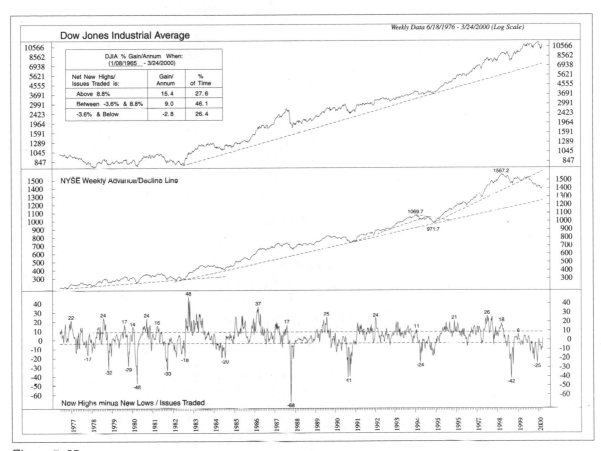

Figure 5–25

Confirmed Messages

Like new highs alone, net new highs as a percentage of issues invariably peak before the market, lending bullish significance to new highs in the indicators and bearish significance to divergences. The confirmation or divergence is especially notable when it occurs with concurrent confirmation or divergence from indicators based on advances and declines, such as the weekly A/D line shown in the middle clip of Figure 5–25. After the bottom of 1982, for example, the weekly net new highs percentage and the weekly A/D line both broke out to new highs, strong confirmation that the market lows had been reached. Prior to the market peaks of 1990 and 1999, both were divergent, emphasizing the warning of weakness forthcoming in the major averages.

The A/D lines for the indices shown in Figures 5–13 through 5–16 can likewise be used in conjunction with the stocks reaching new highs and new lows, based on the

T A B L E 5–4

Breadth Indicator Readings Near Market Bottoms

| Date of Market Bottom | Daily Net New Highs/Issues Traded | | New Highs—New Lows/Issues Traded | |
	Low w/in Three Mos. Prior to Bottom (%)	Date of Indicator Low	Low w/in Three Mos. Prior to Bottom (%)	Date of Indicator Low
10/07/1966	−31.0	08/30/1966		
05/26/1970	−47.9	05/26/1970		
11/23/1971	−10.6	11/23/1971		
12/06/1974	−28.0	09/16/1974		
02/28/1978	−5.2	01/13/1978	−13.7	01/13/1978
04/21/1980	−19.8	03/27/1980	−47.6	03/28/1980
08/12/1982	−7.9	08/12/1982	−18.3	08/12/1982
07/24/1984	−9.7	05/30/1984	−19.9	07/24/1984
10/19/1987	−17.0	10/19/1987	−68.1	10/19/1987
10/11/1990	−19.4	08/23/1990	−40.9	08/24/1990
08/31/1998	−20.9	08/31/1998	−42.2	09/04/1998*
Mean	**−19.8**		**−35.8**	
Median	**−19.4**		**−40.9**	

* Indicator low occurred after market low.

stocks that make up the respective indices. The additional perspective can be gained by using the absolute number of new highs and new lows or by using those totals as percentages of the number of issues in the index.

But just as no two market cycles are exactly alike, no two periods of divergence are quite the same. And there have been cases when periods of divergence have cleared up without a bear market in the major averages. In 1994, the breadth indicators were bearish and divergent, yet the major averages avoided a bear market, experiencing nothing worse than a correction. It could justifiably be argued, however, that the correction would eventually have turned into a bear market had there not been an interest rate decline starting at the end of the year. History shows that declining interest rates and general improvement in monetary conditions are usually required for a bullish resolution to a divergent period. NDR analyst Sam Burns used the 90-day A/D ratio to identify 17 periods of divergence since 1966, including 12 periods resolved without a bear market. And of those bullish resolutions, 10 occurred with interest rates declining, as shown in Table 5–5.

T A B L E   5–5

Breadth Divergences

Divergence Date	Bear/Resolution Date	Time (Months)	Rates Declining? (Y/N)
November 67	Resolved 7/68	8	N
May 72	Bear market starts 1/73	8	Y
April 75	Resolved 1/76	9	Y
March 80	Resolved 7/80	4	N
January 81	Bear market starts 4/01	3	N
August 82	Resolved 11/82	3	Y
October 83	Bear market starts 11/83	1	N
August 84	Resolved 12/84	4	N
November 85	Resolved 3/86	4	Y
June 86	Resolved 10/86	4	Y
November 88	Resolved 4/89	5	Y
November 89	Bear market starts 7/90	8	Y
April 92	Resolved 8/92	4	Y
February 94	Resolved 8/95	18	Y
February 96	Resolved 4/96	2	Y
May 97	Resolved 8/97	3	Y
May 98	Bear market starts 7/98	2	Y
October 98	Current		

Notes: Mean time to top (5 cases) = 4.4 months. Mean time to resolution (12 cases) = 5.7 months. Divergence occurs when the DJIA 90-day percentage change minus the NYSE 90-day A/D ratio rises above 8.0. Divergence ends when it is resolved or a bear market begins, whichever comes first. Resolution occurs when the DJIA minus the A/D difference falls to 1.2 or below. Time column indicates months from divergence date to resolution date or start of bear market. Rates declining column based on interest rate indicator shown in Figure 8–8.

MOMENTUM

Confirmation and divergence can also be assessed in terms of momentum, with confirmation consistent with improving momentum and divergence consistent with weakening momentum. A common method of gauging breadth momentum is to monitor the percentage of stocks in an index, such as the NYSE, that are above a widely watched moving average, such as a 200-day moving average. The breadth momentum confirms when the percentage breaks to new highs in conjunction with new highs in the major indexes, and it is divergent when its highs are lower highs. Alternatively, the approach can be applied to a group universe, with the breadth momentum measured by the percentage of groups above their moving averages.

Another way to gauge breadth momentum is to compare an A/D line to its moving average, the approach used in Figures 5–12 through 5–16. The S&P 500, for instance,

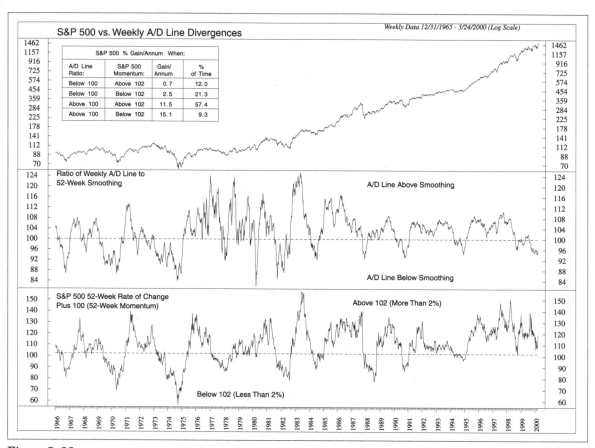

Figure 5–26

tends to perform better than normal when the NYSE weekly A/D line is above its 52-week moving average and worse than normal when it is below the smoothing.

In fact, the influence of the breadth momentum is greater than the influence of the momentum of the S&P 500 itself. The box in the upper left of Figure 5–26 indicates that when the A/D line's breadth momentum has been favorable, the S&P 500 has performed well regardless of the S&P 500's momentum, as measured by its 52-week rate of change. When the A/D line's breadth momentum has been unfavorable, the S&P 500 has performed poorly.

Moreover, under periods of weak breadth momentum, the S&P 500's performance has been worse when the rate of change has been greater than 2 percent than when the rate of change has been less than 2 percent, a fact attributable to the leading tendency of breadth. Weak breadth momentum is a portent of the developing market weakness that tends to occur when the S&P 500's momentum is still positive, but receding. By the time the S&P 500's momentum has turned negative, the market weakness has typically become so pervasive that a market bottom has started to appear on the horizon, with the subsequent market upturn occurring with the A/D indicator still negative, but rising. When the leading A/D indicator has reached positive levels with the lagging S&P 500 momentum gauge still negative, the most impressive gains have tended to occur, as shown by the 15 percent per annum gain with the A/D gauge above 100 and the momentum gauge below 102. Once the momentum has followed with a rise above 2 percent, it has been a good idea to keep an eye on the breadth gauge for evidence of divergence.

But this demonstration doesn't mean that the momentum of the S&P 500, or any other index, cannot be used to confirm developing trends. By using a shorter time frame, such as 4 weeks instead of 52, and by seeking to identify extremely high levels exclusively, you will be able to identify the momentum surges that occur in conjunction with breadth thrusts.

An alternative means toward that end is to compare a moving average of just a few periods with a moving average of more periods, an approach that produces less noise and volatility than the simple rate of change. Similar to the Moving Average Convergence-Divergence method developed by analyst Gerald Appel,[3] the indicator in Figure 5–27 can be used to identify reversals from overbought and oversold conditions. But it can also be used to identify surging momentum on both the upside and the downside. Figure 5–27 generates momentum thrust signals when the ratio of the Value Line Composite's two-day smoothing to its 16-day smoothing reaches 103, or 3 percent when expressed as a percentage. The indicator generates sell signals when the ratio drops below 97, or –3 percent.

Another momentum application is to remove the time consideration and look for gains of a specified percentage from an index's lows and declines of a specified percentage from an index's highs. More times than not, you will identify an emerging advance or a new decline, as the confirmation of reversals tends to perpetuate further momentum and a continuation of the new advance or decline. To recognize the market's upward bias over time, and the fact that a market is more likely to, for instance, rise by 100 percent than to fall by 100 percent (thus dropping to 0), you are likely to have better luck with an indicator that generates sell signals with a percent decline requirement that's shorter than the percent gain required for a buy signal. Examples include the S&P 500 reversal indicator in Figure 5–28 and the shorter-term Value Line Composite indicator in Figure 5–29.

VOLUME

The tape indicators shown thus far are examples within an immense range of possible indicators that use price action or breadth to identify confirmation and divergence. But the bullish assurance provided by confirmation and the bearish warnings provided by

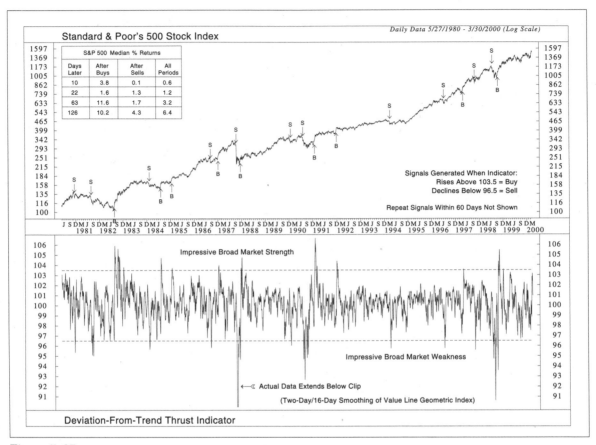

Figure 5–27

divergence can also result from the analysis of market volume, that is, the quantity of shares trading hands. It can serve this purpose because, like market breadth, volume has leading tendencies. In fact, as mentioned earlier, a Dow Theory cornerstone is that volume precedes price. The study of market volume is at the core of technical analysis.

As listed in Table 5–1 and shown in Figure 5–30, the weekly total of NYSE volume tends to lead market tops. Weekly volume has peaked in advance of 9 of the past 10 bull market peaks, indicating the significance of volume divergences. And the leading tendencies are also evident in Figure 5–31, which shows average daily volume. Wheareas the A/D line's downward bias lends greater significance to its confirming new highs, volume has an upward bias over time, which lends greater significance to volume divergences.

It should also be noted that extremely high volume occurs not only during healthy uptrends, when activity is expanding on the upside, but also at market lows, during pe-

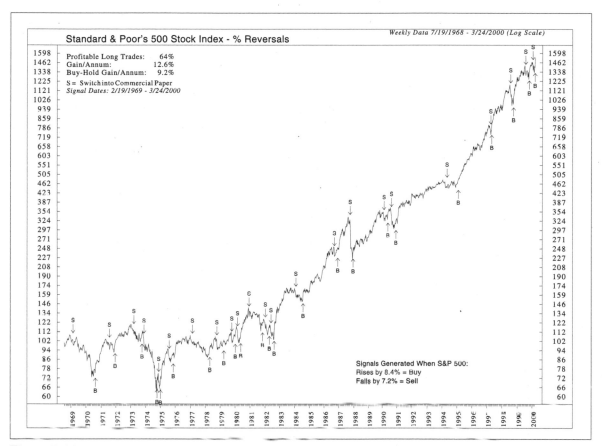

Figure 5–28

riods of extreme panic and frenzied selling. During the crash week of 1987, for example, the NYSE weekly volume total reached 2.3 billion shares, an extreme unmatched for nearly nine years. But in most cases, the volume high reached at a market bottom is surpassed by the volume high reached during the mature stages of the subsequent bull market, again in keeping with its upward bias over time. The key point to remember is that the market tends to perform well when volume is high relative to recent history, and it tends to perform poorly when volume is relatively weak.

It's also essential to keep an eye on the quality of the volume, whether the volume is sending the market shooting upward, crashing downward, or churning sideways. This requires a distinction between advancing volume, which is the volume in advancing stocks, versus declining volume, the volume in declining stocks. A rare and typically bullish development is the upside volume thrust evident when advancing volume ex-

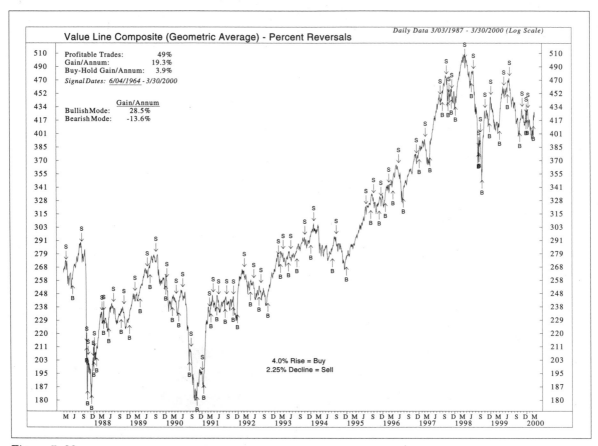

Figure 5–29

ceeds declining volume by 9 times, a development that often occurs in conjunction with a breadth thrust.

But such events, called *9-to-1 up days,* can also occur during continuing declines, as in January 1974 and early 1982, and near market tops, as occurred in 1976 and 1981. In Figure 5–32, 9-to-1 up days are indicated by the arrows without the Bs. The arrows with the Bs identify cases in which two 9-to-1 up days have occurred within three months without an intervening 9-to-1 down day, confirming that the advancing volume is in fact the sign of renewed buying interest and not a false signal. As shown in the chart, those signals have been followed by strong market gains, with the Dow Industrials up by a median of 17 percent over the subsequent six months.

Additional perspective can be gained by combining advancing and declining volume with the number of advancing and declining stocks, which is done in the calculation

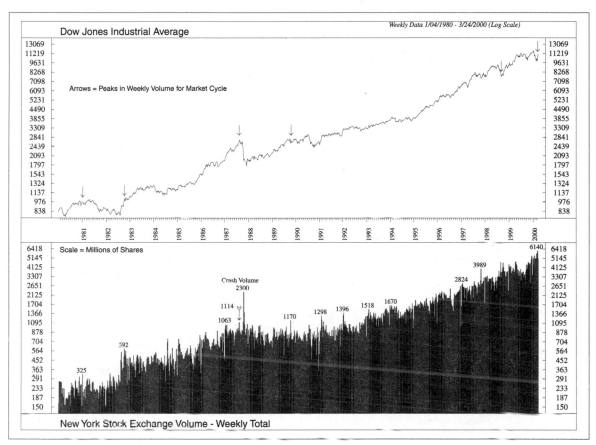

Figure 5–30

of the widely watched market Trading Index (TRIN). I will take a closer look at TRIN when discussing overbought/oversold indicators in Chapter 7, and that will follow a broader look at the market excesses that tend to occur around turning points, the focus of Chapter 6. Both chapters will discuss how to determine when the market has started to correct those excesses, thus addressing the Dow Theory tenet that a trend should be assumed to continue until a reversal has been confirmed.

CYCLES

But before moving on to the topic of market sentiment, another aspect of price action warrants attention: the market's cyclicality. As discussed earlier, historical tendencies are repetitive, which is why insights into the current market action can be gained by

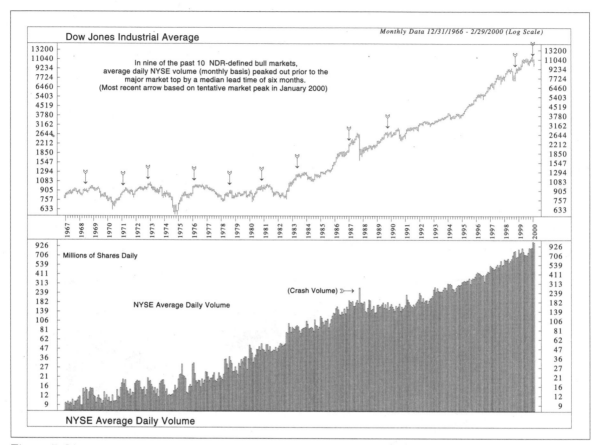

Figure 5–31

watching indicators based on the market's previous responses to like conditions and developments. Cycles recognize that the upward and downward price movements of the major averages tend to occur over similar lengths of time. Time similarities can be seen when looking at, for example, the bull and bear markets in Tables 1–5 and 1–4, tables indicating that the median bull market has lasted 614 days while the median bear market has lasted 363 days.

Cycles also recognize similar movement at specific times within a certain time frame, such as the market's tendency to rise in January. Cyclicality within the calendar year is generally called *seasonality,* indicated by the Dow Industrials' mean monthly change listed near the top of Figure 5–33 and by the percentage of times that the market has gained in each month, as noted in the chart's vertical bars. An alternative perspec-

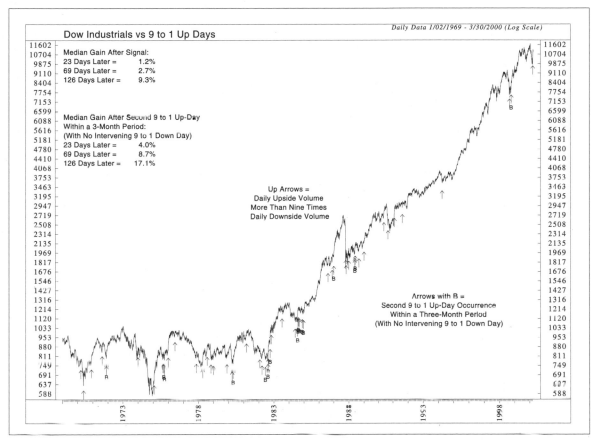

Figure 5–32

tive is shown in Figure 5–34, which plots the average annual pattern since 1900. And Table 5–6 uses the S&P 500's monthly average to rank the one-month gains, as well as the three-month and six-month gains. The impact of seasonality is evident in Table 5–7, which shows that a strategy of staying invested during the seasonally favorable May–September period would have beaten a strategy of investing during the unfavorable October–April period by a factor of 62.

   When the time frame is expanded from one year to four years, you can identify the market's position in what is known as the *four-year presidential cycle*. The cycle is plotted in Figure 5–35, with the year-by-year breakdown shown in Table 5–8. The cycle period is expanded even further in Figure 5–36, which shows the 10-year cycle, and the average performance by year of decade is shown in Table 5–9.

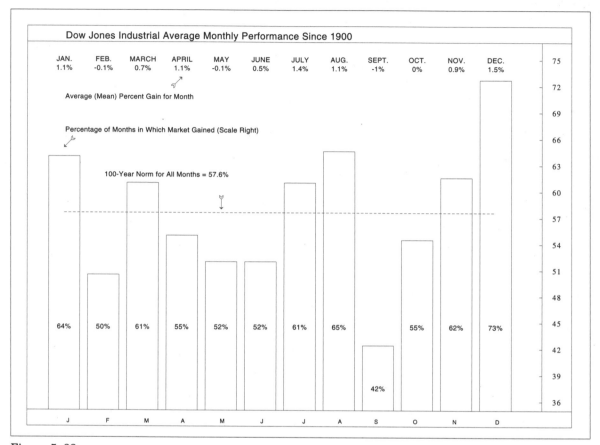

Figure 5–33

In evaluating the 10-year cycle, however, you should consider the wide range in the annual returns by year of decade, as the decade's third year, for example, has included four double-digit down years as well as four double-digit up years. And while there's some rationale to the differing gains during different times of the year and the presidential year, there's no rationale for differing gains during different years of the decade. Also recognize that for a given span of time, the shorter the cycle, the more cases used in calculating the averages, a plus from the standpoint of statistical significance.

Yet, recognizing its limitations, the 10-year cycle can be combined with the four-year and one-year cycles to create a composite forecast for the year ahead. Since Ned Davis began featuring the annual cycle composite in the 1980s, it has indicated sev-

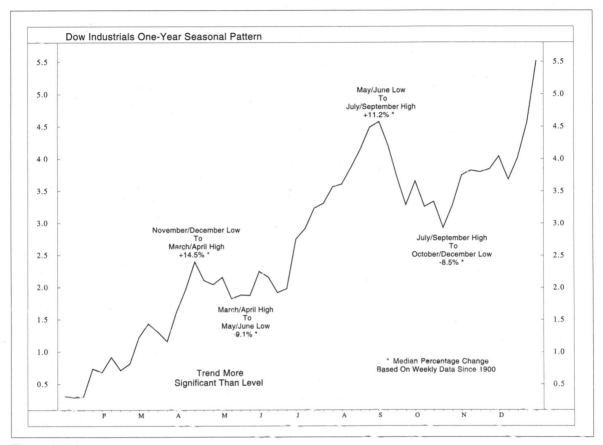

Figure 5–34

eral major turning points with surprising accuracy. If you are serious about using cycles as an integral part of your analytical process, I would suggest tapping into the vast body of knowledge that has been built around cycle research, organized by the Foundation for the Study of Cycles.[4]

Again, the starting point for analysis of the market tape, and for market analysis in general, should be a thorough assessment of the market's underlying health, as measured by indicators that identify confirmation, divergence, and the strength of the market's breadth. You will then be able to determine whether supply is building relative to demand, thereby threatening stock prices, or whether demand is outpacing supply, keeping the uptrend well intact. And you will keep yourself aligned with the primary trend.

T A B L E   5–6

Seasonality of Standard & Poor's 500 Monthly Average (1900–02/29/2000)

Six-Month Gains

Period	Since 1900		Since 1952		Since 1982	
	Mean	Rank	Mean	Rank	Mean	Rank
August–January	3.76	4	4.48	7	5.34	9
September–February	3.28	9	5.30	6	7.46	6
October–March	3.54	7	6.43	3	9.22	4
November–April	4.36	2	7.44	1	9.87	3
December–May	4.42	1	6.97	2	10.22	1
January–June	4.15	3	6.15	4	10.03	2
February–July	3.44	8	5.31	5	9.17	5
March–August	3.73	5	4.24	8	6.66	7
April–September	3.55	6	3.22	10	5.55	8
May–October	2.72	12	2.18	12	4.75	11
June–November	2.79	11	2.74	11	4.43	12
July–December	3.22	10	3.71	9	4.95	10

Three-Month Gains

Period	Since 1900		Since 1952		Since 1982	
	Mean	Rank	Mean	Rank	Mean	Rank
November–January	2.66	3	4.16	1	4.80	4
December–February	2.88	1	4.06	2	5.69	2
January–March	2.77	2	3.89	3	5.95	1
February–April	1.54	7	3.13	4	4.99	3
March–May	1.30	8	2.59	5	3.89	6
April–June	1.26	9	2.06	7	3.75	7
May–July	1.84	6	2.02	8	3.94	5
June–August	2.40	5	1.56	9	2.68	9
July–September	2.47	4	1.08	11	1.76	11
August–October	0.93	10	0.17	12	0.95	12
September–November	0.35	12	1.20	10	1.99	10
October–December	0.75	11	2.59	6	3.27	8

One-Month Gains

Period	Since 1900		Since 1952		Since 1982	
	Mean	Rank	Mean	Rank	Mean	Rank
January	1.77	1	1.65	1	1.74	2
February	0.45	6	0.99	6	2.25	1
March	0.43	7	1.01	4	1.41	5
April	0.58	4	0.99	5	0.92	9
May	0.17	10	0.56	8	1.52	4
June	0.23	9	0.43	9	1.28	7
July	1.25	2	0.94	7	1.03	8
August	0.93	3	0.17	10	0.37	10
September	0.14	11	−0.10	12	0.36	11
October	−0.24	12	0.03	11	0.12	12
November	0.29	8	1.21	3	1.31	6
December	0.57	5	1.28	2	1.63	3

Note: Gains are mean percentage changes in the S&P 500 monthly average.

T A B L E   5–7

Seasonal Switching Strategy 1950–1999

Year	S&P % Change May 1– Sept. 30	Investing $10,000	S&P % Change Oct. 1– April 30	Investing $10,000	Year	S&P % Change May 1– Sept. 30	Investing $10,000	S&P % Change Oct. 1– April 30	Investing $10,000
1950	7.64	10764	15.32	11532	1976	3.54	8037	−6.46	67780
1951	3.70	11162	0.26	11562	1977	−1.94	7881	0.31	67991
1952	5.23	11746	0.33	11600	1978	5.90	8346	−0.76	67474
1953	−5.16	11140	21.03	14039	1979	7.43	8966	−2.77	65604
1954	14.33	12737	17.49	16494	1980	18.04	10583	5.86	69447
1955	15.04	14652	10.79	18273	1981	−12.52	9258	0.22	69603
1956	−6.26	13735	0.86	18430	1982	3.42	9574	36.54	95034
1957	−7.26	12738	2.40	18873	1983	1.00	9671	−3.62	91589
1958	15.24	14679	15.04	21712	1984	3.78	10036	8.27	99160
1959	−1.23	14498	−4.41	20754	1985	1.25	10162	29.35	128264
1960	−1.56	14271	22.03	25325	1986	−1.78	9980	24.66	159892
1961	2.17	14582	−2.23	24760	1987	11.61	11130	−18.80	129834
1962	−13.75	12577	24.04	30713	1988	4.05	11590	13.88	147850
1963	2.72	12919	10.82	34037	1989	12.76	13069	−5.26	140079
1964	5.94	13687	5.86	36031	1990	−7.48	12091	22.64	171798
1965	0.95	13817	1.22	36471	1991	3.33	12494	6.98	183797
1966	−15.92	11617	22.79	44784	1992	0.69	12580	5.36	193647
1967	2.87	11951	0.91	45192	1993	4.26	13115	−1.75	190263
1968	5.21	12573	0.99	45641	1994	2.61	13458	11.24	211654
1969	−10.19	11291	−12.46	39955	1995	13.54	15280	11.94	236919
1970	3.30	11664	23.44	49321	1996	5.07	16054	16.59	276225
1971	−5.40	11034	9.49	54001	1997	18.21	18978	17.36	324184
1972	2.67	11329	−3.24	52252	1998	−8.52	17361	31.28	425605
1973	1.36	11484	−16.71	43520	1999	−3.93	16679	N/A	N/A
1974	−29.64	8080	37.39	59794	**Net gain since**				
1975	−3.93	7762	21.19	72463	**1950**		**$6,679**		**$415,605**

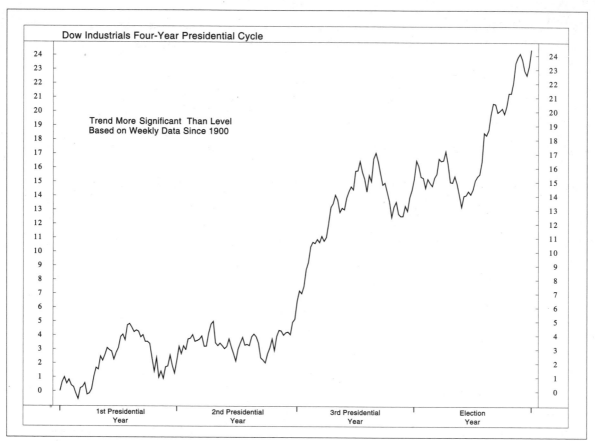

Figure 5–35

T A B L E 5–8

Presidential Cycle (12/31/1888–12/31/1999)

President Elected	Party	Four-Year Cycle Beginning	Election Year	Post-Election Year	Midterm Year	Pre-Election Year
Harrison	R	1888	−2.5	3.5	−13.5	17.6
Cleveland	D	1892	1.8	−20.0	−2.5	0.5
McKinley	R	1896	−2.3	12.6	18.9	6.5
McKinley*	R	1900	14.1	15.7	1.3	−18.4
T. Roosevelt	R	1904	25.6	15.6	3.1	−33.2
Taft	R	1908	37.4	14.1	−12.1	0.7
Wilson	D	1912	3.0	−14.3	−8.6	29.0
Wilson	D	1916	3.4	−30.6	16.2	14.0
Harding*	R	1920	−24.5	7.4	20.9	−1.5
Coolidge	R	1924	18.7	21.9	5.7	30.9
Hoover	R	1928	37.9	−11.9	−28.5	−47.1
F. Roosevelt	D	1932	−15.1	46.6	−5.9	41.4
F. Roosevelt	D	1936	27.9	−38.6	25.2	−5.5
F. Roosevelt	D	1940	−15.3	−17.9	12.4	19.4
F. Roosevelt*	D	1944	13.8	30.7	−11.9	0.0
Truman	D	1948	−0.7	10.3	21.8	16.5
Eisenhower	R	1952	11.8	−6.6	45.0	26.4
Eisenhower	R	1956	2.6	−14.3	38.1	8.5
Kennedy*	D	1960	−3.0	23.1	−11.8	18.9
Johnson	D	1964	13.0	9.1	−13.1	20.1
Nixon	R	1968	7.7	−11.4	0.1	10.8
Nixon[†]	R	1972	15.6	−17.4	−29.7	31.5
Carter	D	1976	19.1	−11.5	1.1	12.3
Reagan	R	1980	25.8	−9.7	14.8	17.3
Reagan	R	1984	1.4	26.3	14.6	2.0
Bush	R	1988	12.4	27.3	−6.6	26.3
Clinton	D	1992	4.5	7.1	−1.5	34.1
Clinton	D	1996	20.3	31.0	26.7	19.5
Up years/total years %			**75.0**	**57.1**	**57.1**	**78.6**
Total percentage gain			**254.4**	**98.1**	**120.2**	**298.5**
Mean gain per year			**9.1**	**3.5**	**4.3**	**10.7**
Median gain per year			**9.8**	**7.2**	**1.2**	**15.2**

Notes: Percentage change from year to year based on Standard & Poor's 500 Stock Index. Before 1919 study uses S&P 500 monthly average prices (based on Cowles Commission estimates). After 1919, study uses S&P 500 closing prices. *Death in office; [†]Resigned; D = Democrat; R = Republican.

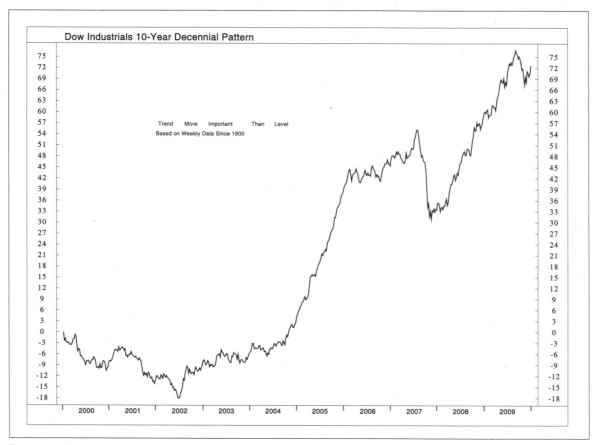

Figure 5–36

T A B L E   5–9

Standard & Poor's 500 Stock Index Gains per Year (%)

Decade	| 1st	2d	3d	4th	5th	6th	7th	8th	9th	10th
					Year of Decade					
1881–1890						8.5	−6.6	−2.5	3.5	−13.5
1891–1900	17.6	1.8	−20.0	−2.5	0.5	−2.3	12.6	18.9	6.5	14.1
1901–1910	15.7	1.3	−18.4	25.6	15.6	3.1	−33.2	37.4	14.1	−12.1
1911–1920	0.7	3.0	−14.3	−8.6	29.0	3.4	−30.6	16.2	14.0	−24.5
1921–1930	7.4	20.9	−1.5	18.7	21.9	5.7	30.9	37.9	−11.9	−28.5
1931–1940	−47.1	−15.1	46.6	−5.9	41.4	27.9	−38.6	25.2	−5.5	−15.3
1941–1950	−17.9	12.4	19.4	13.8	30.7	−11.9	0.0	−0.7	10.3	21.8
1951–1960	16.5	11.8	−6.6	45.0	26.4	2.6	−14.3	38.1	8.5	−3.0
1961–1970	23.1	−11.8	18.9	13.0	9.1	−13.1	20.1	7.7	−11.4	0.1
1971–1980	10.8	15.6	−17.4	−29.7	31.5	19.1	−11.5	1.1	12.3	25.8
1981–1990	−9.7	14.8	17.3	1.4	26.3	14.6	2.0	12.4	27.3	−6.6
1991–1999	26.3	4.5	7.1	−1.5	34.1	20.3	31.0	26.7	19.5	
Mean	**3.9**	**5.4**	**2.8**	**6.3**	**24.2**	**6.5**	**−3.2**	**18.2**	**7.3**	**−3.5**
Total	**43.4**	**59.1**	**31.2**	**69.2**	**266.5**	**78.0**	**−38.2**	**218.4**	**87.2**	**−41.7**
Number of Observations	**11**	**11**	**11**	**11**	**11**	**12**	**12**	**12**	**12**	**11**

Notes: S&P 500 monthly average prior to 1919 based on estimates from Cowles Commission. Starting 1919 table uses S&P 500 closing prices.

E N D N O T E S

1. Dan Sullivan, *The Chartist,* P.O. Box 758, Seal Beach, CA, 90740

2. Sherman McClellan, Sherman McClellan & Associates, 2250 Moreno Dr., Los Angeles, CA 90039

3. Gerald Appel, Signalert Corp., 150 Great Neck Road, Great Neck, NY 11021

4. Foundation for the Study of Cycles, 214 Carnegie Center, Suite 204, Princeton, NJ 08540

REFERENCES

Edwards, Robert D., and John Magee. 1991. *Technical Analysis of Stock Trends.* Enhanced Ed. Boston: International Technical Analysis.

thesized, weighed and finally expressed in the one precise figure at which a buyer and seller get together and make a deal." When the hopes and guesses reach their extreme of optimism, the market reaches a top, as the market's liquidity is insufficient for further gains. When the fears and moods reach their extreme of pessimism, the market bottoms out, as the market's liquidity creates a buffer against further weakness.

In *Being Right or Making Money* (1991), Ned Davis explains the relationships between optimism and illiquidity and pessimism and liquidity: "Think of an extreme in liquidity as the direct opposite of an extreme in psychology. If everyone decided that the Dow Industrials would rise . . . they would rush out and buy stocks. Everyone would become fully invested, the market would be overbought, and nobody would be left to buy, in which case the market wouldn't be able to go any higher. . . . On the other hand, if everyone was pessimistic . . . the weak and nervous stockholders would sell, the market would be sold-out, and nobody would be left to sell, in which case the market wouldn't go down any more. Whereas increasing optimism and confidence produce falling liquidity, rising pessimism and fear result in rising liquidity."

To illustrate how market peaks tend to form in the midst of extremely optimistic popular opinion and how market troughs tend to occur in conjunction with extremely pessimistic popular opinion, Davis's book expanded upon the work of analyst Paul Montgomery[1] to show how the cover stories of major news magazines have been contrarian indicators. Davis showed that when a bull has appeared on a magazine cover, the advance has often been in its final stage, whereas a bear on a cover has been a precursor to a new bull market.

SENTIMENT EXTREMES

The evidence of public sentiment can, in fact, take many forms. This was apparent in the 1990s, when the stock market's popularity exploded in tandem with its remarkable run of outperformance. The S&P 500 gained 15 percent per annum during the decade versus its historical return of 7 percent per annum since 1926. And during the decade there appeared to be a growing tendency for soap operas, talk shows, and sporting events to be replaced by CNBC and its moving ticker on daytime TVs in public venues, such as lunch counters, waiting rooms, and furniture stores. The decade also saw the creation of the TheStreet.com and its many clones, all benefiting from the revolutionary incursion of the Internet into daily life. For most of the time, these various vendors of financial news carried bullish headlines, keeping the public's interest rising in conjunction with their expanding paper profits. "Record high in the Dow," a phrase that could not once be used between 1929 and 1953, became a common part of the market vocabulary, with 1995 including 69 records. That averaged out to a record high every 3.7 trading days, or more than one a week.

Also phenomenal is the fact that none of the decade's years included fewer than 10 record highs. Figure 6–1 shows how the century ended with an unprecedented number of record highs. Like an athlete on drugs that mask the body's warnings that it's time to slow down, the stock market fed on the public's fascination with easy profits. The euphoria enabled the market to defy its historical tendency to consolidate after periods of strength. The chart's box indicates that while the Dow Industrials tend to post strong gains in years with record highs, the subsequent years have typically been weak. Considered at the time a new rule of the "new paradigm" and the "new economy," history will show that the 1990s were a truly exceptional exception to the rule, as we will see a reversion back to the norm of fewer and more sporadic record highs.

In fact, early signs of the reversion process became evident in the second half of the decade, as they were in the late 1920s and late 1960s. In each period, the peak in record highs indicated a peak in long-term momentum. The 1925 peak in records culminated a quarter century of gains that accrued in conjunction with the country's emergence as an industrial power, and the record highs diminished as the momentum carried the advance into 1929. The 1964 peak in records marked the peak of a postwar consumer boom

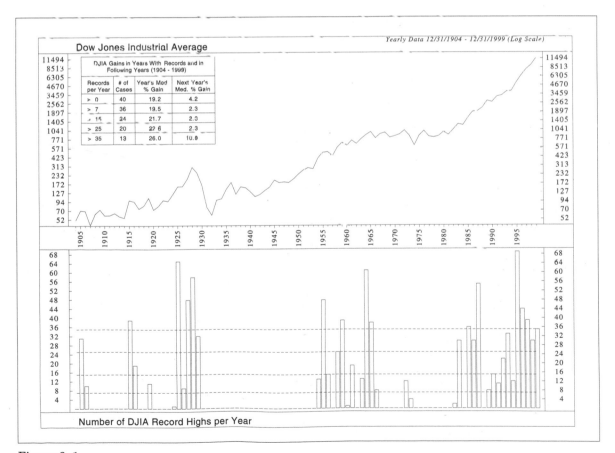

Figure 6–1

that likewise carried the market into the early 1970s with fewer records, as glaring breadth divergences warned of the market's inevitable demise. Likewise, the 1995 peak in records represented the pinnacle of momentum associated with the boom of information technology and new paradigm productivity enhancements. Two years later, the market breadth reached a long-term peak along with several measures of sentiment. And by 1999 the divergence had become glaring enough for me to provide clients with a special report on 40 signs of a sentiment peak, featuring indicators of breadth, sentiment, and others. A continuing return to normality was all but inevitable as the century drew to a close.

Of the sentiment extremes prevalent near the end of the decade, none was as telling as the extreme in stocks as a percentage of household financial assets, shown in Figure 6–2. Household stock ownership ended 1999 at record of 43 percent, nearly double its 40-year

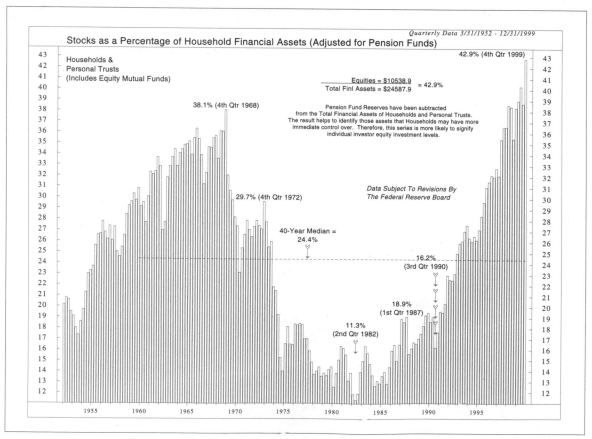

Figure 6–2

norm and nearly triple its levels around the market lows of 1990. Throughout the decade, the percentage rose steadily as the market was able to maintain a long-term uptrend, fend off major bear market threats and assure the public that the stock market was a safe place for their savings. Investment clubs grew in popularity, as the public sought ways to take advantage of the market uptrend and enhance their stock selection. From a total of about 7000 at the beginning of the decade, the number of clubs rose by nearly six times to a total of more than 36,000 at the end of the decade, as shown in Figure 6–3.

More significantly, the public found mutual funds to be an easy way to take part in this stock market boom, and inflows surged, as shown in Figure 6–4. The rising inflows themselves helped perpetuate the market's rise, as well as the growth of the mutual fund industry. And as the fund industry grew and became more competitive, the public flocked into 401-k plans offering index funds and other mutual fund choices.

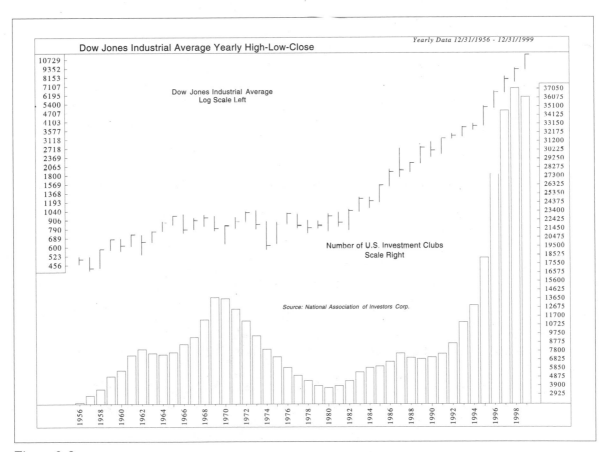

Figure 6–3

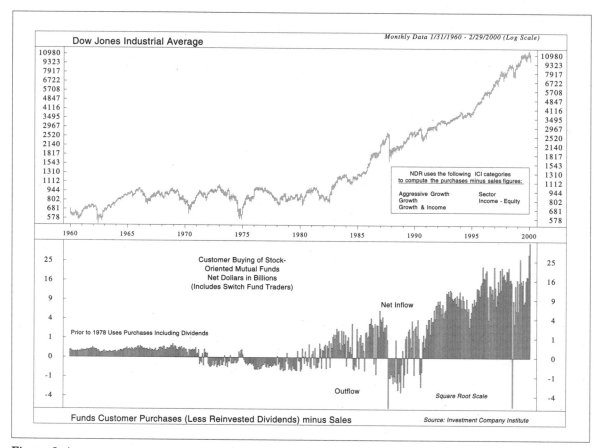

Figure 6–4

It wasn't long before index funds were taking on the appearance of the passbook savings accounts of earlier days, and viewed as such by a public that had forgotten about the potential for major bear markets and capital depreciation. After all, the market had snapped back from the 1987 crash, and it had been more than 15 years since a bear market of even 100 days. Why not save for the future by taking the low-risk buy-and-hold approach of sending part of each paycheck into an index fund of large-cap growth stocks with steady earnings and plenty of staying power?

By the end of the decade, this attitude had created a huge gap between capitalization-weighted indices like the NASDAQ Composite, dominated by big growth stocks like Microsoft and Intel, and broader market indices like the Value Line Composite, small-cap indices, and breadth gauges. The breadth divergences and narrow leadership were their most prominent since the late 1960s, when household stock ownership

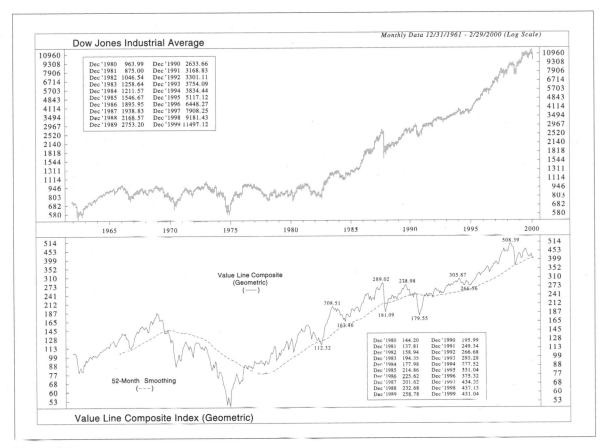

Figure 6–5

peaked, the large-cap "Nifty 50" dominated, and the stage was set for the rocky period of ongoing breadth divergence that culminated in the 1973–1974 bear market. The divergence between the major averages and the broad, geometrically averaged Value Line Composite began to look like it did in the earlier period, as shown in Figure 6–5 and as I discussed in the context of breadth in Chapter 5.

EXCESSIVE VALUATION

Even more dramatic in the late 1990s than in the early 1970s was the willingness of investors, both public and institutional, to bid stocks to extremely high valuation multiples, in many cases unprecedented and astronomical. This was reflected by the S&P 500 price to trailing 12-month earnings ratio using the bottom-line earnings that corpora-

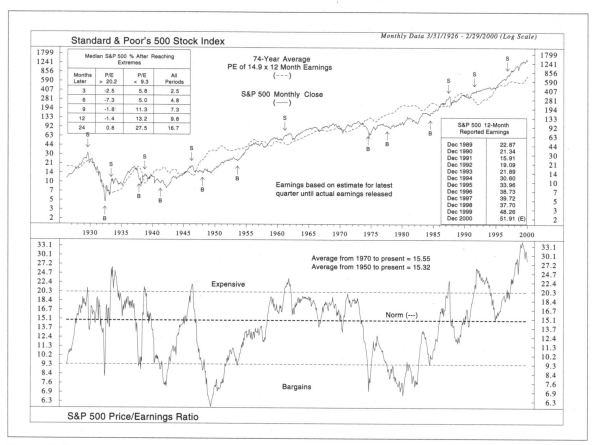

Figure 6–6

tions report in their financial statements, shown in Figure 6–6. And it was also indicated by the S&P 500 price to operating earnings ratio, which has a higher denominator
since operating earnings exclude the write-offs that depress reported earnings. That ratio is shown in Figure 6–7.

The extremely high earnings multiples were a sign of widespread optimism and an
attitude of complacency toward the potential for more than corrective downside price action. A return to record highs was a given. And the so-called buy the dip mentality fos-
tered an environment in which growth stocks remained in vogue despite price-to-earnings ratios that rose to levels that were increasingly distant from their historical norms.
The market was discounting future earnings growth that, apparently because of "new
paradigm" productivity gains, was expected to maintain its strength indefinitely.

A view also arose that the equity risk premium had vanished, and this became the
basis for lofty projections for the future level of the Dow Industrials. Traditionally, stock

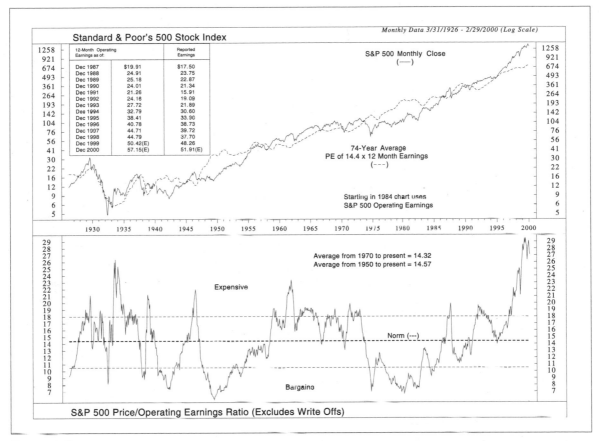

Figure 6–7

market analysts have assigned a 2 percent risk premium to stocks over a long-term bond yield, accounting for the justifiable view that stocks are more risky than bonds. The yield plus the risk premium equals the required rate of return. And that rate of return is the discount rate that's plugged into dividend discount models, which are popular tools among the Wall Street fundamental analysts whose stock forecasts can influence rapid price swings. Let's take a closer look at how they work.

Dividend Discount Models

Essentially, the purpose of a dividend discount model is to determine a stock's value by using the required return (again, the bond yield plus the risk premium) to discount all future cash flows back to the present, a process that can occur once an expected annualized growth rate of dividends is determined. All else being equal, a relatively low discount rate held down by a low risk premium, combined with a relatively high dividend growth rate, produces a relatively high valuation, indicating that high prices are justified. This can be seen using the standard dividend discount model formula that P (the current market price) equals $D1$ (next year's dividend based on the expected dividend growth rate G) divided by R (the required rate of return) minus G (the dividend growth rate), or $P = D1/(R - G)$. The higher a stock's price above its valuation, the greater its overvaluation and the greater the risk of a price decline. The lower a stock's price below its valuation, the greater its undervaluation and the greater the potential for rising prices.

Table 6–1 illustrates how a dividend discount model can be applied to the S&P 500, stemming from an estimate for expected 12-month reported earnings. With the earnings estimate, next year's dividend can be derived by multiplying the estimate by the historical dividend payout ratio, which is the ratio of dividends to earnings. This example uses a payout ratio of 50 percent, which tells us that historically, S&P 500 companies have paid out half of their earnings as dividends. The market's value can then be determined based on whatever discount rate and growth rate you select.

As you can see, there's no shortage of guessing going on here. First of all, you need an earnings estimate, something that only the most ambitious can hope to derive without help from a professional analyst. Among Wall Street institutions, it's common to see entire departments dedicated to valuation estimates on individual companies, yet even among the pros the margin of error is vast. Standard & Poor's compiles analyst estimates to determine consensus estimates, and those numbers can facilitate attempts to determine the S&P 500's valuation. But rarely are those estimates on target.

The guesswork continues as the expected earnings estimate is used to derive the dividend payout by applying the historical dividend payout ratio. During the 1990s, the dividend payout ratio steadily dropped, rendering useless the price-to-dividend ratio (often cited in its inverse form as the dividend yield). In fact, this is why the dividend payout ratio in Table 6–1 emanates from earnings, not dividends. If rather than a 50 percent payout ratio, you would apply the five-year average of 40 percent, your expected payout would be lower, as would your valuation resulting from the dividend discount model.

The problem with using dividends at all was elucidated by professors Eugene Fama and Kenneth French (1999), who related the waning importance of dividends to profitability and the growth in the number of publicly traded companies. They pointed out that in 1978, 67 percent of public companies paid dividends, and no more than 10 percent of all companies were unprofitable. By the end of the century, the percentage of dividend-paying companies had dwindled to just 21 percent, while the percentage of unprofitable companies had risen to 30 percent. Moreover, from 1963 to 1997, the assets of companies that had never paid a dividend grew by an average of 16 percent a year on average, while the assets of dividend-paying companies grew by an average of 9 percent per year.

These statistics suggests that rapid growth and profitability have been consistent with low or nonexistent dividend payouts while slow growth and a lack of profitability

T A B L E 6–1

Dividend Discount Model–Standard & Poor's 500 Stock Index
Estimated earnings* = $51.92; payout ratio† = 50%; "payout"‡ = $25.96

Long-Term Earnings Growth Rate, %	Discount Rate§																
	6.00%	6.25%	6.50%	6.75%	7.00%	7.25%	7.50%	7.75%	8.00%	8.25%	8.50%	8.75%	9.00%	9.25%	9.50%	9.75%	10.00%
3.00	865	799	742	692	649	611	577	547	519	494	472	451	433	415	399	385	371
4.00	1298	1154	1038	944	865	799	742	692	649	611	577	547	519	494	472	451	433
4.50	1731	1483	1298	1154	1038	944	865	799	742	692	649	611	577	547	519	494	472
4.75	2077	1731	1483	1298	1154	1038	944	865	799	742	692	649	611	577	547	519	494
5.00	2596	2077	1731	1483	1298	1154	1038	944	865	799	742	692	649	611	577	547	519
5.25		2596	2077	1731	1483	1298	1154	1038	944	865	799	742	692	649	611	577	547
5.50		3461	2596	2077	1731	1483	1298	1154	1038	944	865	799	742	692	649	611	577
5.75			3461	2596	2077	1731	1483	1298	1154	1038	944	865	799	742	692	649	611
6.00				3461	2596	2077	1731	1483	1298	1154	1038	944	865	799	742	692	649
6.25					3461	2596	2077	1731	1483	1298	1154	1038	944	865	799	742	692
6.50						3461	2596	2077	1731	1483	1298	1154	1038	944	865	799	742
6.75							3461	2596	2077	1731	1483	1298	1154	1038	944	865	799
7.00								3461	2596	2077	1731	1483	1298	1154	1038	944	865
7.50										3461	2596	2077	1731	1483	1298	1154	1038
8.00												3461	2596	2077	1731	1483	1298

Note: Price = next year's payout divided by (discount rate − growth rate). A standard risk premium used in practice is 2 percent over long-term Treasuries. All rates shown are nominal rates. The long-term average annual growth rates of reported earnings per share for the S&P 500 are: since 1926: 5.10 percent; since 1950: 6.20 percent; since 1960: 6.90 percent; since 1970: 7.50 percent; since 1980: 6.00 percent; since 1990: 8.60 percent.

* Estimate for reported earnings per share from S&P for Q4 2000.

† The assumed payout ratio is based on the long-term average dividend payout ratio.

‡ The "payout" (EPS × payout ratio) is the cash assumed to be returned to shareholders, either via cash dividends or share repurchases.

§ The discount rate is generally a long-term Treasury rate plus a risk premium for stocks.

have been consistent with relatively high dividends, in keeping with the uptrend in growth indices versus value indices during the 1990s. To Fama and French, the statistics reflect a disenchantment with dividends by the growing ranks of new public companies finding the need to enhance their growth by reinvesting earnings rather than paying them out as dividends. The tendency had a greater impact as the number of public companies exploded, evident in the uptrends in stock offerings and issues traded during the 1990s.

But Fama and French also pointed out that the dwindling interest in dividends was no less evident among large firms, which is the message of the dropping dividend payout ratio in Figure 6–8. Concurrent developments were the growth in share repurchase programs, sometimes called *dividend surrogates* since they enabled management to reward shareholders by repurchasing stock rather than paying dividends, and cash-for-stock merger and acquisition activity, which rewarded the shareholders of target firms with a "liquidating dividend." The retirement of stock was itself a bullish influence from a supply/demand standpoint, as I will discuss later. Throughout the 1990s, capital appreciation was king, and companies knew that they would be more attractive to investors by doing what they could to enable investors to benefit from that growth. If the market had been going nowhere, the stable income from dividends would be more appealing.

Given the diminished role played by dividends and the resulting problems in using them to measure valuation, an alternative approach is to simply ignore dividends altogether, instead focusing on earnings. When this is done, it is generally preferable to use operating earnings rather than reported earnings, which are subject to accounting gimmicks. When a nonrecurring write-off reduces the bottom line in one year but not in the next, the year-to-year change in earnings will rise even if the firm's profitability did not improve. Since operating earnings assess the profit picture as if the write-offs were never taken, they are less prone to presenting a distorted picture of earnings growth.

However, analysts may seek even more clarity by moving their focus higher up on the income statement and assessing income prior to depreciation, amortization, interest, and taxes, known by the acronym of EBITDA (earnings before interest, taxes, depreciation, and amortization) and generally referred to as *cash flow*. What complicates this analysis are the numerous definitions of cash flow and its various calculations. Reported and operating earnings better lend themselves to comparisons among companies (known as *cross-sectional analysis*). And when looking at the S&P 500, reported earnings have the advantage of a data history that dates back to the 1920s.

A User-Friendly Alternative

To reduce the need for estimates and determine the market's valuation without the need to use dividends, I prefer a user-friendly alternative to the dividend discount model, the

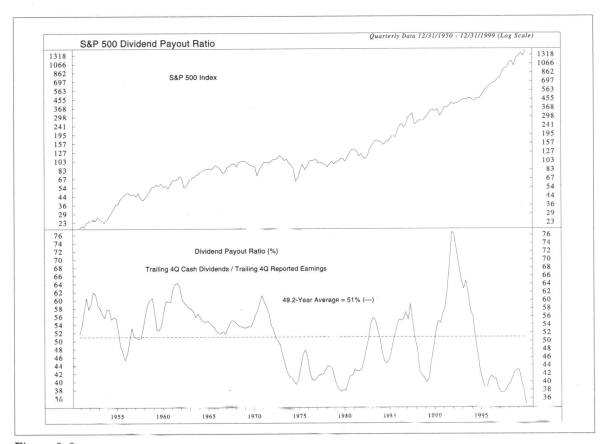

Figure 6–8

ratio of the long bond yield to the S&P 500 earnings yield. In Figure 6–9, the ratio uses reported earnings and a composite long bond yield, though viable alternatives would be a 30-year bond yield, a 10-year note yield, or a T-bill yield, as shown in Figure 6–10. When the ratio is extremely high, it indicates that investors are optimistic about future earnings growth and thus willing to pay high prices despite the relatively attractive income that could be guaranteed by purchasing a bond, note, or bill. In 1999 the bond yield was twice as high as the earnings yield, indicating that investors saw limited downside and unlimited upside. In reality, in contrast to the expectations, the ratio indicated limited upside, unlimited room for disappointment, and substantial downside. In other words, the extremely high bond yield to earnings yield ratio indicated an extremely high risk/reward ratio.

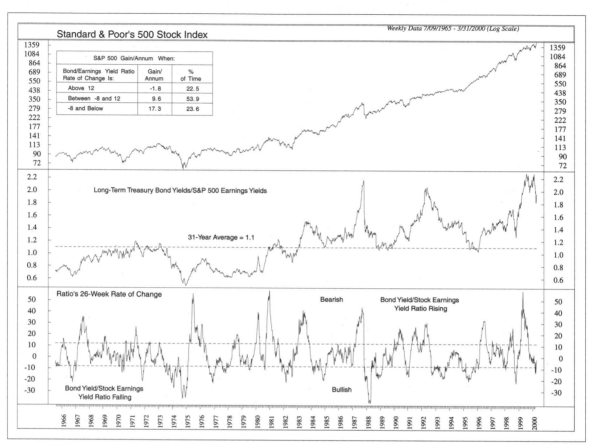

Figure 6–9

In fact, if the ratio is compared to its 10-year norm, it can be used like a dividend discount model, though unfortunately, you must again rely on assumptions. In this case, the assumption is that the market would be fairly valued at the ratio's 10-year average and that the ratio would not be likely to exceed its previous highs or lows. When overvalued conditions are indicated by an extremely high ratio, the maximum upside potential is represented by the ratio's 10-year high while the downside risk is represented by the ratio's 10-year norm. When undervalued conditions are indicated by an extremely low ratio, the maximum downside potential is indicated by the ratio's 10-year low while the upside reward is represented by the 10-year norm.

By holding the bond yield and earnings constant, you can determine the S&P 500 level that would return the ratio to the norm, or you can make that calculation after first plugging in bond yield and year-ahead earnings estimates. Similar to the dividend discount model in Table 6–1, this valuation approach lends itself to a matrix, as shown in

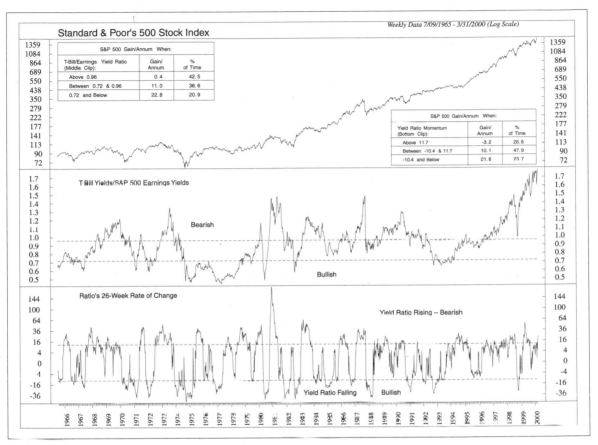

Figure 6-10

Table 6–2. The matrix enables you to see the variations in the risk levels, reward levels, and price changes needed to reach fair value, variations that occur with changes in the bond yield and current or expected earnings. Also note that the ratio's secular trends can be normalized with a 26-week rate of change, which illustrates shorter-term extremes, as shown in the bottom clips of Figures 6–9 and 6–10.

Other Valuation Indicators

Yet another spin on the valuation question can be provided by an indicator similar to the model that Fed Chairman Alan Greenspan discussed in a July 1997 monetary policy report to Congress. This model is based on the historical tendency for the S&P 500 earnings yield (S&P 500 earnings/S&P 500) to track the 10-year Treasury note yield, using the consensus estimate for year-ahead earnings. If the earnings yield equals the interest

T A B L E 6–2

Bond Yield/Earnings Yield Ratio
Estimated Earnings (12/2000)* $51.92

Bond Yield/ Earnings Yield Ratio	S&P 500 Value When Long-Term Treasury Yield† Is:								
	5.50%	5.75%	6.00%	6.25%	6.50%	6.75%	7.00%	7.25%	7.50%
2.2	2077	1987	1904	1828	1757	1692	1632	1576	1523
2.1	1982	1896	1817	1745	1677	1615	1558	1504	1454
2.0	1888	1806	1731	1661	1598	1538	1483	1432	1385
1.9	1794	1716	1644	1578	1518	1461	1409	1361	1315
1.8	1699	1625	1558	1495	1438	1385	1335	1289	1246
1.7	1605	1535	1471	1412	1358	1308	1261	1217	1177
1.6	1510	1445	1385	1329	1278	1231	1187	1146	1108
1.5	1416	1354	1298	1246	1198	1154	1113	1074	1038
1.4	1322	1264	1211	1163	1118	1077	1038	1003	969
1.3	1227	1174	1125	1080	1038	1000	964	931	900
1.2	1133	1084	1038	997	959	923	890	859	831
1.1	1038	993	952	914	879	846	816	788	761
1.0	944	903	865	831	799	769	742	716	692

* Estimate from S&P.
†Composite of Treasury yields maturing in more than 10 years.

rate, then price times the interest rate should equal earnings. So when the terms are rearranged to solve for earnings, an implied earnings level can be plotted, indicated in Figure 6–11 as the solid line in the middle clip. When the implied earnings are more than 25 percent above the estimated earnings, the indicator shows the market overvalued; when the implied earnings are below the estimate, the market is considered undervalued.

Earnings are such a reflection of investor sentiment that risk and reward can even be assessed using earnings alone. Figure 6–12 shows that when earnings growth is high and euphoria omnipresent, the market tends to perform poorly. When earnings growth is weak and fear abundant, the market tends to perform well. This is evident when comparing the year-to-year earnings growth rate to its 60-month moving average, shown in the middle clip.

The differing performance also reflects the degree to which the market discounts the future. The strongest gains tend to occur when an earnings recovery is expected. By the time the "news is out" and the earnings momentum is in full gear, the market has discounted the news and has started to look ahead to the next decline in earnings momentum. This forward-looking tendency can also be seen in the chart's bottom clip,

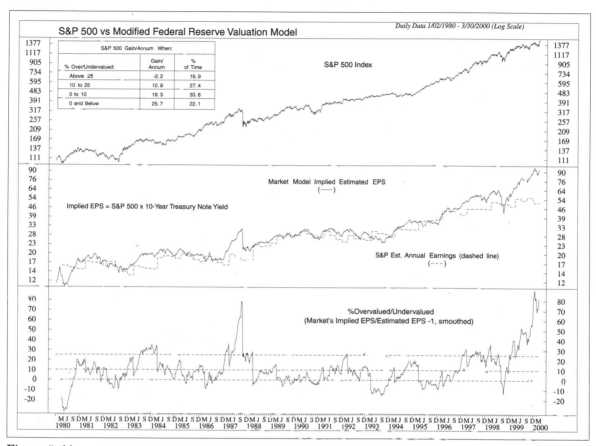

Figure 6–11

which plots earnings growth with its historical linear regression line indicating the average earnings growth rate. By the time earnings have peaked, the market has already started looking ahead to the earnings declines, the price has dropped, and thus the price-to-earnings ratio has been a relatively low 11.4. By the time earnings have bottomed, the market has already started looking ahead, the price has risen, and thus the price-to-earnings ratio has been a relatively high 16.9.

To an armchair investor tuned into CNBC or the other sources of financial news that discuss favorable earnings news in bullish terms and unfavorable earnings news in bearish terms, it may seem counterintuitive or illogical that rapid earnings growth is consistent with weak market performance and that earnings peaks are consistent with low P/Es. And it may seem equally odd that the historical record shows weak earnings growth consistent with strong market performance and earnings troughs consistent with high P/Es. But this simply demonstrates that as a participant in the cycles of mass psychology—the ups

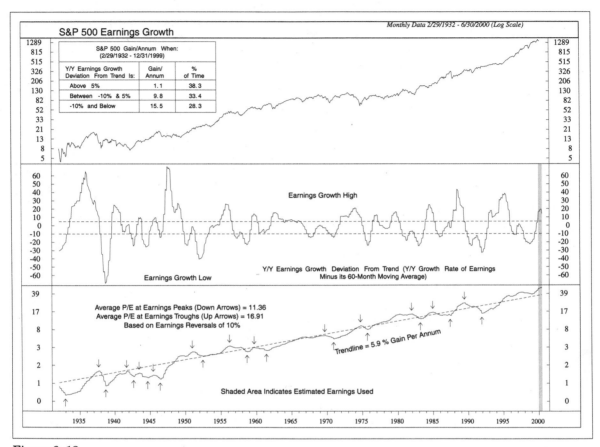

Figure 6–12

and downs that create supply/demand imbalances and bull and bear markets—it's essential to recognize that the market is most risky when all the good news is out, leaving virtually unlimited room for disappointment. The market is least risky when all the bad news is out, leaving virtually unlimited room for positive surprises. As measures of long-term sentiment, indicators based on earnings, and valuation in general, can help you gauge the market's long-term risk relative to its potential upside reward.

LIQUIDITY EXTREMES

It should also be recognized that valuation extremes correspond with liquidity extremes. After bidding the market to expensive extremes, investors can be considered cash-poor and illiquid, as all of their spending power has been used up. After selling the market to inexpensive extremes, investors can be considered cash-heavy, liquid, and able to put their money to work in buying stocks at bargain prices. And these long-term swings in investor liquidity tend to be reflected by the liquidity of equity mutual funds, as fund managers tend to hold an inordinate amount of cash around market bottoms and a relatively small amount of cash around market peaks.

The contrarian indication of mutual fund cash holdings is evident in the mutual funds cash-to-assets ratio, shown in Figure 6–13, which was very high at the bottoms in 1970, 1974, 1982, and 1990, and very low at the tops in 1973 and 1976. The relative cash reduction was especially dramatic during the second half of the 1990s, reflecting the increasing popularity of indexing and the growth of complacency during the long bull market. The low cash-to-assets ratio reflected the view that market risk had diminished to such an extent that there was little need for a cash cushion.

The cash-to-assets ratio can also be affected by interest rates, since fund managers have more incentive to hold cash when the cash returns are greater. Interest rates also

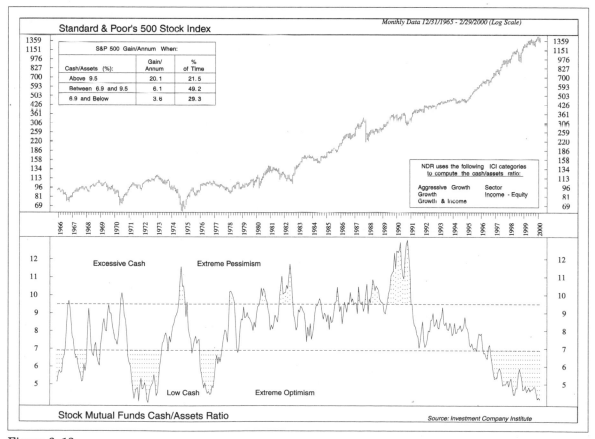

Figure 6–13

influence money market mutual fund assets, which tend to rise when rates are rising and the market is dropping. Extremely high levels represent potential for buying by switch fund traders in particular, as mutual fund traders often waste little time in switching from cash to their favored funds, and vice versa at the onset of market downturns. The appeal of switching has increased with the growth of on-line trading vehicles and capabilities and with the increase in switching options available in 401-k accounts and others.

But the main point to keep in mind is that high cash levels represent bullish liquidity and buying potential while low cash levels represent low liquidity and selling potential. And for a more comprehensive picture of liquidity, it can help to combine the mutual funds cash with other cash pools, the approach taken by NDR's Available Liquidity Forecast indicator in Figure 6–14. This indicator adds the monthly equity fund cash to-

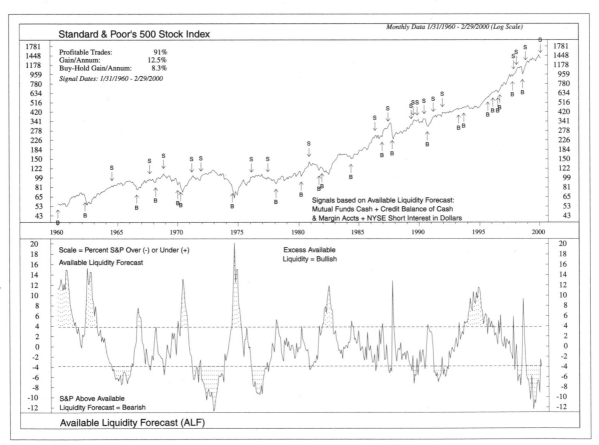

Figure 6–14

tal to the credit balances (dollar amounts) in cash and margin accounts, plus the dollar amount of NYSE short interest determined by multiplying the short interest ratio by average daily dollar volume.

When a regression formula is applied, the indicator determines the linear relationship between the cash total and the S&P 500, with the bottom clip comparing the difference between the S&P 500's current level and its potential level determined by the regression formula. When the S&P 500 is far above where it should be based on the available liquidity, the indicator is at very low levels, the market is illiquid, and the uptrend is at risk, the situation in the mid-1960s, early 1970s, and late 1990s. When the S&P 500 is far below where it should be based on the available liquidity, the indicator is at very high levels, the market is very liquid and a strong advance is likely, the situation during the market-bottom years of 1962, 1970, 1974, 1983, 1987, 1994, and 1998.

OFFERINGS AND SUPPLY

During periods of low liquidity, it can be especially problematic when relatively large amounts of new supply are flowing on to market, since the potential buyers of that new supply will be limited in a fully invested market. Conversely, after a market decline has produced large hordes of cash, a lack of new stock supply can set up a scenario in which, on the first signs of an improving outlook, cash moves back into the limited stock supply, sending prices skyward. In advance of the 1973 peak, for example, liquidity was very low while initial public offerings were numerous, as shown in Figure 6–15. Since a high amount of IPOs suggests that companies see a market for the speculative buyers who tend to buy their stocks, it indicates that extreme optimism is prevalent. At the same time, the offerings add to the supply of stock. And the greater the supply, the greater the market's vulnerability to a downturn in demand.

Based on a concept from analyst Norman Fosback,[2] the IPO monthly total can be used as a "thermometer" to produce high-temperature warnings any time the total of new issues rises from less than 28 to at least 62. Although the indicator does not include buy signals, a lack of new issues can nevertheless be considered a sign of limited new supply and widespread pessimism, as reflected by the lack of new issues around the market bottoms in 1974, 1987, 1998, and other years.

A broader illustration of the supply trend is provided in Figure 6–16, which shows the 13-week total of the dollar amount of IPOs as well as secondary offerings. In a typical secondary, a block of stock is redistributed directly from an underwriter on behalf of a corporation or corporate insider seeking to raise funds or simply to unload shares due to a worsening fundamental outlook for the stock. While a large number of secondary offerings is thus a sign of bearish smart money sentiment, it also indicates an increase in the stock supply above and beyond the supply expansion caused by IPOs. A high and rising

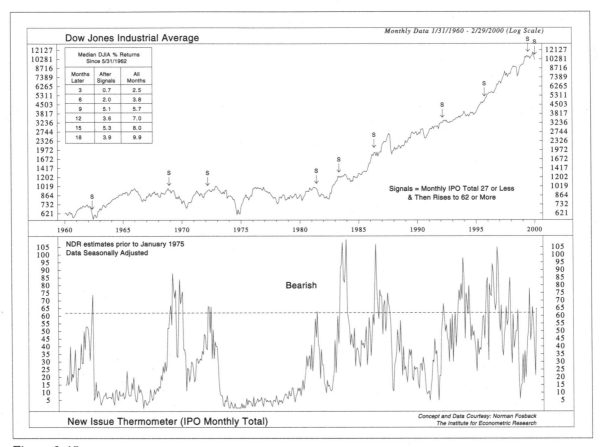

Figure 6–15

total of IPOs and secondary offerings therefore reflects wrong-money speculation, right-money pessimism, and most important, a dangerous flood of new supply.

When watching offerings, however, you should recognize that the trends have strong seasonal tendencies, as illustrated in Figure 6–17. By comparing the month-to-month percent changes in offerings, you can see the tendency for offerings to pick up in the February–March and September–October time frames and drop off in July–August and December–January. You may recall from Chapter 5 that those periods of rising offerings are generally the market's weakest of the year while the periods of falling offerings are generally the strongest. In fact, the monthly seasonality of offerings is generally inverse to the monthly seasonality of the market, shown in Figure 5–33 in Chapter 5. It cannot be known if this is a sign of corporations and insiders correctly anticipating the market's seasonal tendencies, launching offerings prior to strength and

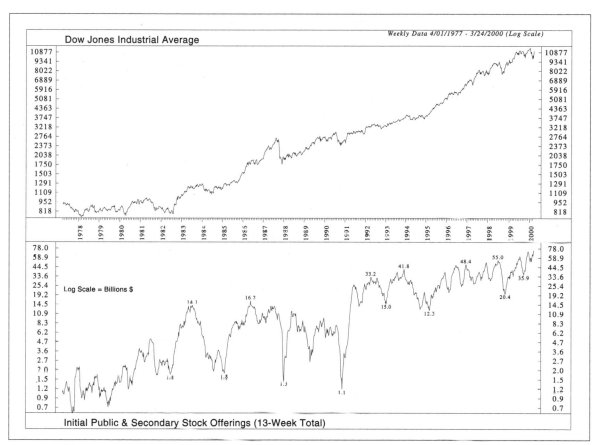

Figure 6–16

pulling back prior to weakness. But the significant observation is that the market is generally weighed down by the new supply and buoyed by the lack thereof.

SUPPLY AND DEMAND

By watching the trend and level of stock offerings, you can therefore gain perspective on a major source of stock supply. But if the demand is sufficient to meet the new supply, the market can continue to rise despite, for instance, a flood of IPOs. To determine whether or not demand is keeping pace with supply, Figure 6–18 compares the six-month supply total with the six-month total of net inflows to equity mutual funds. Shown in Figure 6–4 and as discussed earlier, mutual fund inflows are a gauge of the public's demand for stock. Figure 6–18 indicates that the market has tended to run into

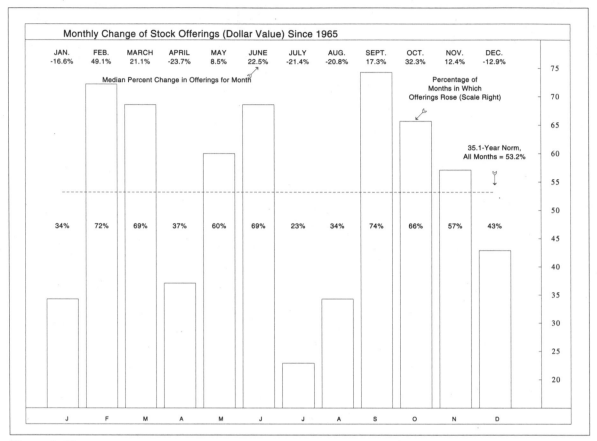

Figure 6–17

trouble once the six-month total of offerings has exceeded the six-month total of inflows by about $3 billion.

Another measure of supply and demand is the net amount of corporate stock sales and purchases discussed earlier and shown in Figure 6–19 on a seasonally adjusted quarterly rate. During periods of heavy merger and acquisition activity that include an abundance of stock buy-backs, the corporate demand helps propel the market higher, in the process reducing the supply of stock and increasing the liquidity of those receiving cash for the retired stock. Corporate demand and stock retirement were major positive influences on the market during the second half of the 1980s and again in the late 1990s.

Figure 6–19 also shows that there have been several long periods in which corporate buying has been light relative to stock offerings, with negative supply/demand im-

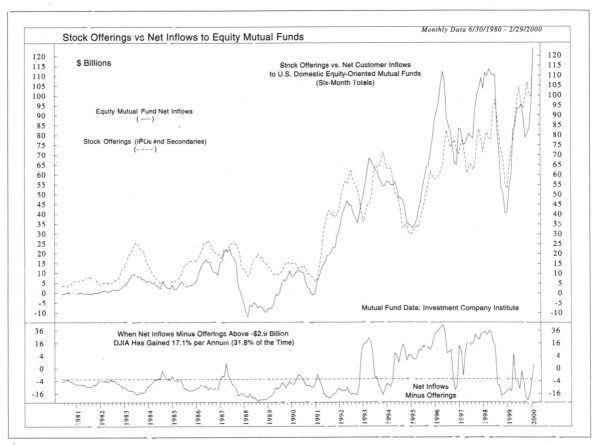

Figure 6–18

plications. The risk during such periods is that investors will eventually use up their cash reserves to buy the new and secondary issues, becoming illiquid and creating a demand vacuum. In the absence of corporate buying, a cash-poor public would leave the market almost void of potential buyers.

I say "almost" because there's another group to keep an eye on, a group that does most of its heaviest buying at the end of a market advance. This group is made up of the foreign buyers of U.S. stocks, still a relatively minor demand influence based on the dollar amount of purchases, yet important to watch from a sentiment standpoint and important to watch when assessing global money flows. Figure 6–20 shows, for example, that foreign buying has been light around market bottoms and heavy around market peaks, and it stood at record highs at the end of 1999.

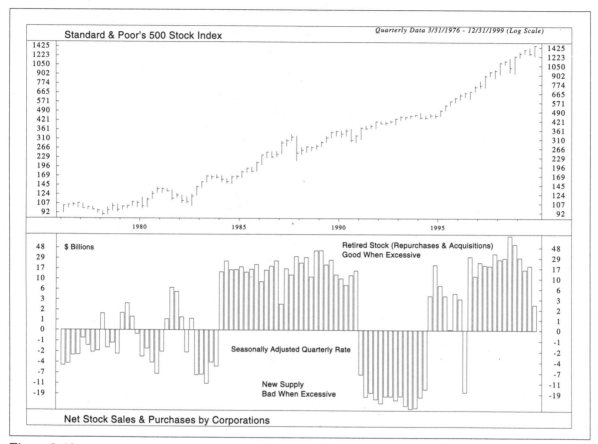

Figure 6–19

As shown in Figure 6–21, most of the foreign buying was by Europeans encouraged by the performance of U.S. stocks, especially when priced in terms of a U.S. dollar that was high and rising relative to the euro. Also in 1999, as shown in Figure 6–22, U.S. investors were pulling money out of Europe, apparently in response to the region's currency weakness and the more impressive stock market performance in the United States. Had the dollar been declining in conjunction with U.S. stock market weakness, in absolute terms and especially relative to other markets, the charts would have almost certainly shown heavy foreign outflows from the U.S. market and greater interest in foreign stocks by U.S. investors.

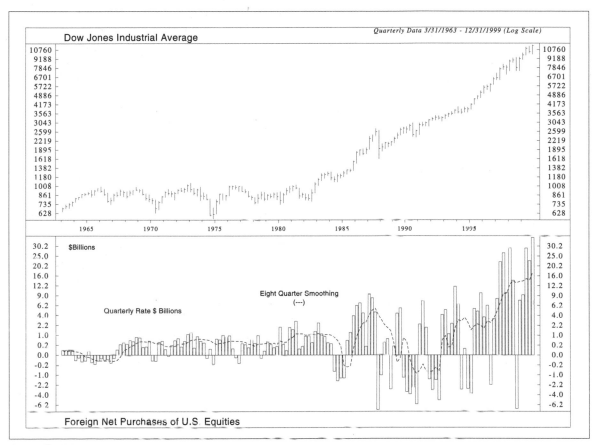

Figure 6–20

Whatever the gauge of supply and demand, liquidity or valuation, it should not be used for market timing, since the sentiment extremes can be used only in hindsight. Rather, the value of these long-term indicators is that they place the current market action in a long-term perspective, enabling you to weigh the risk versus the potential reward. Your assessment of the risk/reward balance will help shape your investment approach, keeping it relatively conservative during risky periods and allowing for a relatively aggressive approach during low-risk periods. But the long-term transitions in sentiment are not without their shorter-term mood shifts, which can be monitored by using other sets of indicators. Those will be examined in Chapter 7.

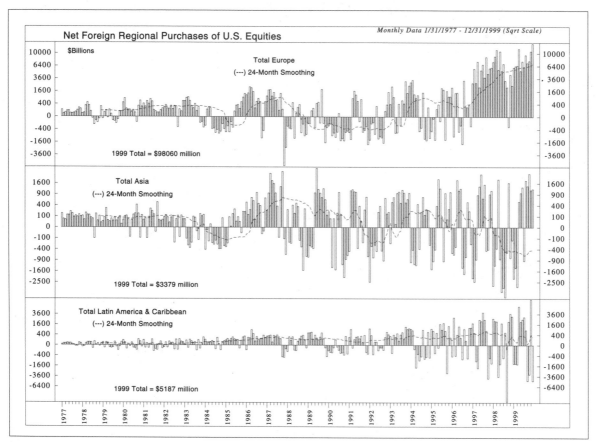

Figure 6–21

E N D N O T E S

1. Paul Montgomery, Universal Economics, Legg Mason Wood Walker, Inc., 600 Thimble Shoals Blvd. #110, Newport News, VA 23606.

2. Norman Fosback, The Institute for Econometric Research, 2200 SW 10th Street, Deerfield Beach, FL, 33442.

REFERENCES

Davis, Nathan E. (Ned). 1991. *Being Right or Making Money*. Venice, FL: Ned Davis Research, p. 19.

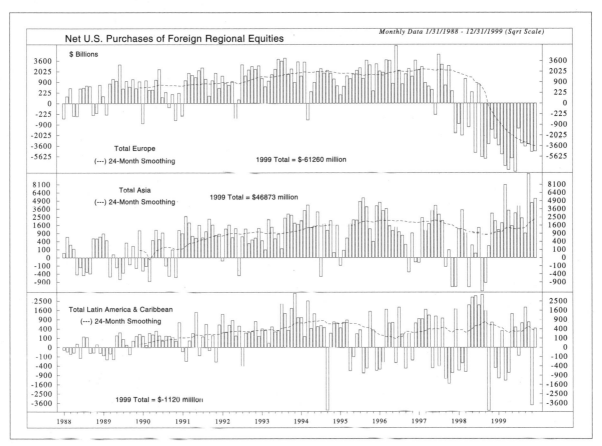

Figure 6–22

Edwards, Robert D., and John Magee. 1991. *Technical Analysis of Stock Trends*, enhanced ed. Boston: International Technical Analysis, p. 19.

Fama, Eugene F., and Kenneth R. French. 1999. Disappearing Dividends: Changing Firm Characteristics or Increased Reluctance to Pay?

CHAPTER 7

Shorter-Term Sentiment
Watching for Market Reversals

During periods in which the market rises unimpeded by anything more than a correction, confidence builds, risk aversion fades, and eventually a state of complacency is reached in which the market is viewed as invincible, the point at which, in reality, it is most vulnerable. And the opposite applies to market declines. Chapter 6 discussed indicators that can be used to identify the long-term sentiment extremes. But in addition, sentiment extremes are typically characterized by contrasting activity among different groups of market players, activity that lends itself to market indicators.

At a market peak, for example, the most exposed are the speculators using margin and derivatives, part of a broader group loosely deemed the unsophisticated "public," though in many cases this group includes crowd-following professional traders and institutional investors. Meanwhile, in response to the need to keep pace with the continued market advance expected by their clients, mutual fund managers are holding relatively little cash, as discussed in Chapter 6. And opinion surveys are showing an abundance of bulls. At the same time, pessimism is evident in the activity of those closest to the corporate boardrooms and the trading floors of major exchanges. These are smart-money players, including specialists, hedgers, and corporate insiders.

INDICATORS OF TRADING ACTIVITY

Since several of the indicators shown in this chapter fluctuate between extremes with far more frequency than most of the long-term indicators in Chapter 6, they can be used not only for indicating major peaks and troughs, but also for signaling the onset of corrections within long-term uptrends or rallies within long-term downtrends. They can be

161

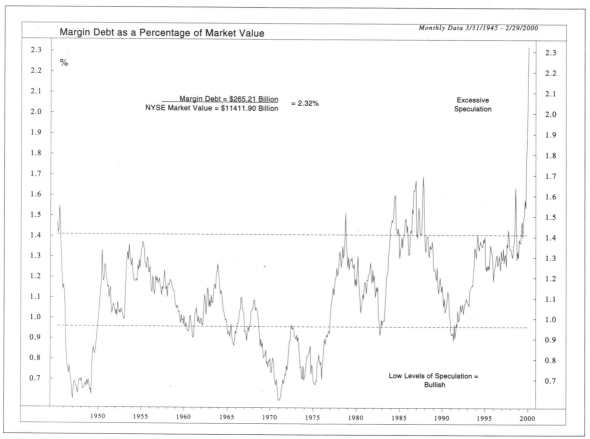

Figure 7–2

To illustrate, the short interest gauge in Figure 7–3 uses an annualized version of the conventional short interest ratio, an approach attributable to Norman Fosback. Rather than the previous month's volume used in the conventional ratio, the annualized ratio uses the average volume for the previous 12 months, eliminating seasonal biases. The NDR indicator compares the annualized ratio to its 16-month smoothing, thereby determining if shorting is excessive, with bullish implications, or light, with bearish implications.

Figure 7–4 makes the distinction between shorting by the public and shorting by specialists, the exchange members who serve as market makers to match buy and sell orders. Whereas the public tends to be wrong at extremes, the specialists represent smart money, typically adding to their short positions in advance of market declines and limiting their shorting ahead of new advances. Not only are the specialists close to the

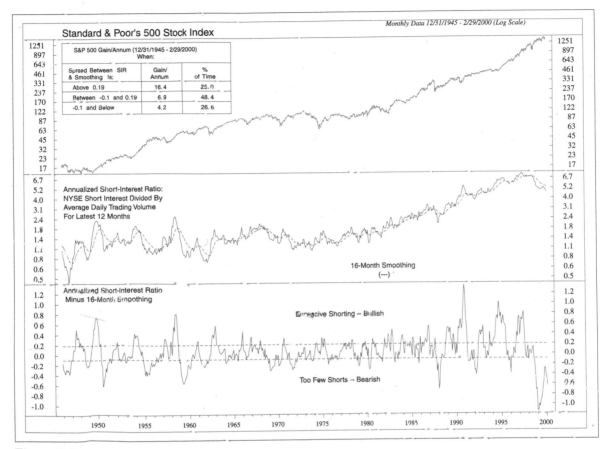

Figure 7–3

trading action, but their function requires that they maintain an orderly market, which helps explain why they often take positions that are contrary to those of the public. By comparing specialist shorting and public shorting, a right-money/wrong-money indicator can be developed.

The relative amount of shorting by the two different groups is measured by the NYSE public to specialist short ratio, which is shown in the middle clip of Figure 7–4 with its 11-week smoothing and bands placed one standard deviation above and below the ratio's 62-week mean. The chart also includes a deviation-from-trend indicator in its bottom clip, based on the ratio of the 10-week smoothing to the 55-week smoothing. At high readings the indicators show that the public is bearish relative to the specialists, which is bullish, and at low readings the indicators shows that the public is bullish relative to the specialists, which is bearish. Signals are generated as described on the chart,

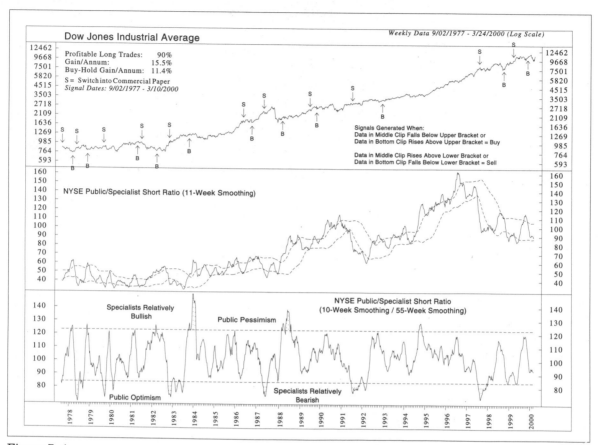

Figure 7–4

although it should be noted that the indicator is more effective at signaling market bottoms than market tops.

Right-money shorting is featured exclusively in Figure 7–5, which is based on the short ratio for NYSE members. This group includes the specialists as well as floor traders and off-floor member firms trading for themselves, all of whom tend to be correct in stepping up their shorting before the market turns downward and cutting back before the market turns upward. Since these professionals tend to be early, the indicator generates buy signals when the normalized ratio follows a period of smart money optimism by reversing upward. Sell signals are produced when this deviation-from-trend measure follows a period of smart money pessimism by turning downward. As with all indicators based on short interest, it's important to recognize the potential distortions caused by irregularities in the levels of derivatives activity and program trading, a major influence before and during the 1987 crash.

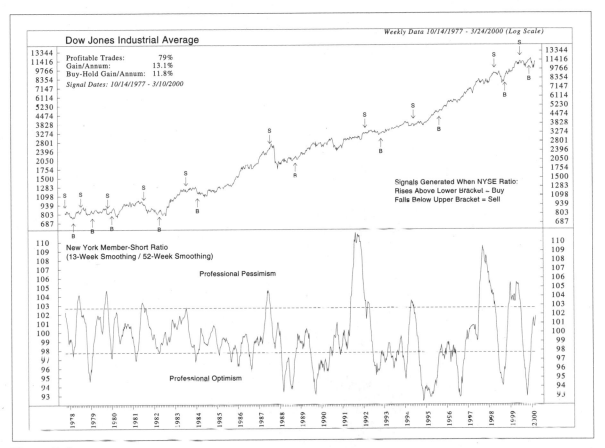

Figure 7–5

Smart Money Indicators

Another way to measure smart-money sentiment is to monitor the Commitments of Traders (COT) data reported by the Commodity Futures Trading Commission (CFTC), which requires all futures trading firms to report the number of outstanding positions in size categories that enable the CFTC to distinguish the open interest of small traders from that of large traders. The latter group is subdivided into large speculators and commercials, who deal directly in the commodity that underlies the futures contract. Since they are often offsetting cash positions in the physical commodity, the commercials are also known as *hedgers,* and they represent smart money because of their access to information on the underlying asset.

The hedgers' net long position in S&P 500 futures contracts, in thousands of contracts, is the basis for the COT Index for Commercials shown in Figure 7–6. Scaled from

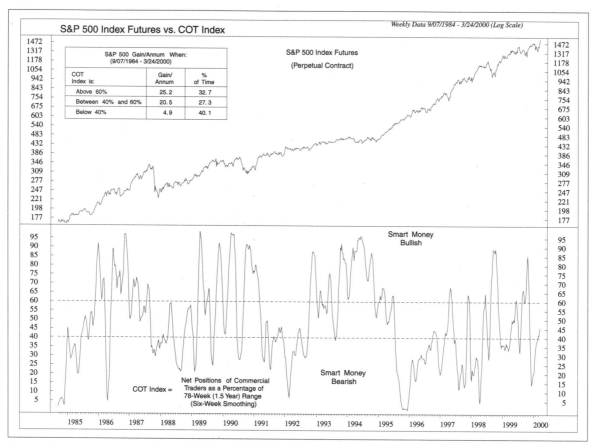

Figure 7–6

zero to 100 percent bullish, the current net position is expressed as a percentage of the range over the preceding one-and-a-half-year period. As shown in the box, the sentiment of the commercials has tended to correspond with the performance of the market, demonstrating the indicator's role as a smart-money gauge.

For an alternative perspective on smart-money sentiment, keep an eye on selling by corporate insiders, a group that includes officers, board members, and owners of at least 10 percent of an equity class of securities. Figure 7–7 illustrates the five-week smoothing of insider sales as a percentage of insider trades, based on data from Vickers Stock Research Corp.[1] Useful for anticipating extremes in individual securities as well as the market in the aggregate, insider selling tends to fall ahead of market bottoms and rise in advance of market peaks, with their selling so influential that it helps to set the topping process in motion. In fact, insider selling has a proven record as a leading indicator, and Table 5–1 indicates that peaks in insider selling have led six of the past seven bull market peaks.

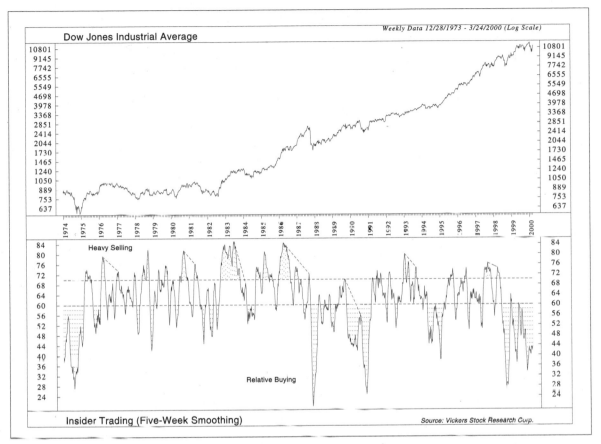

Figure 7–7

Like shorting activity, however, insider selling can occur for reasons that have nothing to do with the outlook for individual stocks or the market as whole, resulting in fluctuations that are of little use in developing a market view. This helps explains why it is difficult to use insider selling with signals or modes. But at extremes, insider selling can be a useful indicator, issuing strong warnings with selling peaks and bullish indications when selling is absent, the condition soon after the market bottoms of 1987, 1990, and 1998.

Put/Call Ratios

Along with the right-money insiders, members and specialists, and the wrong-money public, keep an eye on the actions of the option traders, in this case a wrong-money group that tends to be extremely exposed to puts relative to calls at market bottoms and calls relative to puts at market tops. Whereas a *put* is a speculative bet on a falling market, a *call* is a speculative bet on a rising market. When put/call ratios reach their high extremes, traders are most aggressively bearish, at which point the pool of potential sellers is tapped out. When put/call ratios reach their low extremes, traders are most aggressively bullish, and anyone who has wanted to make a bullish bet has already done so.

As with most other wrong-money sentiment indicators, the indicator's extremes should be viewed from a contrarian standpoint, and you should prepare yourself to take the opposite position when an extreme is apparent. But since the actual extreme can be identified only in hindsight, you should delay acting until the indicator signals that the ratio has started to reverse, at which point you should align yourself with the newfound shift in sentiment. This approach of acting after extremes is used with the three put/call indicators shown in Figure 7–8. Each produces buy signals after the put/call ratio reverses below the indicator's upper band and sell signals after the put/call ratio reverses above the indicator's lower band.

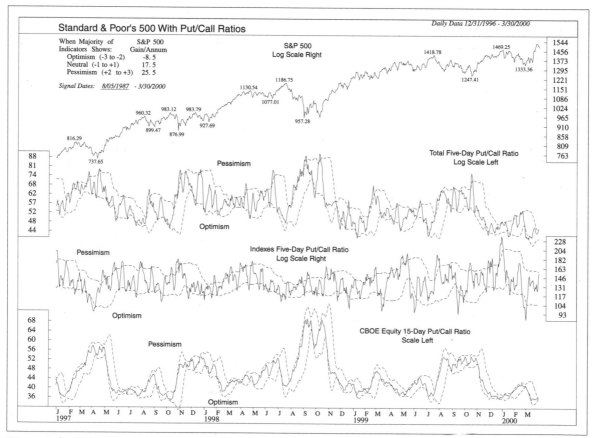

Figure 7–8

The approach is used in the second clip with the total five-day put/call ratio, which includes all of the equity options traded on the AMEX and CBOE, including index options. It is used in the third clip with the five-day put/call ratio for indexes, which is based on the S&P 100 Options Index, the AMEX Major Market Index, the S&P 500 Options Index, the Value Line Index Options, and the New York Stock Exchange Index Options. And it is used in the bottom clip with the 15-day smoothing of the Chicago Board of Options Exchange Equity Put/Call Ratio, a measure based on all traded CBOE stock options, not including indexes. As indicated in the chart's upper-left-hand corner, the market has tended to decline when all three indicators have been on sell signals and the market has tended to rise impressively when all three indicators have been bullish.

It should be noted that these put/call ratios are volatile, as illustrated by their fluctuations over the time span shown in Figure 7–8. And put/call ratios in general are most useful for short-term timing. But I find them to be especially useful for confirming the messages of the short-term overbought/oversold indicators.

OVERBOUGHT/OVERSOLD INDICATORS

Also known as contratrend indicators, overbought/oversold indicators must be handled with care since they use many of the same data series used in the most reliable breadth and trend-following indicators. The market is overbought when buying demand has been exhausted, liquidity is low, and buyers are ready to take profits. Yet from a longer-term perspective, a very overbought reading can be evidence of strong breadth, or even a breadth thrust. In those cases, the overbought condition usually is followed by a temporary pause within a bullish uptrend.

When the market is oversold, selling pressure has been exhausted, liquidity is high, and sellers are ready to move back into the market at the cheaper levels. But during extended declines, an oversold condition may result only in a bear market rally, and it's not until an extremely oversold condition is reached that the market is ready to form a bottom and launch a new bull market. In a bull market, the most overbought readings occur early on, in conjunction with a breadth thrust. In a bear market, the most oversold readings occur at the end of the decline, in conjunction with a high-volume selling climax. It is therefore a long-term bullish sign when conditions become either extremely overbought or extremely oversold, while the more run-of-the-mill overbought conditions have short-term bearish implications and the ordinary oversold conditions have short-term bullish implications.

All of this can be seen in Figure 7–9, which shows extremely oversold conditions at the bottoms in 1982, 1984, 1987, 1990, and 1998, followed by swift and decisive pendulum swings to extremely overbought readings early in the subsequent bull markets. But for the vast majority of the time, this indicator is most useful for its short-term

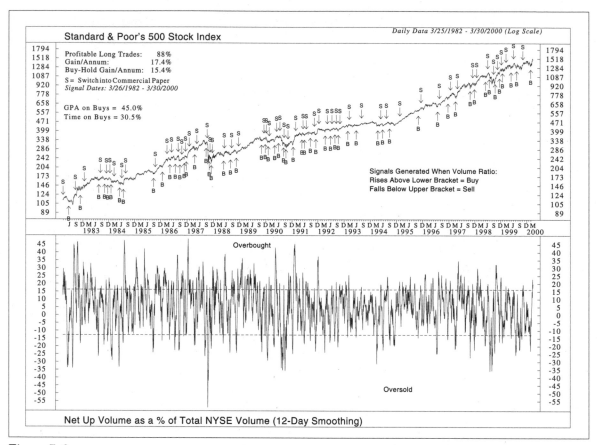

Figure 7–9

contratrend signals, produced using the daily net advancing volume on the New York Stock Exchange as a percentage of total NYSE volume.

This indicator is developed by subtracting the volume of stocks closing lower from the volume of stocks closing higher and then smoothing the net up volume figure with a 12-day moving average. The total NYSE volume is likewise smoothed with a 12-day moving average, and the ratio of the smoothed net up volume to the smoothed total volume is determined. When the indicator moves above the upper parameter, the market is overbought. And sell signals are generated when it drops out of the overbought zone, indicating that the extreme demand has given way to profit taking. When the indicator moves below the lower parameter, the market is oversold. And buy signals occur when the indicator rises out of the oversold zone, indicating that the selling has been exhausted and replaced by renewed demand.

Like the signals of most short-term overbought/oversold indicators, the indicator's signals appear to be most accurate during trading ranges. During long-term uptrends, such as occurred during the 1990s, the indicator is most useful for its buy signals, indicating when the "buy the dip" sentiment is likely to reinvigorate the advance. The results shown in Figure 7–9 include an impressive per annum gain with the indicator on buy signals. And it shows how you would have done by using signals not for shorting the market, but for switching into commercial paper, a risk-averse alternative to the risky strategy of shorting the market for short-term profits during a long-term uptrend.

The Trading Index

Probably the most widely recognized of all overbought/oversold indicators is a gauge that includes not only the volume data used in Figure 7–9, but also advances and declines. It is known by several names, including the *Arms Index,* after Richard Arms, who popularized its use. It is also known as *MKDS,* the *Trading Index,* or *TRIN,* which is probably its most common name. By comparing the amount of volume required to advance a stock to the amount of volume required to produce a declining stock, the Trading Index indicates bullish conditions when less volume is required to produce an advancing stock than to produce a declining stock, typically the situation when the market is oversold. Conditions are bearish when heavy volume is required to advance relatively few issues, with much less volume required to produce a declining stock than an advancing stock. At those times, the TRIN readings indicate that the market is churning and laboring to move higher, the sign of an overbought market.

You can calculate the Trading Index by dividing the ratio of advancing issues to declining issues by the ratio of advancing volume to declining volume, or you can use the widely quoted readings of the calculated TRIN. For the indicator in Figure 7–10, the 1 p.m. and 4 p.m. EST TRIN readings are averaged, and the result is then smoothed over 40 days. The higher the smoothed TRIN reading, the more oversold the market; the lower the smoothed TRIN reading, the more overbought the reading. And like the indicator in Figure 7–9, signals are generated when the indicator reverses from its overbought and oversold levels. But this indicator additionally recognizes that an extremely oversold reading is the sign of a high-volume selling climax and a market bottom, and thus a buy signal is also produced if the 40-day TRIN reaches the extremely high level. Such signals do not require a drop back below the high level. In the same way for a sell signal, the reversal requirement is waived if the 40-day TRIN reaches an extremely low level, indicating manic buying.

An alternative approach to using TRIN is shown in Figure 7–11, which uses volatility bands to generate signals on the 40-day TRIN for not only the NYSE, but also the NASDAQ and AMEX. While sell signals are produced by upward reversals from over-

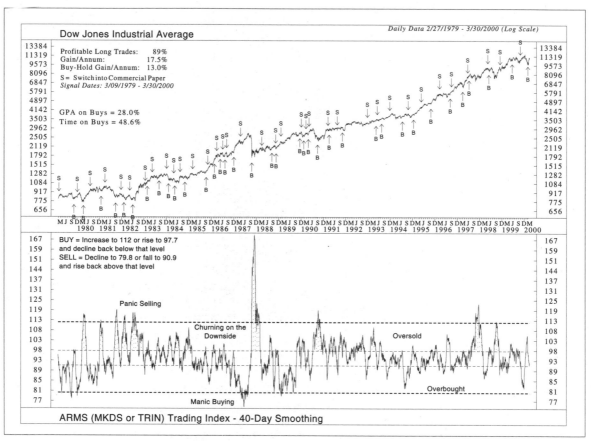

Figure 7–10

bought levels, buy signals are generated by downward reversals from oversold levels, with the indicator signal moving to zero if the indicator returns to an extreme reading without having first moved to the opposite extreme. The composite of the three signals is used as an indicator for the NASDAQ Composite, which has performed exceptionally well when the weight of the evidence has been bullish and poorly when the weight of the evidence has been negative.

RSI and Stochastics

Two other popular vehicles for measuring overbought and oversold conditions are the Relative Strength Index (RSI) and stochastics, both shown in Figure 7–12. Developed by J. Welles Wilder, Jr.,[2] the RSI, in this case a 40-day RSI, is calculated by dividing the aver-

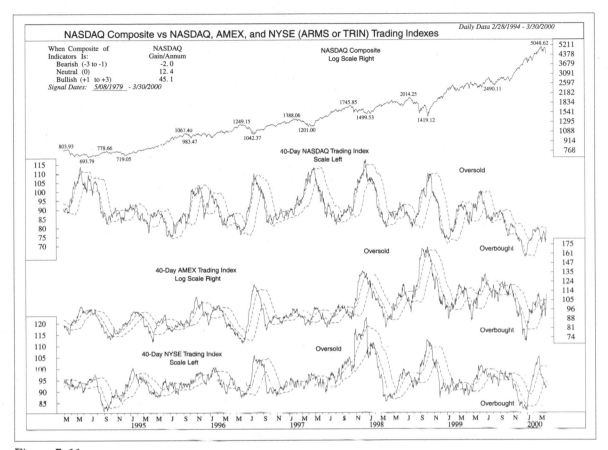

Figure 7–11

age point gain for the up days during the 40-day period by the average point gain for the up days plus the average point loss for the down days during the 40-day period. Despite its name, the Relative Strength Index is less a relative strength measure than a gauge of price momentum and the market's overbought/oversold balance. Whereas RSI indicators express momentum in a range of 0 to 100, momentum indicators based solely on rates of change can reach −100 percent on the downside but are unlimited on the upside.

Indicators based on stochastics likewise oscillate in a range of 0 to 100. And like the RSI, stochastics techniques indicate overbought conditions at high readings and oversold conditions at low readings. Developed by George C. Lane,[3] stochastics indicators are used to determine whether stocks have been closing near the high end or low end of their price ranges for the period in question. The stochastics formula, which Lane dubbed %K (a smoothed version is called %D), can also be applied to market indi-

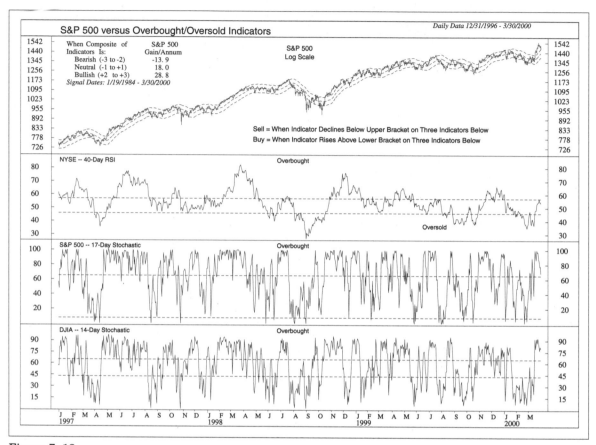

Figure 7–12

ces by determining the index's lowest theoretical intraday low during the specified period, subtracting it from its latest close, dividing that spread by the period's highest intraday high minus the period's lowest intraday low, and then multiplying the result by 100 (%K = 100 * [latest close minus x-periods low/x-periods high minus x-periods low.])

Figure 7–12 uses a 17-day stochastic on the S&P 500 and a 14-day stochastic on the Dow Industrials. In each case, a buy signal is generated when the stochastic rises above its lower parameter, indicating that, after closing near the bottom of its range, the market index has started to move upward. The most effective sell signals are generated when the stochastic falls below the upper bracket, indicating that, after closing near the top of its range, the market index has started to head downward.

During uptrends these indicators tend to reach overbought levels and stay there for some time, which is why it's essential that a sell signal not be generated until a decisive reversal from an extreme is indicated. Even then, it's possible that instead of continuing toward oversold levels, the indicator will quickly return to an overbought level. This whipsaw tendency is the indicator's drastic stochastic flaw. But as with the TRIN indicators in Figure 7–11, the indicators in Figure 7–12 adjust by reverting to zero when such whipsaws occur.

Stochastics indicators can, however, generate timely buy signals after bottoms. And they can provide accurate perspective on the overbought/oversold balance when used on a composite basis with an RSI indicator, the approach taken in Figure 7–12. The chart's indication is bullish when at least two of the three indicators are on buy signals (and none on sell signals) and bearish when at least two of the three indicators are on sell signals (and none on buy signals).

VOLATILITY INDICATORS

Similar in concept to overbought/oversold indicators are indicators based on volatility. But volatility indicators are frequently misunderstood, perhaps because the term is often bandied about with negative connotations. Volatility is often discussed in terms of market risk, as measured by standard deviation and other statistics. And while volatility tends to increase during market declines, extremely high volatility is usually a good sign, occurring around market bottoms. Readings of low volatility are typically negative, often occurring in conjunction with the churning indications of TRIN indicators and other signs of the overbought conditions that tend to be present at market tops. To use volatility as a market indicator, it's thus essential to keep in mind that volatility tends to be very low at market tops, rising as the market declines, peaking around the market bottoms and during the early stages of the new advance, and then gradually receding as the advance matures.

Again, the breadth data is a good starting point for developing volatility indicators, and Figure 7–13 is based on the spread between weekly advances and weekly declines on the NYSE. The difference is added up over a 14-week period, producing what is called the *14-week Plurality Index*. The index is then compared to bands placed 10 percent on either side of the index's 52-week exponential smoothing, with buy signals generated when the index follows a sell signal by rising above the upper band, indicating that volatility is high relative to its long-term trend. Sell signals appear when the index follows a buy signal by dropping below the lower band, indicating that volatility is low relative to its long-term trend.

As shown by the indicator's early sell signals, the indicator has some of the same timing drawbacks faced by overbought/oversold indicators during long-term uptrends. But the informational value of extremely high readings is reflected by the extremes reached in conjunction with the broad market bottoms of 1980, 1982, 1987, 1990, and 1998, indicated by the Dow Industrials and especially the Value Line Composite.

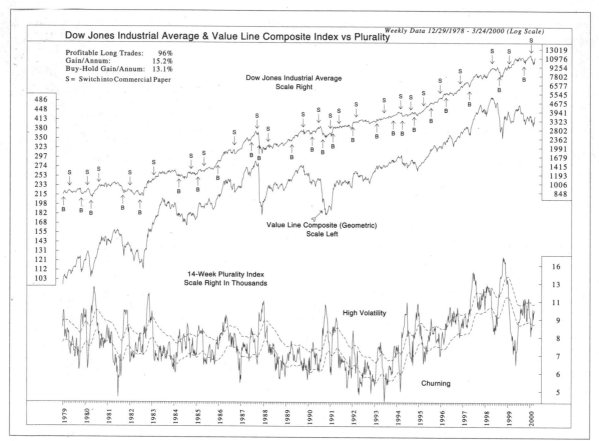

Figure 7–13

Likewise, the market's tendency to perform well after high volatility readings can be seen in an indicator that measures volatility based not on the difference between advances and declines, but on the change in the S&P 500, irrespective of the direction of the change. Derived from an indicator developed by Marty Zweig, Figure 7–14 plots the 100-day average of the S&P 500's absolute change. When the indicator has been above the upper parameter, the situation at numerous market bottoms dating back to 1940, the S&P 500 has gained about 17 percent per annum, as compared to its 8 percent per annum gain over all periods since then and its 2 percent per annum gain when low volatility has been indicated by volatility readings below the lower parameter.

The relationship between volatility and market performance is also illustrated in Figure 7–15. It features the deviation from trend of the CBOE Volatility Index, commonly known as the *VIX Index*. A popular volatility gauge among short-term traders,

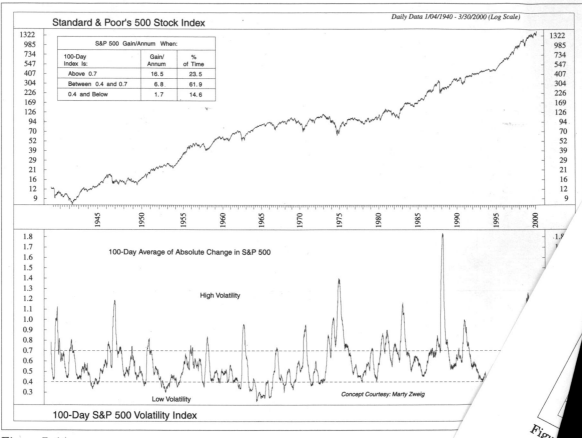

Figure 7–14

the VIX Index is based on option volatility. Specifically, it is th
volatilities of the nearest strike prices for OEX puts and c
months.[4] When the ratio of the index's eight-day smoothing t
above the upper parameter, buy signals are generated. Sel
the ratio drops below the lower parameter, indicating lo

Intraday Volatility

For long-term perspective, however, a better picture
Intraday Volatility Index shown in Figure 7–16. A
working with it in recent years, I have been intr
turning points in the context of longer-term tr

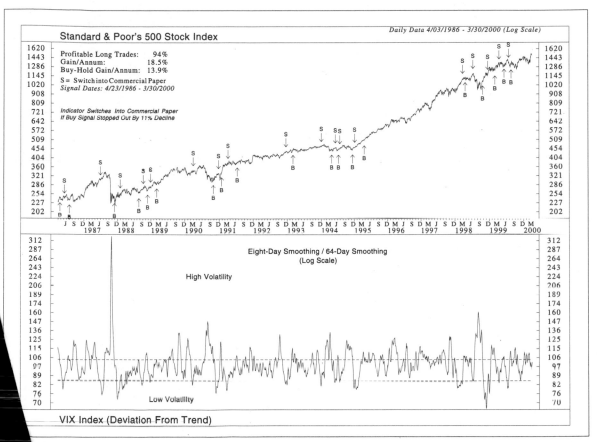

Standard & Poor's 500 Stock Index

Daily Data 4/03/1986 - 3/30/2000 (Log Scale)

Profitable Long Trades: 94%
Gain/Annum: 18.5%
Buy-Hold Gain/Annum: 13.9%

S = Switch into Commercial Paper
Signal Dates: 4/23/1986 - 3/30/2000

Indicator Switches Into Commercial Paper
If Buy Signal Stopped Out By 11% Decline

Eight-Day Smoothing / 64-Day Smoothing
(Log Scale)

High Volatility

Low Volatility

VIX Index (Deviation From Trend)

e 7–15

the intraday high and low of the Dow Jones Industrial Average smoothed over
ays; the data history dates back to 1928, with the longer-term trends reflected by
ement of bands placed 20 percent above the spread's one-year average and 20
below the one-year average. In addition, to indicate extremely high volatility,
band is placed 110 percent above the one-year average.

chart's lower box indicates that when the index has been below the lower
market has performed poorly since 1928, and the subpar performance dur-
atility periods has been a consistent tendency over numerous time frames.
1970s and 1980s, however, the market performed best with volatility be-
ands. But for the rest of the time, high volatility has been consistent with
ressive market returns, as indicated by the market's per annum gain of
th volatility more than 20 percent above the one-year average. And when

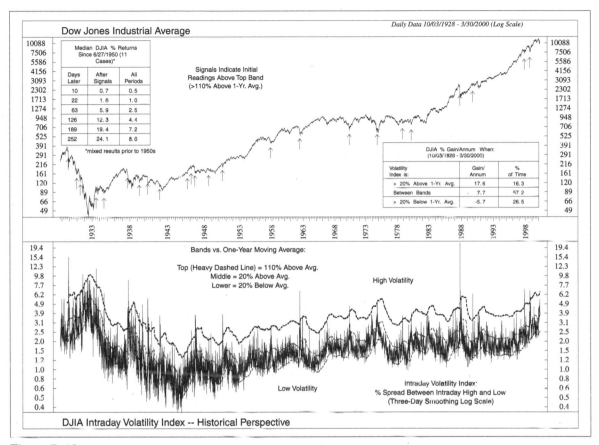

Figure 7–16

extremely high volatility has been indicated by an index reading of more than 110 per-cent above the one-year average, a market bottom and a good buying opportunity have usually been indicated. Although the responses to the extreme volatility readings were mixed prior to the 1950s, the market has since performed better than normal over the subsequent incremental periods following the extreme readings, as indicated in the chart's upper box.

Of course, there are exceptions to the rules of any indicator. But the chart's message is that, in general terms, the demise of major advances has often occurred with waning intraday volatility, the subsequent declines have started with the index in the low volatil-ity mode, volatility has picked up quickly on the downside, and then it has peaked with the selling climax that has often occurred around major bottoms. Volatility has remained high as the market has taken off with strong upside momentum, as this has often been the

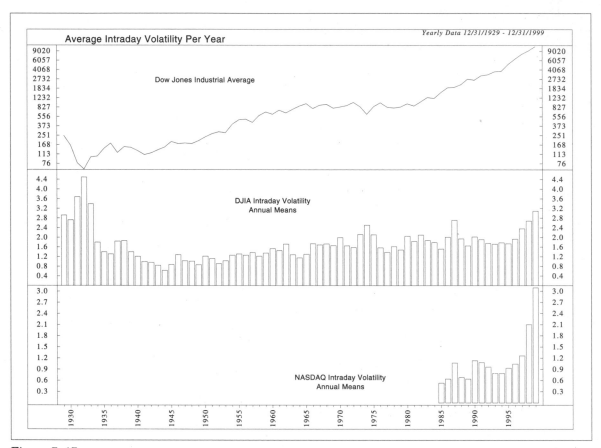

Figure 7–17

time when the market has amassed its most impressive gains. And then it has receded again as the advance has matured, with the cycle starting over.

The long-term perspective provided by the chart's bands is consistent with Figure 7–17, which plots the average level of intraday volatility for each year starting in 1929, plus the NASDAQ's intraday volatility starting in 1985. And the illustrations of DJIA volatility are consistent with the average annual levels of volatility indicated by the standard deviation of the DJIA's one-day rate of change and the number of 5 percent reversals per year. Reflecting the "so bad it's good" implication of extremely high volatility, 1929, 1974, 1987, and 1998 were the four years in which all three volatility measures indicated an average standard deviation of at least 1.1, at least 10 turning points for 5 percent moves, and average intraday volatility of at least 2.5 percent on the DJIA. Each of those years included an NDR-defined bear market bottom.

These long-term perspectives also shed light on the view that volatility has increased as a result of the advent of day trading and after-hours trading, and as a result of the whirlwind expansion in the breadth and depth of market information available on the air and on line. Some stock movements have even been attributed to the unsubstantiated opinions tossed around in on-line chat rooms. All of these factors may help explain the overall time compression evident in everything from the time required for trade settlement to the speed in which news is announced and digested. It may even help explain why the most recent three bear markets were three of the four shortest bear markets since 1900. If volatility has in fact moved to a higher and rising range, then history would suggest that future bottoms will occur at much higher volatility levels, as will be indicated by a continued uptrend in the upper moving band of Figure 7–16.

It can also be argued that in the same way that the proclivity of "record highs" supported the optimistic sentiment of the 1990s, a continued prevalence of the word *volatility* would contribute to mounting fear. Remember that volatility indicators are in fact sentiment indicators, as rising volatility is consistent with the mounting fear that culminates in deeply oversold conditions and market bottoms, while falling volatility is consistent with the spreading complacency and optimism that tend to produce market peaks.

INDICATORS BASED ON OPINION

This examination of sentiment indicators has thus far demonstrated how sentiment is reflected by the differing actions of investors in the aggregate, and by the contrasting actions of different investor groups. For a direct reading of what investors are thinking about the market outlook, regardless of their actions, the best approach is to look at indicators that gauge public opinion. The most widely followed of those indicators are the advisory service opinion surveys updated by Investors Intelligence,[5] which tabulates the percentage of advisors who say they are bullish, the percentage saying they are bearish, and the percentage of those who are long-term bullish but looking for a short-term correction.

Figure 7–18 shows the percentage of bearish advisors smoothed over four weeks, with high readings indicating widespread pessimism and low readings indicating complacency. The chart's bottom clip shows the percentage of bullish advisors smoothed over two weeks. In this case, high readings indicate abundant optimism while low readings indicate pessimism. At times, such as in 1976, an abundance of bulls and a lack of bears have correctly warned of a major peak, while at others time, such as in 1994, a large bearish contingent and a scarcity of bulls have accurately pointed to good times ahead for the market. But at other times, the readings have been volatile or indecisive.

One way to get a better handle on these data is to combine them with the ratio of bulls to the total of bulls and bears. While the ratio allows the extremes in advisory opinion to become more evident, it is still tricky to use since high optimism levels have often

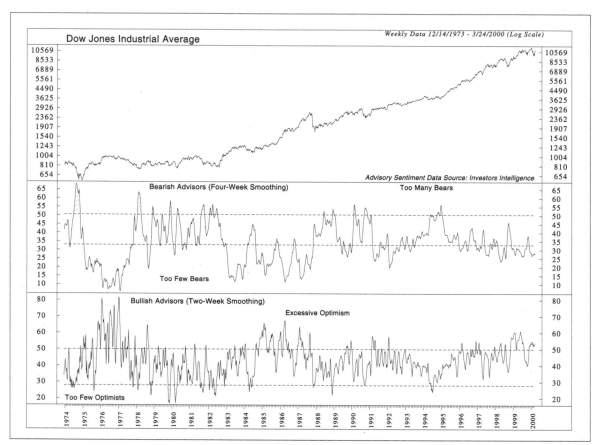

Figure 7–18

been reached well before market peaks. In fact, the initial increases in advisory optimism can help fuel an advancing market by herding more buyers into the market. Since
market peaks typically occur over long periods of distribution and divergence, the distinction needs to made between optimism that's bullish from a demand standpoint and
optimism that indicates a sentiment extreme. But that distinction can be made only
subjectively. For signals, you may need to overlay an indicator that reflects conditions
normally found around market peaks and market bottoms. When extreme optimism is
evident and the indicator is warning of top conditions, you can be more confident that
the optimism is in fact a sign of speculative excess. When extreme pessimism is evident
and the indicator is at levels consistent with market bottoms, you can be more confident
that rather than a bearish influence on selling pressure, the pessimism is in fact the indication of an oversold condition.

   Ned Davis has used this approach to produce what he has called *dynamic brackets,*
shown in Figure 7–19. In this case, the overlayed indicator is the 26-week rate of change

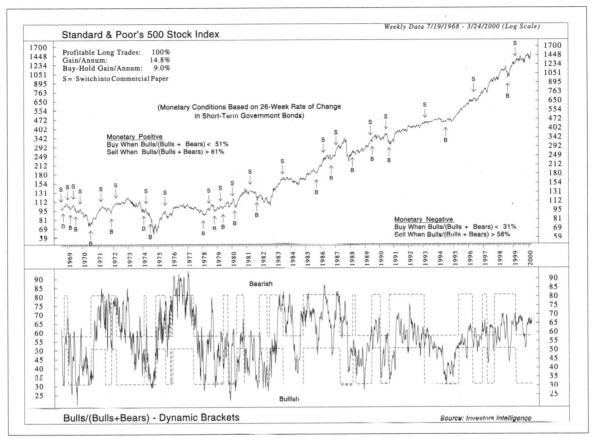

Figure 7–19

of short-term government bonds, which tends to be low around market peaks and high around market bottoms. The brackets shift depending upon the signal of the bond momentum indicator (to be discussed in more detail in Chapter 8). When the bond momentum indicator is bullish, a market top requires more optimism, and a market bottom requires less pessimism, than would be needed for a reversal with the bond momentum indicator on a sell signal. When the bond momentum indicator is on a sell signal, a market top requires less optimism, and a market bottom requires more pessimism, than would be required with the bond momentum indicator bullish.

Even with the overlay, however, the signals can lack precision, and the sell signals still show a tendency to be early. When assessing market opinion, you should therefore compare the message of advisory service sentiment to the messages of other types of opinion polls. Figure 7–20 presents the sentiment of brokers and advisors, plotting the Consensus Index based on surveys conducted by Consensus Inc.[6] Although the data is volatile, reflecting opinions about the short to intermediate term, signals can be gener-

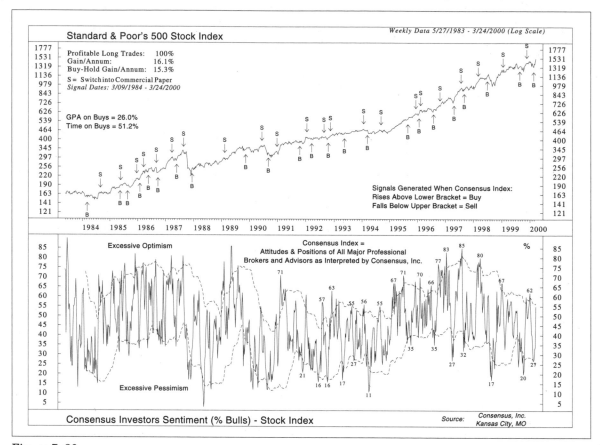

Figure 7–20

ated with wide volatility bands that move with the longer-term cyclical shifts in the data. Sell signals are generated when the index reaches a high optimism reading and reverses below the upper band, and buy signals are produced when the index drops to a high pessimism reading and reverses above the lower band. Again, since many of this indicator's signals, especially the sell signals, have been far from precise, the indicator should not be used in isolation.

A similar approach is used with the even more volatile Bullish Consensus Index on stock index futures, based on surveys of futures traders conducted by Market Vane Corp.[7] As shown in Figure 7–21, this indicator's volatility bands are closer together and move in shorter cycles, enabling the indicator to signal rallies and corrections within the longer-term trends.

While the advisory service sentiment, Consensus Index, and Bullish Consensus Index are all based on the sentiment of investment professionals, the sentiment of "Main Street" is reflected by the data from the American Association of Individual Investors

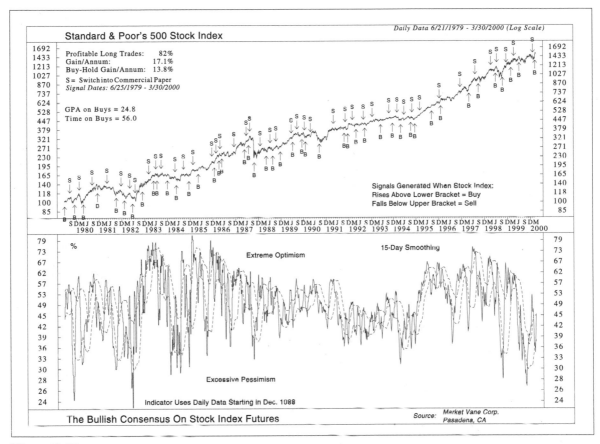

Figure 7-21

(AAII), an investment association.[8] The AAII polls its members on their six-month market predictions, resulting in bulls and bears percentages similar to those from Investors Intelligence. Figure 7–22 shows the two-week average of the ratio of the association's bulls to the total of its bulls and bears. This indicator makes no attempt to generate trading signals, with the box simply indicating that, on an annualized basis, the market has performed worse when these public investors have been bullish, indicated by a ratio above the upper bracket, than it has when this group has been bearish, indicated by a ratio below the lower bracket.

For keeping the sentiment messages long term in their perspective, I have found that using the sentiment indicators on a mode basis is usually preferable to using them on a signal basis, especially given the tendency for sell signals to be early. When indicators based on opinion and predictions are used, it's essential to keep in mind that what people say and what they do can be entirely different. They may say they are bearish but remain fully invested, thus helping to prolong the advance and making the

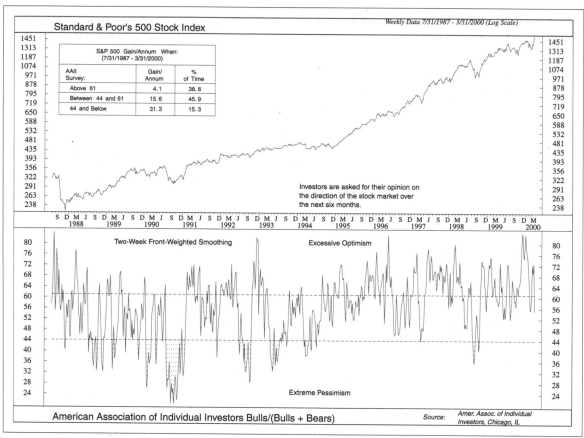

Standard & Poor's 500 Stock Index — Weekly Data 7/31/1987 - 3/31/2000 (Log Scale)

AAII Survey:	Gain/Annum	% of Time
Above 61	4.1	38.8
Between 44 and 61	15.6	45.9
44 and Below	31.3	15.3

S&P 500 Gain/Annum When: (7/31/1987 - 3/31/2000)

Investors are asked for their opinion on the direction of the stock market over the next six months.

Two-Week Front-Weighted Smoothing — Excessive Optimism — Extreme Pessimism

American Association of Individual Investors Bulls/(Bulls + Bears)   Source: Amer. Assoc. of Individual Investors, Chicago, IL

Figure 7–22

high optimism warning appear early in retrospect. Conversely, during a period when the consensus view is bearish, few may be willing to act on their opinions. In contrast to tape indicators based on actual market activity, opinion indicators are a step removed from the price action. Bullish or bearish sentiment may influence the market, but it does not necessarily mean that stock prices will respond accordingly or that the extremes in sentiment will correspond to extremes in the market.

RISK/REWARD PERSPECTIVE

The major benefit of a sentiment assessment is that it can enable you to place the current market action in the framework of risk and reward. It can help you determine whether a favorable risk/reward balance warrants an aggressive approach or whether an unfavorable risk/reward balance warrants a high cash position. The challenge is reaching a sentiment conclusion that's accurate. Subjective signs and anecdotal evidence are usually abundant when things get out of hand. During the manic and dangerously divergent NASDAQ run at the end of 1999 and start of 2000, for example, it was typical to read headlines and hear the exclamations of yet another record high on the NASDAQ, with hardly a mention of yet another day of new lows exceeding new highs on the NYSE. At such times, you will hear the oft-told story of the cab driver giving out stock tips.

But the best approach is to rely on indicators based on data that can be viewed from a historical perspective. As discussed in this and the preceding chapters, those indicators include the longest-term valuation indicators, the shortest-term overbought/oversold indicators, the opinion surveys, and everything that gauges and compares the differing actions and behaviors of various groups of traders and investors, including the mutual fund managers, public speculators, specialists, hedgers, and insiders. When the shorter-term indicators agree with the long-term indicators, the message is strongest. When they disagree, consider the shorter-term indications within the longer-term context. And remember that for much of the time, the indicators will be indecisive or neutral, with little bearing on the market outlook. In those cases, you will need to stay focused on the tape indicators and the monetary indicators, which are examined in the next chapter.

E N D N O T E S

1. Vickers Stock Research Corp., 226 New York Avenue, Huntington, NY 11743.
2. J. Welles Wilder, Trend Research, P.O. Box 128, McLeansville, NC 27301.
3. George Lane, Investment Educators, 719 S. 4th St., Watseka, IL 60970.
4. Implied volatility is the future market volatility expected by options traders and used in the pricing of options.
5. Investors Intelligence, 30 Church St., New Rochelle, NY 10801.
6. Consensus, Inc., P.O. Box 411128, Kansas City, MO, 64108.
7. Market Vane Corp., P.O. Box 90490, Pasadena, CA 91109.
8. American Association of Individual Investors, 625 Michigan Ave., Chicago, IL 60611.

REFERENCES

Zweig, Martin E., and Morrie Goldfischer. 1994. *Martin Zweig's Winning on Wall Street*. New York: Warner Books.

CHAPTER 8

Monetary and Economic Indicators

Benefiting from an Accurate Assessment
of the Fed's Intentions

In addition to an understanding of tape conditions and market sentiment, an accurate market assessment requires that you stay on top of changes in Fed policy and the economic indicators that affect those changes. Better yet, if you can get yourself inside the minds of the Federal Reserve Board governors, you will be better able to anticipate the changes in policy.

The flows, quantities, and costs of money are known collectively as the *monetary environment,* and the status of this environment is a major influence on the decisions of stock market investors. When the Fed is accommodative, maintaining a policy that helps keep the money supply high and rising, and interest rates low, the stock market tends to benefit. When the Fed is restrictive, limiting money supply growth and pushing interest rates higher, the market tends to encounter problems. While interest rates have the most direct impact on market performance, an evaluation of money supply growth will enable you to place current interest rate trends and Fed policy shifts in a long-term context.

The basic point to remember is that the value of money is determined by its purchasing power, as explained by Gwartney and Stroup (1997): "The value of a unit of money—a dollar, for example—is measured in terms of what it will buy. Its value, therefore, is inversely related to the level of prices. An increase in the level of prices and a decline in the purchasing power of a unit of money are the same thing. If the purchasing power of money is to remain stable over time, the supply of money must be controlled. Assuming a constant rate of use, if the supply of money grows more rapidly than the real output of goods and services, prices will rise. In layman's terms, there is 'too much

191

money chasing too few goods.'" Extreme examples of money supply growth sending prices skyward include the inflationary experiences of Germany in the 1920s and Russia in the 1990s.

MONEY SUPPLY

Currently in developed countries, money supply growth is managed by the central banks. They can stimulate economic growth by taking actions that increase the money supply growth; and they can keep economic growth from becoming excessive, thus limiting inflation, by making moves that restrict the money supply growth. For its part, the U.S. Federal Reserve Board can control money supply growth by changing its reserve requirement and by changing the discount rate in conjunction with a change in the Fed funds target rate.

When the Fed changes the Fed funds target rate, it is announcing its intent to keep the Fed funds rate, the rate that banks charge each other for short-term loans, in line with its target rate by selling and buying U.S. government securities in the open market. Such an action is one example of an *open market operation,* the term that describes the Fed's purchases and sales of bonds, notes, and bills. Open market operations are far and away the means employed most often by the Fed in its effort to control the money supply.

To increase the money supply and implement its policy without affecting the Fed funds rate, the Fed can buy bonds originally issued by the Treasury, thus obtaining a stake of the national debt. While the sellers can choose to cash the Fed's check, thereby increasing the currency in circulation, their more likely choice is to deposit the check with a commercial bank. Either way, the money supply increases, with the new bank reserves enabling the bank to make additional loans and further expand the money supply.

Under fractional reserve banking, a bank need only maintain reserves equivalent to the percentage of its short-term deposits mandated by the Fed's reserve requirement, which was 10 percent in early 2000. The money supply thus expands as a bank loans out those deposits that it does not keep on reserve, with the borrowed funds in turn deposited in another bank. That bank in turn loans out as much as it can, and the process continues. Banks tend to loan out almost all of their reserves exceeding those that they must hold based on the reserve requirement.

By purchasing U.S. securities, then, the Fed increases the monetary base, defined as the sum of currency in circulation and the bank reserves (vault cash plus reserves on deposit with the Fed). And when it does so, the multiplier effect increases the money supply. In 1999, the effect was increasing M1, the most narrow money supply aggregate, by about $2 for each dollar in securities purchased. The opposite applies when the Fed sells the government bonds, reducing the monetary base, and in turn the money supply, by about $2 for each dollar in securities sold. And while the M1 multiplier was thus around 2, the multiplier for the broader M2 was about 8, and the multiplier for the even broader M3 was about 11.

It is important to recognize that M1 has been subject to distortions over the years. It is made up of currency in circulation, checkable deposits, and traveler's checks; M1's expansion in the 1980s was largely a result of the advent of interest-earning checking accounts, which gave it a savings component. In the 1990s, money market deposit accounts gained appeal relative to those accounts, with a negative effect on M1. And the monetary aggregate has also been affected by the growth of currency held overseas.

For analytical purposes, M2 is a better monetary aggregate, as it includes everything that's in M1, plus money market mutual funds, savings accounts (including money market deposit accounts), and small-denomination time deposits at banks, savings and loan associations, credit unions, and other depository institutions. Thus including cash as well as assets that can be converted into cash and checking account funds, M2 comprises liquid funds, those with a savings appeal and those without. M3 includes everything that's in M2 plus time deposits with large denominations, money market funds with large minimum balances, repurchase agreements (overnight loans to commercial banks from their customers), and overnight eurodollar deposits (dollar deposits at non-U.S. financial institutions).

None of the monetary aggregates include the assets of stock and bond mutual funds, which have become liquid alternatives for saving. And it remains to be seen how the "Ms" will be affected by the continued growth in the use of debit cards, e-banking, and future financial innovations. But for assessing the outlook for interest rates, economic growth, and Fed policy, relevant information can still be gained by watching the money supply, M2 and M3 in particular, and by gauging the money supply growth after accounting for inflation.

This is done in Figure 8–1, which illustrates real M2 money supply growth starting in 1915. The chart supports the adage that "money moves markets," as the liquidity produced by Fed easing shows up first in the form of rising stock and bond prices, followed later by increased economic activity. Primarily through its open market operations, the Fed can set the process in motion, with the money supply growth typically rising in tandem with an advance in stock prices. This is reflected by the DJIA's gain of about 12 percent per annum when money growth has been decisively positive. The market's returns have been about half that when money supply growth has been mildly positive. And the returns have been marginal when the growth rate has been no higher than 1 percent.

A more comprehensive perspective on money supply growth can be gained by comparing it to data on economic output, thus determining whether liquidity is sufficient for the needs of the economy as well as the financial markets. In Figure 8–2, the year-to-year change of industrial production is subtracted from the year-to-year change of the real money supply, in this case M3. When the spread is high, the real money supply is growing

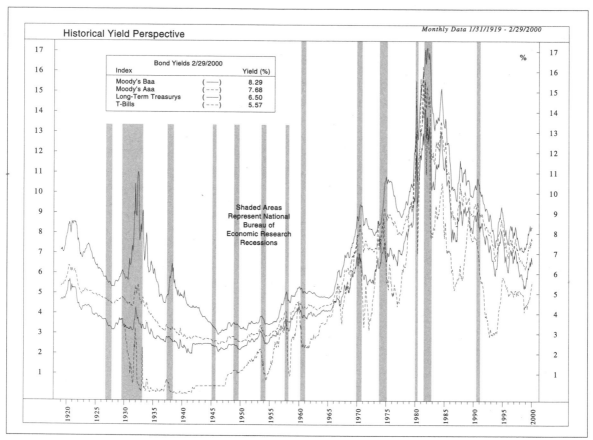

Figure 8–3

early to middle 1990s, when market valuations were reasonable. But it wasn't until real money supply growth began expanding that the market would gain the momentum for the impressive advances of the early 1950s and late 1990s.

INTEREST RATES

Also with Figure 8–3, you can make comparisons between long-term interest rates and short-term interest rates as represented by T-bill yields. When the long-term rates are well above T-bill yields, the yield curve is steep, the Fed is typically accommodative, the markets expect economic strength, and stock prices tend to benefit. Generally during those times, there will be a narrow spread between the yields of the lower-quality Moody's Baa corporate bonds and the yields of higher-quality Aaa bonds, which would normally be much lower relative to the corporate bond yields. When investors are willing to buy lower-quality bonds, thus reducing their yields, optimism is high as investors exhibit little concern for the greater default risk associated with the lower-quality bonds.

When short-term rates are close to or above long-term rates, the yield curve is flat or inverted, the Fed is typically restrictive, the markets expect economic weakness, and stock prices tend to perform poorly. Usually during those periods, widespread risk aversion keeps the yields of the lower-quality bonds rising relative to the yields of the high-quality bonds, which benefit from the desire for safety.

In Chapter 9, I will demonstrate how you can use yield spreads in assessing the appeal of stocks relative to bonds and cash, and the appeal of growth stocks relative to value stocks. The chapter will also show that credit spreads can be used to gauge the relative attractiveness of small-cap stocks and large-cap stocks.

But in considering the general question of how the monetary environment stands to affect the stock market, you can use the specific interest rates in isolation to obtain the vast majority of the information that you will need as a complement to the indicators based on money supply growth. And when examining interest rates, start with the Fed and its role in manipulating the money supply.

While the Fed's most common policy tool is the open market operation, as I have discussed, its least common approach is to alter the reserve requirement, the percentage of deposits that banks must hold in reserve. By raising the requirement, the Fed can limit bank loans and money supply growth; by reducing it, the Fed can encourage loans and money supply growth. In practice, however, changing the reserve requirement can have unexpected results, so the Fed rarely resorts to making such changes.

More common than reserve requirement changes are changes in the Fed funds target rate and the discount rate, the rate that banks pay on loans from the Federal Reserve. While increases in those rates are restrictive moves, cuts in the rates are accommodative. Since in theory, banks will borrow from the Fed when they are running out of reserves, the Fed can encourage banks to keep their reserves from dwindling by raising the discount rate and making it more expensive for them to borrow. By dropping the discount rate, the Fed can encourage banks to borrow and loan out their reserves.

In reality, banks borrow from the Fed only if they are in serious trouble, as they instead borrow from other banks at the Fed funds rate. Considering that borrowings from the Fed account for less than 0.01 percent of the available loanable funds of commercial banks, the Fed's discount rate changes tend to have more of a symbolic impact than anything else. During the 1990s, the Fed's changes in the discount rate became more predictable as the central bank began to announce changes in the Fed funds target rate.

From the Fed's perspective, the limited-discount window borrowing is a good thing. The Fed tries to discourage that borrowing and instead encourages banks to borrow from each other in the Fed funds market, at a rate that will almost always be close to the Fed funds target rate that the Fed has established. The Fed therefore keeps the discount rate in line with the Fed funds target rate, since a lower discount rate would encourage banks to borrow from the discount window. As discussed earlier, the Fed keeps the Fed funds rate in line with its target rate by using open market operations.

However, the discount rate does not necessarily move in lockstep with the Fed funds target rate. Prior to announcing the changes in the discount rate, the Fed typically announces the Fed funds target rate changes more frequently and in smaller increments, as shown in Figure 8–4. And even when no rate announcement has been made, the Fed has been able to influence monetary conditions with statements regarding its policy bias, effectively unleashing the "bond vigilantes" to fine-tune the Fed's monetary intentions by sending bond yields higher or lower. In keeping with Fed chairman Alan

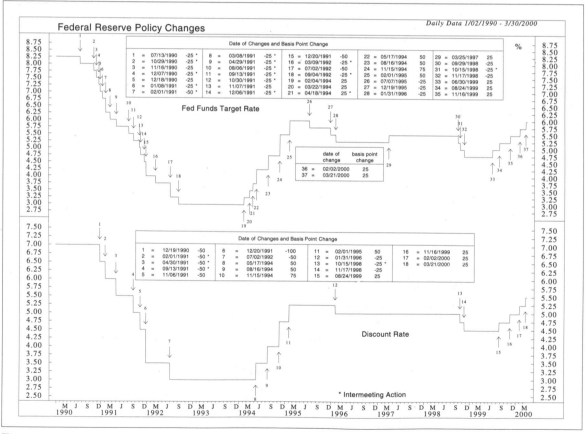

Figure 8–4

Greenspan's predilection to remain "preemptive" in fighting inflation, the Fed has thus been able to enhance its monetary repertoire with such statements, which tend to sway interest rate expectations and, in turn, the interest rates themselves.

It is changing expectations, in fact, that best explain changes in interest rates, and it is this sensitivity to expectations that best explains why interest rates can be used to develop effective stock market indicators. Long-term bond yields in particular are quick to detect a changing inflation outlook, as the yields of long-term bonds carry the largest inflation premiums. The longer the bond's maturity, the greater the markup to compensate investors for the risk that inflation will erode the purchasing power of their future cash flows. And when interest rates rise in anticipation of future inflation, stock prices generally fall as investors mark down the value of the promised future earnings. A dollar of future earnings erodes when inflation is expected to rise.

Another way to consider the impact of rising interest rates is to look at them defined as the *required rate of return,* which is the nominal interest rate plus the risk premium. As discussed in Chapter 6, the required rate of return is R in the dividend discount model formula, in which the expected dividend is divided by the spread between R and the dividend growth rate G. It is possible that when higher inflation is anticipated, increasing the required rate of return, a firm's value will remain intact since the firm will be able to pass on the increased costs by raising prices, offsetting the higher R with a higher G. If a firm is not able to raise prices, and G remains constant while R rises, the spread between them will widen, the model's denominator will rise, and the firm's value will drop. And the negative impact on the firm's value will intensify if the higher rates affect earnings to such an extent that G declines.

Some firms, such as firms with limited financing needs, are better able to handle higher interest rates than are others. But in the aggregate, rising interest rates have a negative impact on stock prices, while falling interest rates have a positive and generally more immediate impact. This is reflected by indicators that call the major indices using interest rates—short-term rates as well as long-term rates.

The Impact of Rate Changes

One of the better-known indicators is called the "three steps and a stumble" sell rule, highlighted several decades ago by analysts Edson Gould, Norman Fosback, and others. The rule holds that the market will "stumble" after three successive moves by the Fed to increase any combination of the discount rate, the reserve requirement, or the margin requirement, that is, the cash amount that must be put down in order to buy stock on margin. The corollary is the "two tumbles and a jump" buy rule, which calls for the market to "jump" after two successive Fed cuts in the discount rate, reserve requirement, and/or margin requirement.

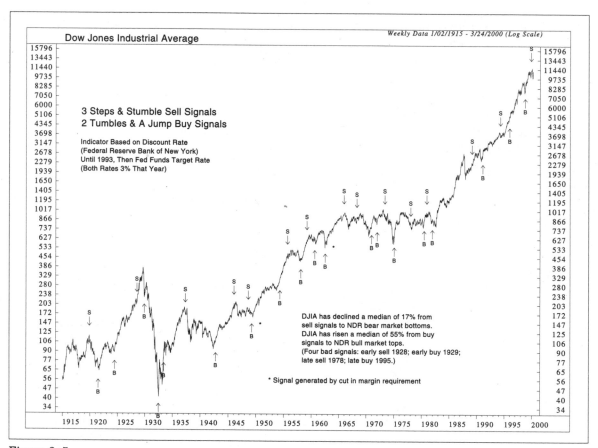

Figure 8–5

Evident in Figure 8–5, the historical record includes several very timely signals, especially buy signals, again reflecting the tendency for Fed ease to have a more immediate impact than Fed restraint. But it should be noted that in recent history, the indicators have been driven by the discount rate only, as the last margin requirement change was in 1972 and the last reserve requirement change was in 1992. And as the discount rate itself has faded in significance as a gauge of Fed policy, the Fed funds target rate has become the major barometer of Fed easing or restraint. In fact, the NDR adaptation in Figure 8–5 uses the Fed funds target rate in lieu of the discount rate starting in 1993.

Moreover, there really is nothing magic about three restrictive moves or two easing moves. And the rules make no distinction between small moves and large moves, or between moves that occur with rates at high levels and those that occur with rates at low levels. The significant point is that the greater the Fed restraint, both in magnitude and persistence, the worse the implications, at least until that point in time when so much restraint has occurred that the market starts to benefit from an expectation that the next rate hike will be the last.

Table 8–1 lists the DJIA's average gains over various periods following an initial discount rate increase, the second of two increases, the third of three increases, and so on, showing that since 1917, the market has generally performed worse as the number of rate hikes has increased, with the performance really deteriorating after four rate hikes. Table 8–2 provides a somewhat different picture using the prime rate since 1979. It shows that after six months have passed since the fifth increase, the market has started to hold up better, as suggested as well by the performance after the sixth increase. But the mean returns for the subsequent periods have still been worse than the buy-and-hold returns for the respective periods.

Conversely, the greater the magnitude and persistence of Fed ease, the better the implications, at least until that point in time when so much easing has occurred that the next rate cut is expected to be the last. And with the Fed's increased disclosure and the proliferation of Fed watching, accelerated by speculation cast about in the financial media, the market's tendency to look ahead appears to be greater than ever, even if the accuracy of those expectations is no better than ever.

T A B L E 8–1

Market Performance after Discount Rate Increases
(12/21/1917–3/14/2000)

	No. of Cases	DJIA Percent Gain after				
		22 Days	63 Days	126 Days	190 Days	252 Days
1st increase	21	0.90	0.92	2.00	4.54	8.57
2d increase	16	1.25	−2.53	2.32	2.87	4.46
3d increase	13	−1.83	1.19	6.37	3.98	3.75
4th increase	9	2.03	1.59	−1.05	−0.14	−2.98
5th increase	6	0.57	0.07	−4.85	−3.05	−4.63
6th increase	3	−1.65	−3.31	−5.90	−3.30	−4.90
Mean		**0.21**	**−0.34**	**−0.18**	**0.82**	**0.71**
Buy/hold		**0.63**	**1.85**	**3.73**	**5.73**	**7.79**

Note: The number of discount rate increases equals consecutive increases until an intervening discount rate cut is encountered at which point the count is started over. Days = market days.

T A B L E 8–2

Market Performance after Prime Rate Increases (4/30/1979–3/14/2000)

	No. of Cases	DJIA Percent Gain after				
		22 Days	63 Days	126 Days	190 Days	252 Days
1st increase	15	0.33	−1.20	2.85	3.86	8.37
2d increase	11	−2.53	−1.63	−2.17	0.33	4.01
3d increase	10	−0.12	0.90	−0.65	4.49	8.75
4th increase	9	−1.26	−3.20	0.74	5.16	5.03
5th increase	8	−2.79	−0.43	2.49	4.46	6.03
6th increase	6	0.32	3.73	7.46	8.42	10.66
Mean		**−1.01**	**−0.30**	**1.79**	**4.45**	**7.14**
Buy/hold		**1.15**	**3.43**	**6.95**	**10.80**	**14.68**

Note: Only consecutive hikes in the prime rate are counted. A decrease in the prime rate restarts the count. Days = market days.

In the case of rate declines, the tables of the discount rate since 1914 and the prime rate since 1979 are consistent with the two tumbles rule. Table 8–3 shows the strongest gains occurring after two discount rate cuts. But the market has continued responding impressively until the fourth cut, after which the market gains have been less impressive. Table 8–4 shows that with the prime rate, the second cut has produced the most consistent gains over the three longest time periods, and the third cut has been the last followed by market gains outperforming the buy-and-hold gains for each subsequent period.

In addition to the number of hikes or cuts in a widely followed interest rate, you can get a sense of magnitude by watching for reversals indicated by a percent increase from a bottom or a percent decline from a top. In Figure 8–6, buy signals are generated when the prime rate's monthly average reverses downward by about 4 percent (that's *percent*, not percentage points) and sell signals are produced by upward reversals of 7.5 percent, with the indicator then calling for a switch into commercial paper. Not only will the move into commercial paper prevent capital losses, but the total returns will be boosted by the uptrend in the interest rate.

After reversals in the Fed funds and discount rates, banks tend to adjust the other short-term rates accordingly. By passing along the rate changes via the prime rate, the banks affect short-term business and consumer loans, thus influencing spending and investment activity. Banks also know that they can raise their lending rates when the demand for loans is fervid. The demand for business loans is illustrated in Figure 8–7 by the 13-week rate of change of commercial and industrial loans, including nonfinancial commercial paper since 1983.

T A B L E 8-3

Stock Market Performance after Discount Rate Cuts
(12/18/1914–11/16/1998)

	No. of Cases	DJIA Percent Gain after				
		22 Days	63 Days	126 Days	190 Days	252 Days
1st cut	21	3.49	6.43	11.17	13.54	19.92
2d cut	17	4.25	10.61	12.73	18.37	28.40
3d cut	12	2.77	8.65	12.09	18.31	23.08
4th cut	10	2.70	8.85	10.09	15.61	23.01
5th cut	9	1.10	1.43	1.10	3.24	8.09
6th cut	7	4.31	7.68	8.81	12.52	12.03
Mean		**3.10**	**7.28**	**9.33**	**13.60**	**19.09**
Buy/hold		**0.64**	**1.84**	**3.71**	**5.67**	**7.61**

Note: The number of discount rate cuts equals consecutive cuts until an intervening discount rate increase is encountered at which point the count is started over.
Days = market days.

T A B L E 8-4

Market Performance after Prime Rate Declines (1/29/1979–3/14/2000)

	No. of Cases	DJIA Percent Gain after				
		22 Days	63 Days	126 Days	190 Days	252 Days
1st decline	15	0.34	4.69	7.00	10.47	13.97
2d decline	12	1.95	7.68	11.53	15.15	19.62
3d decline	11	2.55	4.63	7.72	11.63	16.66
4th decline	7	1.47	9.11	9.77	8.60	12.76
5th decline	7	3.85	7.89	10.23	9.77	14.38
6th decline	7	5.75	6.97	8.98	6.52	15.97
Mean		**2.65**	**6.83**	**9.21**	**10.36**	**15.56**
Buy/Hold		**1.15**	**3.38**	**6.90**	**10.65**	**14.47**

Note: Only consecutive cuts in the prime rate are counted. An increase in the prime rate restarts the count. Days = market days.

Although loan demand tends to be volatile, perspective can still be gained by comparing the rate of change to its 89-week smoothing. As shown in the chart's box, the market's performance has been relatively weak when loan demand has been above the smoothing, suggesting that banks are compelled to match the increased demand by

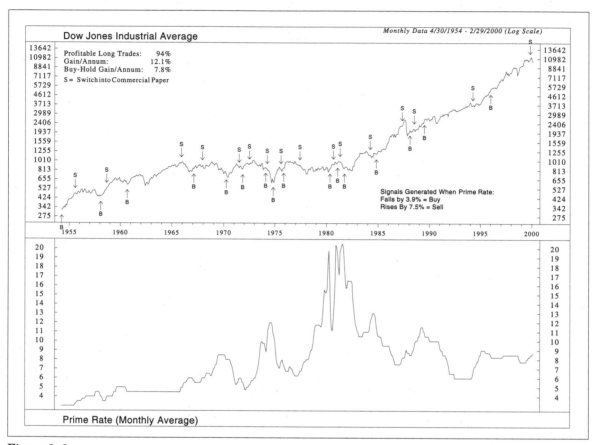

Figure 8–6

making loans more expensive. In contrast, the market has performed relatively well when loan demand has been below the smoothing, compelling banks to make their loans cheaper in order to remain competitive.

Using Long-Term Rates

Continuing with the assessment of interest rates themselves as stock market indicators, Figure 8–8 takes an approach similar to that of the prime rate indicator in Figure 8–6. This indicator generates signals based on reversals in the composite long-term Treasury bond yield, a composite of Treasury bonds with more than 10 years to maturity. While buy signals are generated by downward reversals of about 9 percent, sell signals are produced by upward reversals of about 12 percent.

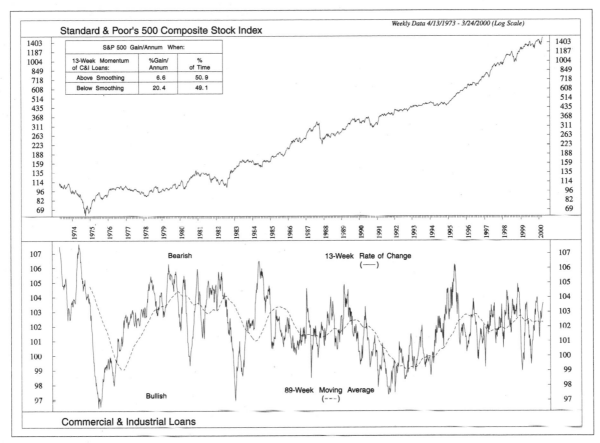

Figure 8–7

You will notice that in both the prime rate chart and the bond yield chart, the percent move needed for a sell signal is greater than the percent move needed for a buy signal. This difference recognizes that a relatively small percentage point increase can represent a large percent rise when the yield is at a low level, while a relatively large percentage point decrease can represent a small percent decline when the yield is at a high level. The higher percent requirement for sell signals is also a reflection of the market's tendency to react more slowly to rising rates than to falling rates. Since both charts enable you to identify the level at which a new signal would be generated, they are useful for answering the question of what it would take for the interest rate trend to become a positive or negative market influence.

It is important to keep in mind that the stock market is less concerned with interest rate levels than it is with interest rate trends, which is why your luck will be better with

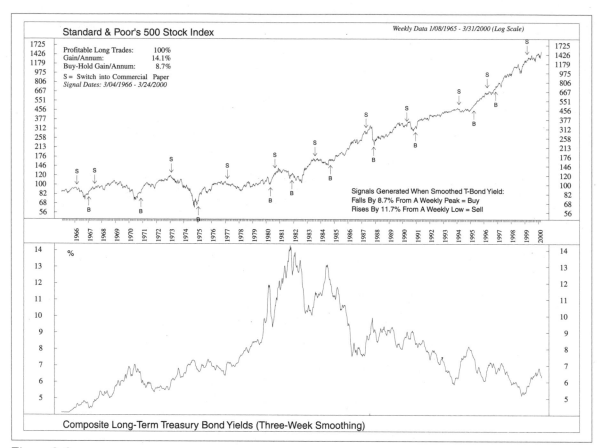

Figure 8–8

interest rate indicators that produce signals based on rate changes than it will be with indicators based on the attainment of specific rate levels. The market significance of bond yield trends is evident in Tables 8–5 and 8–6, based on the yields on bonds with more than 20 years to maturity. During interest rate uptrends defined by gains of at least 15 percent in the S&P long-term government bond yield (Table 8–5), the DJIA's average correction has been twice as severe as it has been during interest rate downtrends defined by bond yield declines of at least 15 percent (Table 8–6). Whereas eight of the 12 corrections have exceeded 10 percent with interest rates rising, eight of the 12 corrections have been less than 10 percent with interest rates falling.

TABLE 8–5

Trough-to-Peak Increases in S&P Long-Term Government
Bond Yields versus Corrections in the DJIA (Weekly data 1968–2000)

15% or Greater Increases in Long–Term Gov't Bond Yields	Corresponding Largest DJIA Corrections during Increases in Bond Yields Dates	DJIA % Decline
08/09/1968–05/29/1970	11/29/1968–05/22/1970	−32.8
03/26/1971–06/18/1971	04/23/1971–06/18/1971	−6.2
12/01/1972–08/03/1973	01/05/1973–07/06/1973	−16.9
10/12/1973–09/19/1975	10/26/1973–12/06/1974	−41.5
01/07/1977–02/22/1980	01/07/1977–03/03/1978	−24.0
06/20/1980–10/02/1981	04/24/1981 09/25/1981	−19.2
11/27/1981–02/12/1982	12/04/1981–02/12/1982	−6.6
11/05/1982–06/01/1984	01/06/1984–05/25/1984	−13.9
04/18/1986–10/23/1987	08/21/1987–10/23/1987	−28.0
08/04/1989–09/28/1990	07/13/1990–09/28/1990	−17.7
09/10/1993–11/25/1994	01/28/1994–03/31/1994	−7.8
01/05/1996–06/14/1996	04/04/1996–05/03/1996	−3.6
Mean		**−18.2**
Median		**−17.3**

Note: A weekly interest rate peak occurred on 10/16/1987, but the date was advanced to 10/23/1987 to reflect a daily interest rate increase during the week of the stock market crash.

Bond Price Indices

Another way to consider the impact of bond yields is to look at the movement of the underlying bond prices, represented in Figure 8–9 by the S&P long-term government bond price index. Instead of showing signals based on percent reversals, this chart simply identifies the point at which the bond prices reach a peak or trough in conjunction with each stock market cycle. It shows that after a trough in bond prices, and thus a peak in yields, a stock market bottom can be expected. And after a peak in bond prices, and thus a trough in yields, a stock market top can be expected. In fact, the bond price index is one of the leading indicators included in Table 5–1 in Chapter 5.

As indicated in the chart, bond prices have peaked in advance of 9 of the past 10 bull market peaks, doing so with a median lead time of 35 weeks. And they have led each of the past 9 bear market bottoms, doing so with a median lead time of 9 weeks. The shorter lead time for bond bottoms is yet another example of how the stock market's positive reaction to falling rates tends to be faster than its negative reaction to rising rates.

T A B L E 8–6

Peak-to-Trough Declines in S&P Long-Term Government
Bond Yields versus Corrections in the DJIA (Weekly Data 1970–2000)

15% or Greater Declines in Long-Term Gov't Bond Yields	Corresponding Largest DJIA Corrections during Declines in Bond Yields Dates	DJIA % Decline
05/29/1970–03/26/1971	06/19/1970–06/26/1970	−4.5
06/18/1971–12/01/1972	09/03/1971–11/19/1971	−11.2
08/03/1973–10/12/1973	08/03/1973–08/24/1973	−5.0
09/19/1975–01/07/1977	09/24/1976–11/12/1976	−8.1
02/22/1980–06/20/1980	02/22/1980–04/18/1980	−12.1
10/02/1981–11/27/1981	10/09/1981–10/23/1981	−4.0
02/12/1982–11/05/1982	05/07/1982–08/06/1982	−9.8
06/01/1984–04/18/1986	09/14/1984–12/07/1984	−6.0
10/23/1987–08/04/1989	10/30/1987–12/04/1987	−11.4
09/28/1990–09/10/1993	06/05/1992–10/09/1992	−7.7
11/25/1994–01/05/1996	07/28/1995–08/25/1995	−2.4
06/14/1996–03/10/2000	07/17/1998–09/04/1998	−18.2
Mean		**−8.4**
Median		**−7.9**

Note: A weekly interest rate peak occurred on 10/16/1987, but the date was advanced to 10/23/1987 to reflect a daily interest rate increase during the week of the stock market crash.

Of course, the lead times can very greatly. While the bond price bottom of 1981 was about a year early, the bond price top of 1998 occurred just a few weeks after the market had bottomed, and thus well before the 1999 peak. Yet in both cases, the reversals would soon have an impact. After the 1981 bond price bottom, the market's downside momentum diminished, and the stage was set for the strong bull market that started in 1982. Soon after the bond peak of 1998, the market breadth began to weaken. In fact, the breadth remained in a downtrend that had started prior to the 1998 bear market, in April of that year.

The key point here is that by using the bond price index, you are able to view the mirror image of interest rates in an integer form that is more consistent with market indices than are the interest rates themselves. You can use the bond index as you would an A/D line or any index of broad market performance. And the index is especially applicable to comparisons that use rate-sensitive indices, such as utilities and financials. Like the bond index, those rate-sensitive indices tend to lead the market, as discussed in Chapter 5, and all of these indices can be used in the same way versus the major market

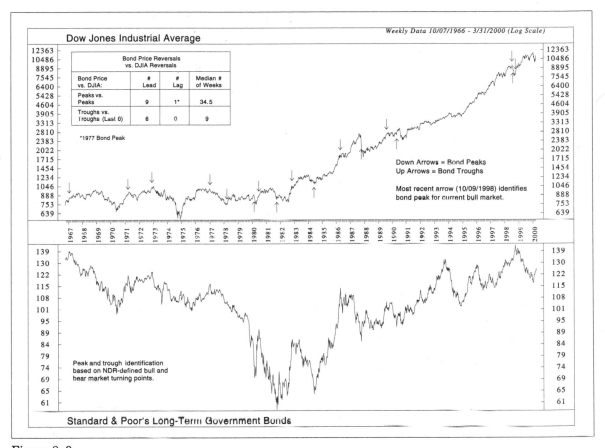

Figure 8–9

averages. The longer-lasting and more decisive the confirmation by the bond index and rate-sensitive indices, the better; the more dramatic and widespread the divergences, the greater the warning.

A good way to assess the magnitude and thrust of an interest rate move is to consider a bond index's percent change not just in relation to extremes, but on an ongoing basis. This approach is taken in Figure 8–10, which plots the six-month rate of change of short-term government bonds. One of my favorite indicators for the simplicity of its message, the indicator shows results in five different modes, indicating that the greater the upward momentum of bond prices, and thus the greater the downward momentum of interest rates, the better the market's performance. The greater the downward momentum of bond prices, and thus the upward momentum of interest rates, the worse the market's performance.

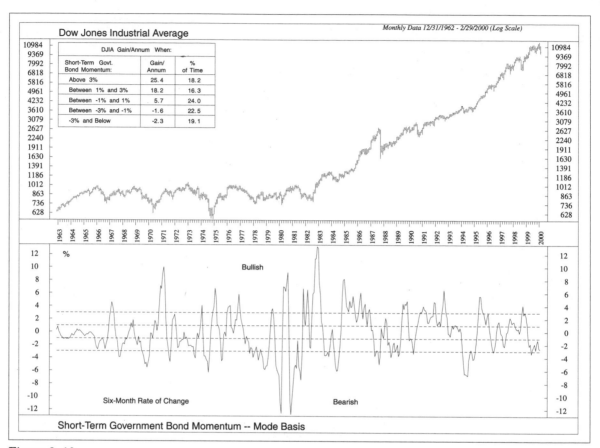

Figure 8–10

The momentum approach can also be used with the interest rates themselves. But due to the potential for rapid moves between modes when rates are at low levels, momentum indicators are better developed using interest rate point changes rather than percentage changes. The indicator in Figure 8–11 uses the year-to-year point change of the 91-day Treasury bill yield, indicating favorable interest rate momentum when the yield is 75 basis points (0.75 percentage points) lower than its level of a year earlier. The indicator describes interest rate momentum as unfavorable when the year-to-year point change is a percentage point higher than its level of a year earlier. It's impressive to note that the rate of change has been in the bullish mode for nearly a third of the time starting in 1966, gaining 23 percent per annum during those periods.

No matter what interest rate or bond price index you choose to use, the implications are the same. Rising interest rates are bad and falling interest rates are good, as the rate

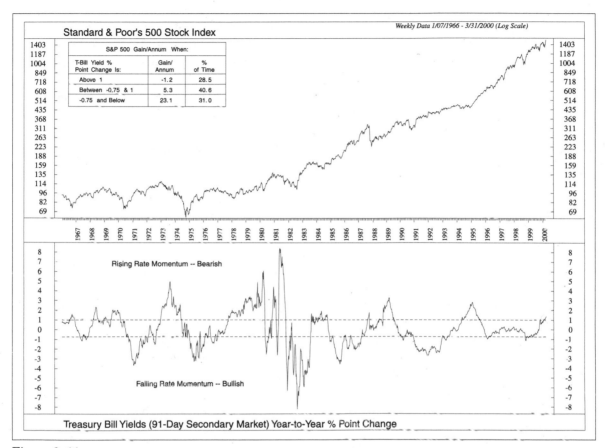

Figure 8–11

trends affect consumer spending, housing affordability, the cost of financing business growth, and corporate profitability. They also affect competing investments in short-term credit instruments, with rising short-term rates making money market mutual funds increasingly attractive investment alternatives.

The rate trends likewise affect the appeal of long-term bonds. While a trend-following approach should be applied to short-term, income-generating credit instruments that roll over frequently, a contrarian approach is needed when timing the purchase of long-term bonds, which are bought for their potential total return—the bond's capital gain plus the reinvested yields. The ideal time to buy bonds is when bond yields are extremely high and peaking, indicating a peak in fears of future inflation. Like so much else in the investment world, bond yields are driven by investor psychology, and when the sentiment reaches an extreme, it's time to look for a reversal. When yields are extremely high and possibly peaking, it's likely that the market is pricing in an unwarranted extrapolation of yesterday's inflation news. At such sentiment extremes, you can lock in the high yield and benefit from the bond's capital appreciation that will occur when yields begin their inevitable descent.

As discussed in Chapter 6, the identification of sentiment extremes is the major reason for watching the ratio of bond yields to earnings yields. And as pointed out when addressing advisory service sentiment in Chapter 7, it is important to consider interest rates when determining whether or not an extreme has been reached in sentiment toward the stock market. Since the risk of investors fleeing the stock market increases as rates ascend, caution is warranted at levels of optimism that are much lower than the optimism heights that could be reached if rates were dropping.

Of course, no indicator is without its drawbacks. As I've pointed out, it can be difficult to pinpoint when an interest rate uptrend will start to have an obvious negative impact on the market. Rising rates have tended to lead market declines, but with varying lead times. And while the bullish impact of falling rates is more immediate and predictable, falling rates will have no effect if the economy is in such dire straits that monetary easing does nothing to encourage borrowing, spending, and investing. That was the case in the 1930s in the United States and in Japan in the 1990s. In both cases, heavy fiscal spending by the government was needed to revive economic activity.

INFLATION ENVIRONMENT

Perspective on the impact of the inflation environment is provided by Table 8–7. It shows that in almost every case, the market has performed well during disinflation, when the year-to-year change of the Consumer Price Index (CPI) has been positive but falling. The condition throughout the 1990s, this environment has usually been consistent with falling interest rates, as shown by the gains in the bond price total returns. Corporate bonds have performed especially well during those periods, reflecting decreased aversion to risk.

Disinflation was not, however, a good omen at the start of the 1930s, as the stock market weakness was a foreboding precursor to the economic malaise and deflation to follow. And the market performed even worse during the subsequent deflation. But the table shows that deflation itself has not been the death knell for stocks. Whether the economy has been deflating, as indicated by a negative and dropping rate of CPI growth, or reflating, as indicated by a negative but rising CPI growth rate, the market has tended to rise, suggesting that the health of the broader economy must also be considered when assessing the threat posed by deflation.

The more consistent negative response is the market's aversion to high and rising inflation. While inflation was relatively stable during the 1960s, enabling the market to

T A B L E 8–7

Asset Returns under Various Inflation Conditions

1. Performance of stocks, Treasury bonds, and corporate bonds total return relative to cash under various price direction environments (Q1/1926–Q4/1999)

Inflation

Dates	Stocks	Treas.	Corp.
Q3/1929–Q1/1930	−16.36	5.09	3.46
Q1/1934–Q3/1934	−13.42	0.87	3.78
Q4/1939–Q4/1941	−20.85	6.97	6.08
Q1/1946–Q2/1947	−11.54	−0.83	0.49
Q3/1950–Q2/1951	12.32	−4.59	−4.12
Q3/1955–Q2/1957	10.43	−9.62	−11.40
Q2/1959–Q1/1970	38.91	−23.04	−18.83
Q3/1972–Q1/1975	−30.62	−10.71	−10.80
Q1/1977–Q2/1980	4.13	−18.61	−18.06
Q1/1987–Q4/1990	−1.91	1.13	3.05
Q2/1998–Q4/1999	23.30	−9.42	−9.03
Gain/annum	**−0.94**	**−2.42**	**−2.13**

Disinflation

Dates	Stocks	Treas.	Corp.
Q1/1926–Q3/1926	18.01	0.16	1.52
Q1/1930–Q3/1930	−25.29	1.76	4.29
Q3/1934–Q2/1938	51.16	19.87	25.80
Q4/1941–Q1/1946	157.77	18.90	15.47
Q2/1947–Q2/1949	2.25	2.27	0.72
Q2/1951–Q3/1954	76.29	5.82	7.38
Q2/1957–Q2/1959	26.43	−3.71	0.17
Q1/1970–Q3/1972	18.99	11.14	15.28
Q1/1975–Q1/1977	14.93	9.88	14.20
Q2/1980–Q1/1987	83.12	31.78	32.98
Q4/1990–Q2/1998	194.08	59.96	52.17
Gain/annum	**12.27**	**3.96**	**4.35**

Deflation

Dates	Stocks	Treas.	Corp.
Q3/1926–Q2/1927	11.6	5.53	2.58
Q3/1030–Q4/1932	−56.05	7.72	5.36
Q2/1938–Q4/1938	17.29	2.08	3.99
Q2/1949–Q4/1949	21.72	1.75	0.47
Q3/1954–Q3/1955	38.79	−3.52	−1.21
Gain/annum	**−0.57**	**2.63**	**2.21**

Reflation

Dates	Stocks	Treas.	Corp.
Q2/1927–Q3/1929	103.39	−6.36	−1.11
Q4/1932–Q1/1934	65.72	4.72	16.27
Q4/1938–Q4/1939	−1.10	5.93	3.96
Q4/1949–Q3/1950	20.88	−0.87	0.52
Gain/annum	**30.41**	**0.56**	**3.56**

2. Performance of stocks, Treasury bonds, and corporate bonds total return relative to cash under various price level environments (Q1/1926–Q4/1999)

	Stocks	Treas.	Corp.	% Time
Price inflation	2.62	1.21	1.77	45.4
Price stability	13.12	1.08	1.12	44.7
Price deflation	2.97	0.86	3.01	9.8
Buy/hold	7.23	1.12	1.60	100.0

Notes: Inflation = CPI Y/Y above zero and rising. Disinflation = CPI Y/Y above zero and falling. Deflation = CPI Y/Y below zero and falling. Reflation = CPI Y/Y below zero and rising. Price Inflation = CPI Y/Y above 3%. Price Stability = CPI Y/Y between −1% and 3%. Price Deflation = CPI Y/Y below −1%. Stocks = S&P 500 Stock Index total return/cash. Treas. = S&P Long Government Bond Index total return/cash. Corp = Long-Term Corporate Bond total return/cash. Cash = 90-Day T-bill total return.

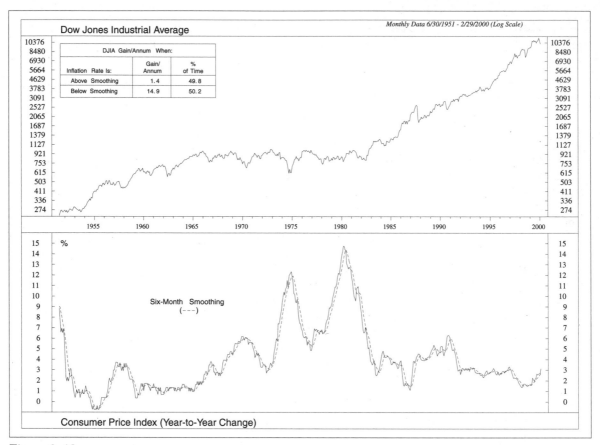

Figure 8–12

rise, equities have otherwise struggled to move higher, or have moved lower, during inflationary periods. The market's tendency to abhor inflation and applaud disinflation
can be seen in Figure 8–12, which shows that the DJIA has performed poorly when the
annual rate of CPI growth has been above its six-month moving average. The DJIA has
gained about 15 percent per annum when the CPI growth has been below the smoothing.

But you shouldn't limit your inflation assessment to the CPI, which has been subject to much debate regarding its accuracy as an inflation gauge. Also keep an eye on the
Producer Price Index (PPI), which measures prices in the manufacturing and distribution stages of production, before the goods reach the consumer. A benefit of watching the
PPI is that it tends to be quicker than the CPI in detecting inflation trends. Based on the
PPI for finished goods, the indicator in Figure 8–13 is similar to the CPI indicator, using
a 12-month smoothing rather than a 6-month smoothing.

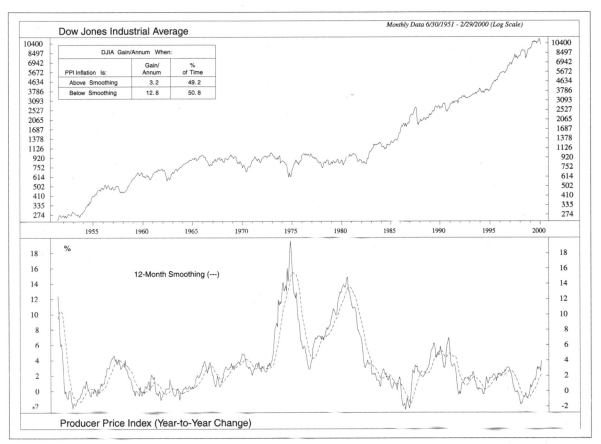

DJIA Gain/Annum When:		
PPI Inflation Is:	Gain/ Annum	% of Time
Above Smoothing	3.2	49.2
Below Smoothing	12.8	50.8

Figure 8–13

An inflation gauge that tends to pick up production-level price pressures even ear-lier than the PPI is the National Association of Purchasing Management Price Index,[1] which is the percentage of purchasing managers who say they are paying higher prices for the products they buy, plus one half of the percentage of purchasing managers indi-cating no change in prices. A component of the broader NAPM Index, the price index is advantageous not only because it is early in indicating the start of inflation trends, but also because the number is reported early in the month. The producer and consumer price indices are typically reported in the third week of the month. Again, the indicator shows the market performing well when price pressures are low and performing poorly when price pressures are high, as shown in Figure 8–14.

One more price index to monitor is the Commodity Research Bureau (CRB) Fu-tures Price Index, which goes directly to the raw material level for a composite reading

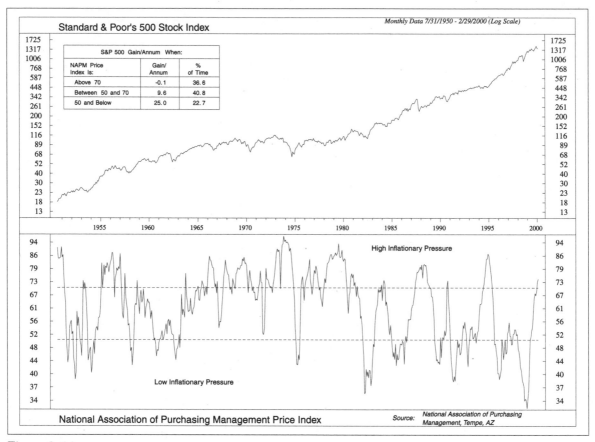

Figure 8–14

on the price of 17 different commodities. In contrast to the other inflation gauges, the in-dex is updated daily, and the index level can even be checked during the day since it is the basis for a futures contract. Figure 8–15 illustrates the index's year-to-year change, smoothed over three weeks, with high readings indicating an abundance of inflationary pressure and low levels indicating a lack of inflationary pressure.

The CRB Index's 17 components include agricultural commodities such as corn, cat-tle, cotton, and seven others; metals commodities gold, silver, platinum, and copper; and energy commodities crude oil, heating oil, and natural gas. It can also be helpful to track each commodity independently, or at least to track the more widely watched and influen-tial commodities like crude oil and gold. But for the purposes of gauging the degree to which inflation trends are adding to market risk or reducing it, the CRB Index should be sufficient, especially if considered along with the CPI, PPI, and the NAPM Price Index.

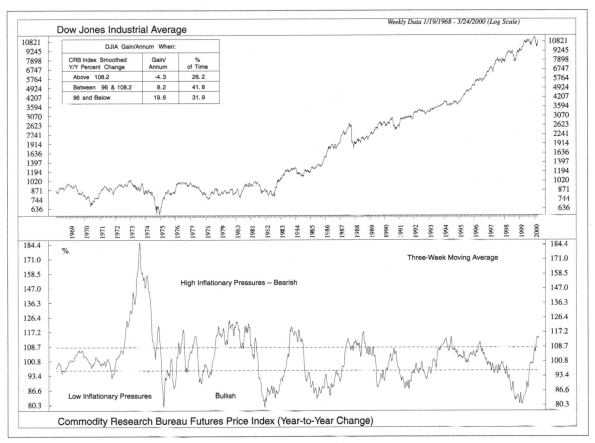

Figure 8–15

In fact, the appeal of a composite approach can be seen in the NDR Inflation Timing Model, shown in the bottom clip of Figure 8–16. Made up of 22 different inflation gauges, the model is designed to call inflation reversals, indicated in the middle clip by the arrows indicating turns in the year-to-year change of the CPI. When the model's reading has been negative, with inflation thus detected by fewer than half of the model's indicators, the DJIA has performed admirably. When the model has been higher than 6, caused by the overwhelming majority of indicators seeing inflation as a problem, the DJIA has performed poorly.

Inflation can therefore be used as an indicator for the market as a whole. But it also has implications for stock selection. During periods of high inflation, relative strength can be expected from stocks that are traditionally viewed as inflation hedges, such as metals mining stocks, industrial materials stocks, and energy stocks. Since interest

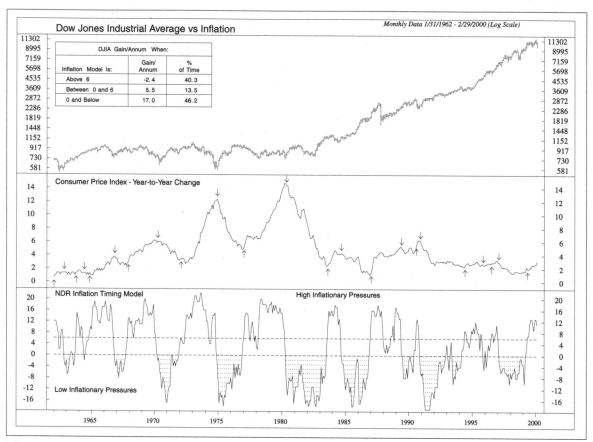

Figure 8–16

rates typically rise during those periods, relative weakness can be expected from financials, utilities, housing stocks, and firms that carry heavy debt loads. During periods of low inflation, the inflation hedges tend to underperform, especially relative to the rate-sensitive sectors. And bonds tend to perform well.

An additional consideration when focusing on inflation is the degree to which it affects price-rearnings ratios. When inflation is high, profits may be inflated as well, boosting the denominator of a stock's P/E ratio. But while a stock may appear to be better valued in such a case, the added profits are considered to be low in quality since they will not be repeated when inflation recedes. In other words, the inflation-produced profits are not operating profits. To compensate for inflation's impact on the denominator, Figure 8–17 adds the inflation rate to the S&P 500 P/E ratio, using the CPI's year-to-year change as an inflation proxy. By comparing this ratio to the unadjusted P/E ratio, you can thus determine whether high inflation has been keeping the P/E ratio unjustifiably low.

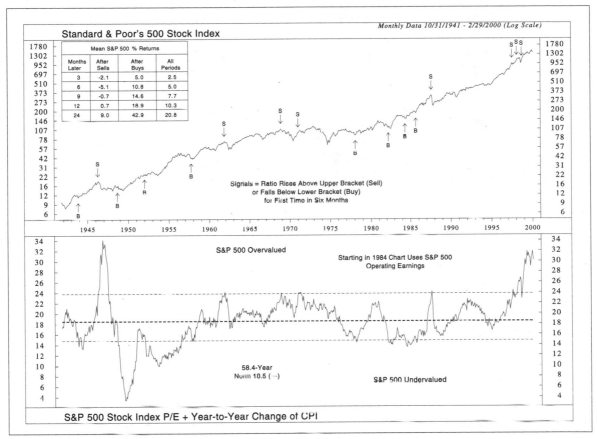

Figure 8–17

    You may notice that the indicator reached extremely high levels after World War II, the result of high inflation. Although the S&P 500 P/E index was nothing extraordinary at 16.5, in 1946 it reached 34 with the inflation adjustment, which helps explain why the market entered a bear market despite what appeared to be decent valuation levels. On the other hand, the inflation rate was low in the early 1960s, but the S&P 500 became so overvalued that the indicator reached overvalued levels anyway.

    In 1999, the market had the worst of both worlds, overvalued levels and rising inflation, with the indicator suggesting that it would only be a matter of time before the market would start to correct its excesses. As shown in the chart's box, the market has performed poorly after sell signals, and it has performed exceptionally well after buy signals, as those signals identify the undervalued levels that could withstand the inflation test. The indicator distinguishes the high-quality undervalued readings from the undervalued readings caused by inflation.

By adding the inflation rate to the price-earnings ratio, you will also be recognizing the interest rate trend, since rates will almost always be on the same trend path as the inflation rate. In fact, the accompanying interest rate rise becomes a threat not only to the illusory profits, but also to the operating profits. The indicator in Figure 8–17 can therefore be used to complement indicators that adjust valuation for interest rates, such as the interest rate to earnings yield ratios shown in Chapter 6.

Again, when bond yields are extremely high relative to earnings yields, bonds represent far better values than do stocks. And when T-bill yields are extremely high relative to earnings yields, investors find T-bills and other low-risk credit instruments more attractive than risky stocks because of the virtually guaranteed income that they produce.

THE U.S. DOLLAR

Also when watching inflation and interest rates trends, keep an eye on the value of the U.S. dollar. A weakening dollar can be inflationary since it causes imported goods to rise in price, making it harder for the Fed to maintain an accommodative policy. At the same time, dollar weakness can be a sign of mounting expectations that the economy will weaken. Since the stock market tends to weaken on those same expectations, it is not unusual to see the dollar and the stock market declining in tandem. And the combined weakness stands to discourage foreign investment in U.S stocks, an additional negative influence.

When the dollar is strengthening, foreign buyers are encouraged, as the market is most likely rising as well. At such times, both the dollar and the stock market are reflecting expectations for economic strength, which usually is good for the broad market. But sorting out the reasons for dollar strength or weakness is far from simple, as the exchange rates with the yen, euro, and other currencies will differ depending upon real and nominal interest rate differentials with the associated countries, relative economic growth, current account and trade balances, political developments, and differing monetary policies. And the dollar's trend can have different relative impacts on different kinds of companies, such as exporters, importers, and multinationals.

But the aggregate impact is illustrated by Figure 8–18, which shows that since 1987, rising dollar momentum has been consistent with strength in the broad market as represented by the Value Line Composite, while falling dollar momentum has been consistent with broad market weakness. The indicator is based on the 14-day smoothing of the 30-day rate of change of the Financial Instrument Exchange (FINEX) dollar index. And since its introduction in July 1989, the indicator has held up well in signaling short- to intermediate-term market moves. When the smoothed momentum has indicated positive dollar momentum, the Value Line Composite has gained 12 percent per annum, whereas the index has lost 4 percent per annum when the momentum has been un-

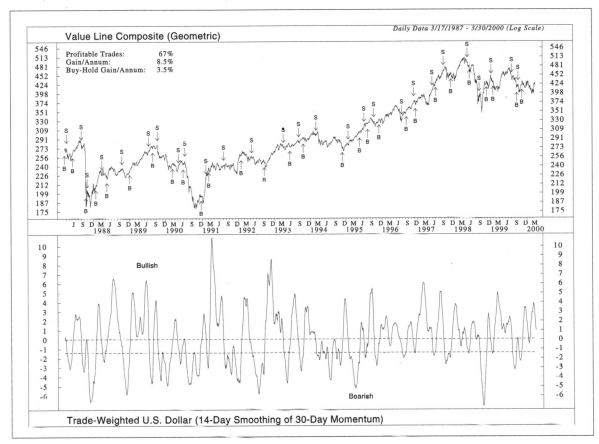

Figure 8–18

changed or negative. Strong dollar momentum thus has bullish implications for the market, while negative dollar momentum tends to have bearish implications.

ECONOMIC INFLUENCES

While the dollar tends to rise in conjunction with bullish expectations for the U.S. economy, so does consumer confidence. Shown in Figure 8–19, consumer confidence can be viewed as a sentiment indicator for the economy. Like sentiment indicators of the stock market, confidence can reach extremely high levels and stay there for a long time, as occurred in the late 1980s and again in the late 1990s. But when the confidence begins to reverse in earnest, typically in conjunction with a stock market decline, it can mark the start of an economic downturn. Conversely, an upturn in consumer confidence can signal the start of an economic advance, as occurred after the recessions of 1973–1975,

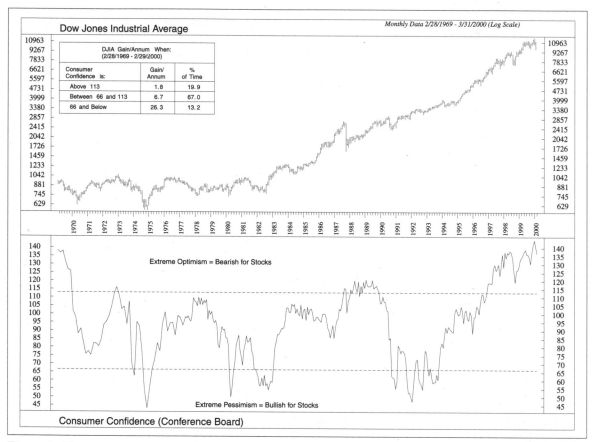

Figure 8–19

1980, 1981–1982, and 1990–1991, although in the last case, confidence didn't start a sustainable rise until 1994.

For stock market analysis, it should be recognized that consumer confidence has a lot to do with the performance of the stock market. The value of the consumer's portfolio is a major influence on the confidence level. Moreover, both the stock market and consumer confidence are leading indicators of the economy. In fact, 2 of the 11 components of the Index of Leading Economic Indicators are the performance of the S&P 500 and the University of Michigan Consumer Expectations Index, which is similar to the Conference Board's index. Since consumer sentiment and stock market performance are both leading indicators of the economy, each is most useful for confirming the other's implications. For instance, an indication of a reversal in consumer sentiment could be used to confirm your sense that a major stock market reversal had occurred. The broader Index of Leading Indicators could be used in the same way for a more comprehensive perspective.

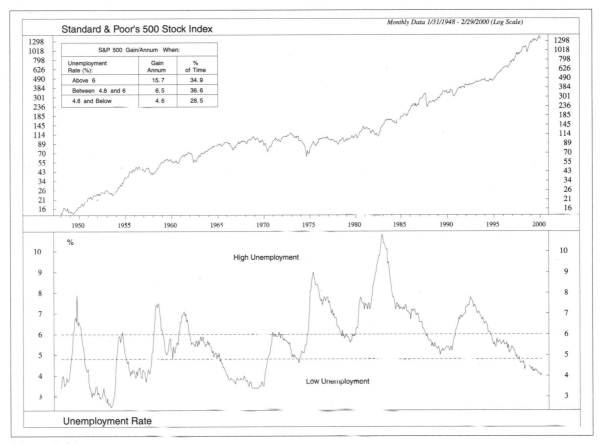

Figure 8–20

As leading economic indicators are confirming indicators for stocks, it follows that coincident and lagging economic indicators are lagging indicators for stocks. Yet, while it would seem nonsensical to use a lagging market indicator as an indicator of the stock market's direction, the unemployment rate is an exception, perhaps because its trends are consistent with the trends of unit labor costs and other measures of wage inflation watched closely by the Fed. Thus affecting inflationary pressures and the Fed's responses to them, the unemployment rate warrants attention. Figure 8–20 shows that since the beginning of 1948, the DJIA has gained 16 percent per annum with the unemployment rate above 6 percent and just 5 percent per annum with the unemployment rate below 4.5 percent.

In watching the indicators featured in this chapter, indicators of economic liquidity, interest rates, inflation, and economic influences, you should be able to gain a sense of the current stage of the economic cycle, and what that implies for risk and reward in the stock market. You should be able to determine whether the economy is in an early

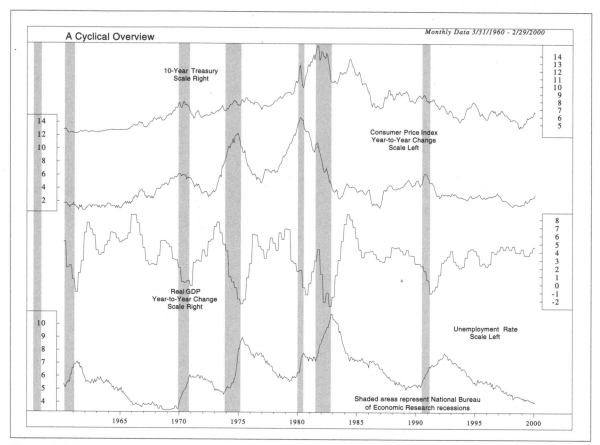

Figure 8–21

stage of economic expansion, in a mature stage, or in one of the relatively infrequent and relatively brief economic recessions, as identified by the shaded regions of Figure 8–21. During a recession, you will see widespread evidence of weak business and consumer demand, reflected by low industrial material prices, low consumer prices, and low inflationary pressures in general. Consumer confidence will be low and falling, unemployment will be rising, and interest rates will be falling.

But at some point prior to the end of the recession, expectations will start to improve, and the Fed's monetary ease will enable the market to bottom out and start to advance in anticipation of profit improvement. The improvement in the market's performance and other leading economic indicators will be followed by an economic trough and a new expansion. When inflationary pressures inevitably return, the Fed will start to tighten again, and the cost of conducting business will start rising faster than profits. As liquidity drains away, short-term interest rates will rise relative to long-term rates, expectations will start to worsen, and the stock market will start to weaken in anticipation of the recession to follow.

As I have stressed several times in this book, no two cycles are quite alike, and there will be times when, as in 1987 and 1994, several conditions will appear conducive to an economic downturn, yet the economy will survive. And it's essential to view the U.S. monetary and economic influences in a global context, recognizing whether U.S. trends are part of broader global trends or exceptions that will prove to be either leading or temporary—that is, they may lead the rest of the world or they may be temporary responses to circumstances unique to the United States.

The bottom line is represented by such adages as "don't fight the Fed" and "money moves markets," as the market significance of Fed policy cannot be underestimated. By watching what the Fed is watching, you will be able to anticipate changes in Fed policy and the likely market ramifications of those changes. On top of your assessment of the market's technical health and sentiment, you will be able to complete your evaluation of the market outlook. You can then get started on acting on that outlook, to be addressed in Part Three.

E N D N O T E S

1. National Association of Purchasing Management, P.O. Box 22160, Tempe, AZ 85285.

REFERENCES

Gwartney, James D., and Richard L. Stroup. 1997. *Economics: Public and Private Choice*, eighth ed. Orlando, FL: Dryden Press.

What to Do with Your Market View

Acting on the Outlook

Maximizing Your Returns through Effective Asset Allocation

You have established a database and the procedures for updating your data. You have used the data to develop indicators based on tape action, sentiment, and monetary conditions. You can then apply your indicators to developing a market outlook. And once you have an outlook, you can apply it to your risk tolerance and financial goals in deciding what to do with your investment funds.

In putting your indicators to use, there is no fail-safe approach. At certain times, the market has a way of outsmarting any human or mechanical system. But in working with both approaches for the past 15 years, I have seen the model-based approaches prove their worth and stand the test of time.

This does not mean, however, that you should use an approach that is entirely model-driven, as a flaw in a model's construction or changing behavior among the indicator components can cause a model to send out misleading messages, or to crash altogether. Rather, the best approach is to control your market outlook as directed by your model.

As discussed in Chapter 3, this model-based approach can be compared to a pilot controlling a jet guided by the plane's autopilot, with the pilot remaining aware of what lies over the horizon (a future Fed meeting, for example), the distance to the ground (the downside potential), and the maximum cruising altitude (the upside potential). While you allow the autopilot (the model) to determine the plane's direction and speed, your continued presence in the pilot seat gives you the option to take the controls during market reversals, during periods of turbulent volatility, and if the autopilot ceases to function—that is, if the model breaks down.

Yet, a reliable model is nevertheless your assurance that you won't get caught up in the hype of the moment and make an investment decision that will prove costly down the road. NDR's Big Mo, for example, was decisively negative toward the market at the end of 1999, ignoring the fervor surrounding the record highs on the NASDAQ and the phenomenal run by technology stocks. You can see this by turning back to any of the five Big Mo charts shown in Chapter 4. The ideal approach is to base your outlook on the model's objective assessment and to then overlay your interpretation of the market's long-term breadth and sentiment conditions, its status within the economic cycle, and the influences that a model may not be able to detect, such as new investment incentives resulting from revised fee structures among mutual funds, new corporate programs that encourage 401-k investing, and changing dividend payout trends.

But a model need not be as complex as Big Mo, which includes hundreds of indicators. As long as the indicators are reliable, a model with 10 or 12 indicators can be very useful. The reliability of the indicators will depend upon the degree to which the indicator has influenced the market historically, and that can be determined using the testing techniques discussed in Chapter 4. While you should make sure that each indicator holds up well after out-of-sample and/or real-time testing, you should apply the same test to the model itself. If your model has 12 indicators, you will typically classify conditions as favorable when the majority of indicators is bullish and unfavorable when the majority is bearish.

Using the mode approach, you might determine that the more favorable the composite message of the individual indicators, the more bullish the outlook; and the more negative the composite message, the more bearish the outlook. This conclusion can be reached either by assigning each indicator a +1, 0, or −1 and then adding them together, or by scaling each indicator from 0 to 100 percent and then determining the average scaled reading. But whatever method you use, don't neglect to apply the same kind of testing to the model that you would apply to the individual indicators. I will provide an example in Chapter 11, in which I will select from the indicators featured in the previous chapters, build the model, combine it with subjective considerations, draw conclusions about the current outlook, and then apply the conclusions in developing an investment strategy.

YOUR ALLOCATION OBJECTIVES

Before moving to that point, let's take a closer look at the issues that need to be addressed, and the options that you will want to consider, when deciding how to put your funds to work. First, you must clarify your objectives. Once you have done so, you can establish a scale that will mandate your strategy, ranging from your most aggressive approach in response to a low-risk outlook to your most defensive approach in response to a high-risk outlook. If your risk tolerance is high and your objective is to maximize your total return over the next year, your response to a low-risk outlook will be far more aggressive than it will be if your objective is to preserve capital.

If you have more than one pool of investment funds, your response to the low-risk or high-risk outlook will be different for each pool. If your analysis tells you that the market outlook is bullish, for example, you might move into small caps with your speculative funds and blue chip stocks with your retirement funds. If your analysis indicates that the bull market is in its late stages, you might switch into blue chips with your speculative funds and bonds or cash with your retirement funds.

While the topic of portfolio construction is beyond the scope of this book, you won't have much trouble finding a wealth of information if you need guidance on how to structure your portfolio to meet your future financial needs and goals. But whatever your risk tolerance, you should be able to enhance your returns by knowing when to adjust your portfolio mix by overweighting or underweighting asset classes relative to your benchmark.

Let's say, for example, that you have determined that your financial objectives would be met by an aggressive portfolio mix of 25 percent large-cap stocks, 40 percent small-cap stocks, 25 percent international stocks, and 10 percent bonds. Table 9–1 shows that from 1975 through 1981, you would have wanted to keep an even higher weighting in small caps, since they were the top-performing of the four asset classes. But from 1985 through 1988, you would have wanted to overweight international stocks, which were the strongest performers. And from 1995 through 1998, you would have benefited by overweighting large-cap stocks, which were the top performers in each of those years. So while an aggressive mix has outperformed the more conservative balanced mix for 66 percent of the time since 1971, and while small caps have been the top performer in 38 percent of those years, those percentages are not high enough to warrant passive, indexed strategies, considering the long periods of outperformance by international stocks and large-cap stocks.

STOCKS VERSUS BONDS AND CASH

The table also shows that in bear market years, such as 1973 and 1974, bonds have been the top performer. The challenge, then, is to identify when an asset class is ready to move into or out of favor, and a good starting point is to compare the outlook for stocks versus bonds and cash, and to do so with an assessment of the economic cycle. As discussed earlier, the glory days for bonds are the depths of a recession, with the falling rates and monetary ease eventually reviving the stock market, and in turn the economy. As the economy warms up and stocks benefit from improving profit prospects, interest rates stabilize, and eventually they start to move higher, to the detriment of the bond

T A B L E   9-1

Comparative Annual Percentage Gains of Various Asset Classes

	Single-Investment				Multi-Investment	
Year	**Large U.S. Stocks**	**Small U.S. Stocks**	**International Stocks**	**Intermediate Gov't Bonds**	**Aggressive Mix**	**Balanced Mix**
1971	14.34	16.50	18.36*	8.73	15.62	14.43
1972	18.91	4.43	22.48*	5.16	12.34	12.46
1973	−14.82	−30.90	−15.24	4.61*	−20.13	−15.01
1974	−26.57	−19.95	−25.47	5.69*	−20.88	−17.51
1975	37.23	52.82*	32.80	7.82	38.71	31.64
1976	23.60	57.38*	13.40	12.87	32.03	25.61
1977	−7.49	25.38*	0.68	1.41	7.69	4.32
1978	6.36	23.46*	16.52	3.49	15.19	12.18
1979	18.24	43.46*	10.95	4.10	24.14	18.31
1980	32.17	39.88*	25.67	3.91	30.33	24.65
1981	−5.11	13.88*	−4.79	9.45	3.63	3.01
1982	21.44	28.01	9.71	29.10*	21.66	21.81
1983	22.45	39.67*	21.93	7.40	27.25	22.33
1984	6.11	−6.67	4.72	14.03*	1.19	4.28
1985	31.60	24.66	40.56*	20.33	29.75	29.07
1986	18.57	6.85	41.89*	15.14	18.61	19.95
1987	5.14	−9.30	16.16*	2.90	1.39	3.33
1988	16.32	22.87	23.29*	6.10	19.54	16.93
1989	31.33*	10.18	16.61	13.29	17.09	17.58
1990	−3.25	−21.56	−17.02	9.73*	−13.30	−8.83
1991	30.40	44.63*	18.28	15.46	31.04	26.69
1992	7.59	23.35*	−5.23	7.19	10.05	7.76
1993	10.04	20.98	22.50*	11.24	17.53	16.06
1994	1.24	3.11	5.08*	−5.15	2.27	0.99
1995	37.45*	34.46	20.72	16.80	29.77	27.05
1996	22.84*	17.62	13.48	2.10	16.19	13.75
1997	33.31*	22.78	15.76	8.38	21.97	19.71
1998	28.54*	−7.31	24.34	10.21	10.14	13.04
1999	21.02	29.79*	24.54	−1.77	22.76	17.74
Mean Gain	**14.02**	**15.10**	**13.54**	**8.58**	**14.61**	**13.22**
Risk (SD)	**16.25**	**23.55**	**15.87**	**7.05**	**15.01**	**12.46**
% time best	**17.20**	**37.90**	**27.60**	**17.20**		
% time better					**65.50**	**34.50**

Notes: All gains based on total return. Large U.S. stocks = Standard & Poor's 500 stock index. Small U.S. stocks = Ibbotson Small-Capitalization stock index. International stocks = Morgan Stanley Capital International world equity index. Intermediate government bonds = Ibbotson intermediate-term government bond index. Aggressive mix = 25% large, 40% small, 25% international, 10% bond. Balanced mix = 25% large, 25% small, 25% international, 25% bond. SD = Standard deviation of annual gains.
* = Best portfolio performance for the period.

market. During such a period of mature economic growth, which described the late 1990s, stocks tend to perform better than bonds. And when the rising rates drag down stock prices, cash becomes the preferred asset class, until that point in time when a bear market is fully recognized and the anticipation of economic weakness sends rates back down, to the bond market's benefit.

The relative performance of stocks and bonds at different stages of economic growth is summarized by the fact that the S&P 500 total return (price plus reinvested dividends) has tended to outperform the bond total return, with the stock/bond ratio rising about 11 percent per annum. This stock market outperformance illustrates why during most periods, most investors maintain a greater exposure to stocks than to bonds. But the degree of outperformance has diminished when weak economic conditions have been indicated by a reading of zero or lower on the NDR Economic Timing Model, a composite of indicators designed to call the economy. Bonds have performed far better than normal during those periods. Conversely, they have performed far worse than normal when a mature expansion has been indicated by a model reading of more than 18, the best mode for stocks and the stock/bond ratio.

Beyond economic conditions, the most important influence on the relative performance of stocks and bonds is the relative valuation of the two, represented by the bond yield to earnings yield ratio shown in Figure 6–9 in Chapter 6. When bond yields are extremely high relative to earnings yields, stocks are overvalued and bonds are undervalued, at least relative to each other and most likely on an absolute basis as well. At such times, the indicator says the time is right to lock in a high yield on bonds that are likely to appreciate in price, and to do so by scaling back in a stock market that is likely to correct its overvalued condition. The benefit of doing so is indicated in Figure 9–1 by statistics showing that when the bond yield to earnings yield ratio has exceeded about 1.5, the ratio of the S&P 500 Total Return Index to the Lehman Brothers Total Return Index has dropped at a –4 percent per annum rate. When stocks have been undervalued relative to bonds, as indicated by a ratio of less than about 1.2, the stock/bond ratio has risen about 11 percent per annum.

The relative appeal of cash can also be included in the relative valuation assessment, especially when T-bill yields are used instead of bond yields. Rather than using a ratio, which can become volatile at the low yield levels that have at times been reached by T-bills, Figure 9–2 uses the spread between the S&P 500 earnings yield and the T-bill yield. When the spread is less than –0.2, the indicator shows that the stock market is overvalued relative to T-bills, which are more attractive for the guaranteed income that they produce. When the spread exceeds 1.3, the stock market is undervalued relative to T-bills, and stocks are thus more attractive than cash.

The chart's box shows that when the spread has been in the upper mode, the per annum return of the S&P 500 Total Return Index has been more than three times the per annum return of the total return indices for bonds and cash. When the spread has been in its lower mode, the per annum gain figures show that T-bills have provided the best

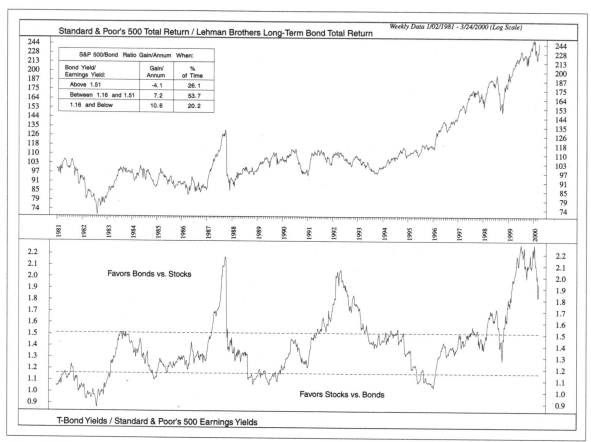

Figure 9–1

total return while the stock total return has been negative. Bonds have done best with the spread in the middle mode, when the stock market tends to be trending downward with falling rates or in the early stages of a bull market, prior to rate increases of significance.

I would also keep an eye on the yield curve, as represented in Figure 9–3 by the spread between the 10-year Treasury yield and the 1-year Treasury yield. When the short-term yield is about the same or higher than the longer-term yield, the returns from cash have been far better than the returns from stocks and bonds. When the 10-year yield has been moderately higher than the short-term yield, the situation with the spread in the chart's middle mode, stocks have been the asset of choice. And when a steep yield curve has been indicated by a wide spread, bonds have been the top performer.

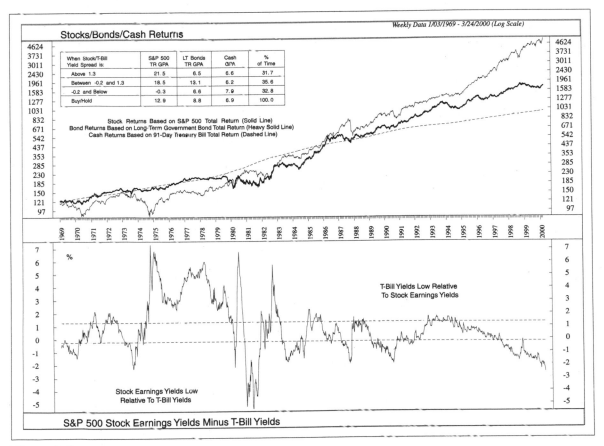

Figure 9–2

I would also keep in mind that most of the monetary indicators featured in Chapter 8 can be applied to the three-way allocation decisions. And at least for the stock/bond ratio, keep an eye on technical indicators that call the ratio itself. You might, for instance, compare the ratio to a moving average or develop an indicator based on the ratio's momentum. As with the stock market alone, your identification of the ratio's trend could prove to be more valuable than anything else.

SMALL CAPS VERSUS LARGE CAPS

Likewise, an accurate assessment of the direction of the ratio of large caps to small caps (or vice versa) could be your most important input when determining whether large caps or small caps can be expected to outperform. But that assessment can be complicated by

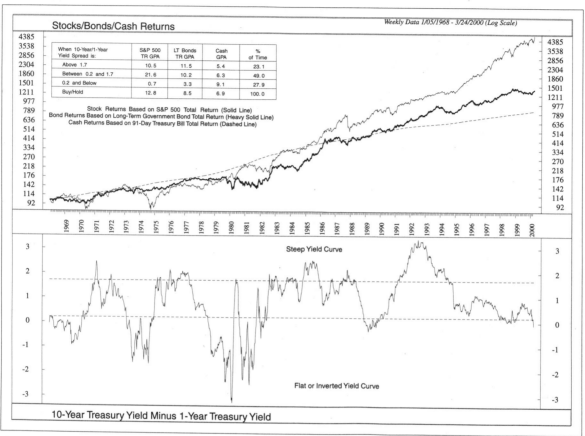

When 10-Year/1-Year Yield Spread is:	S&P 500 TR GPA	LT Bonds TR GPA	Cash GPA	% of Time
Above 1.7	10.5	11.5	5.4	23.1
Between 0.2 and 1.7	21.6	10.2	6.3	49.0
0.2 and Below	0.7	3.3	9.1	27.9
Buy/Hold	12.8	8.5	6.9	100.0

Figure 9–3

the need to distinguish between short-term surges of small-cap outperformance versus the longer-term trends, recognizing, for instance, the tendency for small caps to outperform from mid-December into early January or later.

It's also important to keep in mind that small caps generally have higher betas than do large caps, which means that they are generally more volatile. It means that they take off quickly from market bottoms and sell off sharply from market peaks, typically underperforming during bear markets. As indicated by Ibbotson[1] and Russell total return data used in Table 9–2, small caps have performed worse than large caps in 21 of the past 24 bear markets. Early in a new bull market, you can expect to see small caps start to outperform, with their outperformance especially dramatic in conjunction with the breadth thrusts that send the broad market skyward. Whereas small caps should be avoided when market risk is high, the small-cap opportunities are often excellent when market risk is low at the beginning of a new advance.

T A B L E 9–2

Small-Cap Total Return versus S&P 500 Total Return—Performance During and Following Bear Markets (9/30/1929–12/31/1999)

Bear Market		% Gain		Small-Cap % Gain Months after Bear Market			S&P % Gain Months after Bear Market		
Start	End	Small Cap	S&P 500	Three	Six	Twelve	Three	Six	Twelve
09/30/1929	11/30/1929	−38.5	−30.2	14.2	10.5	−33.4	12.5	19.5	−17.1
04/30/1930	07/31/1932	−76.9	−70.6	23.6	2.5	190.7	16.5	18.6	75.4
09/30/1932	02/28/1933	−40.6	−27.4	172.6	255.2	295.8	73.1	101.4	99.9
02/28/1934	07/31/1934	−31.1	−17.8	14.7	23.5	23.4	2.7	7.4	33.9
03/31/1937	03/31/1938	−75.9	−49.5	57.9	60.7	32.9	38.6	48.9	36.6
11/30/1938	04/30/1939	−25.9	−12.7	24.6	52.2	74.3	11.5	20.2	17.1
09/30/1939	04/30/1942	−18.2	−30.3	10.6	38.1	147.1	14.0	27.7	61.6
05/31/1946	05/31/1947	−40.3	−21.2	13.4	14.4	35.5	7.3	6.4	21.8
06/30/1948	06/30/1949	−20.7	−10.1	14.8	28.7	35.4	11.9	22.4	33.5
01/31/1953	09/30/1953	−11.4	−8.0	1.5	12.2	35.1	7.8	18.7	45.8
04/30/1956	10/31/1957	−13.7	−10.1	6.9	14.2	46.6	2.7	8.1	30.1
01/31/1960	10/31/1960	−7.5	−1.4	17.7	34.0	33.2	16.7	24.3	32.5
12/31/1961	06/30/1962	−20.6	−22.3	3.4	11.0	31.1	3.7	17.3	31.0
02/28/1966	10/31/1966	−20.6	−10.1	25.0	42.4	74.7	8.9	19.2	20.9
12/31/1968	05/31/1970	−47.3	−22.7	4.8	9.5	42.8	7.6	16.2	34.9
04/30/1971	11/30/1971	−19.2	−7.9	27.7	25.1	18.9	14.2	18.2	27.7
01/31/1973	12/31/1974	−42.2	−36.5	39.4	68.3	52.8	23.0	41.8	37.2
09/30/1976	02/28/1978	45.0	−12.0	28.8	47.6	−50.5	13.2	21.7	16.4
09/30/1978	04/30/1980	−58.0	12.5	25.8	44.4	66.3	15.9	22.9	31.1
04/30/1981	08/31/1982	−12.8	−3.1	29.6	50.2	73.4	17.5	27.0	44.1
11/30/1983	07/31/1984	−15.6	−6.7	8.9	22.0	30.6	11.5	21.9	32.2
08/31/1987	10/31/1987	−31.9	−23.3	6.7	24.6	27.2	3.0	5.6	14.7
07/31/1990	10/31/1990	−25.8	−13.8	22.0	44.8	58.6	14.2	25.6	33.4
07/31/1998	08/31/1998	−19.4	−14.5	18.1	16.8	28.4	22.0	30.3	39.8
Mean		**−27.9**	**−18.7**	**25.5**	**39.7**	**57.1**	**15.4**	**24.6**	**34.8**

Notes: Study uses NDR-defined bear market dates for the months in which those moves started or ended. Study is presented using monthly total returns. Small-cap total return data from Ibbotson prior to 1979, Russell thereafter.

You should be leery, then, of a small-cap rally that gets started during the mature stages of a stock market advance and an economic expansion, especially in the presence of conditions that not only are normal for the end of a stock market advance, but also are consistent with small-cap underperformance. For instance, when bond price momentum is negative, as is often the case at the end of a stock market advance and late in an

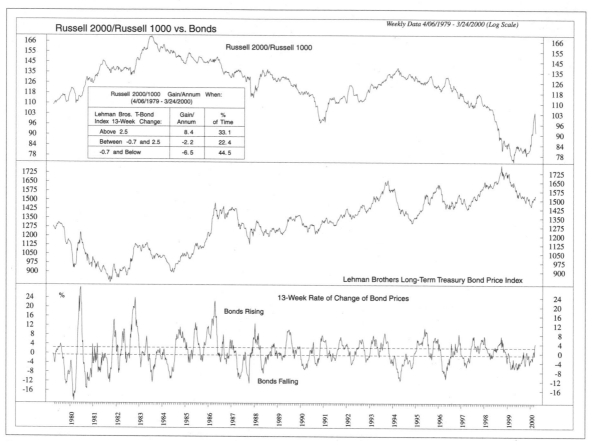

Figure 9–4

economic expansion, the Russell 2000, a widely recognized proxy for small caps, tends to perform worse than the Russell 1000, a proxy for large caps. As shown in Figure 9–4, the ratio of the Russell 2000 to the Russell 1000 has dropped at a per annum rate of about –7 percent when the 13-week rate of change of the Lehman Brothers Long-Term Treasury Bond Index has been negative.

Also late in a cycle, you can expect to see a low risk premium, as measured by the spread between the Moody's Baa bond yield and the 10-year Treasury bond yield, shown in Figure 9–5. The risk premium is narrow when the yield of the higher-risk corporate bond is relatively low versus the yield of the lower-risk Treasury bond, indicating relatively high demand for the higher-risk bonds. At such times, risk aversion is scarce, and the willingness to speculate is high.

For the vast majority of the time, the word *speculation* is synonymous with *small caps*. But history shows that at extremes, the risk premium has been a contrary indica-

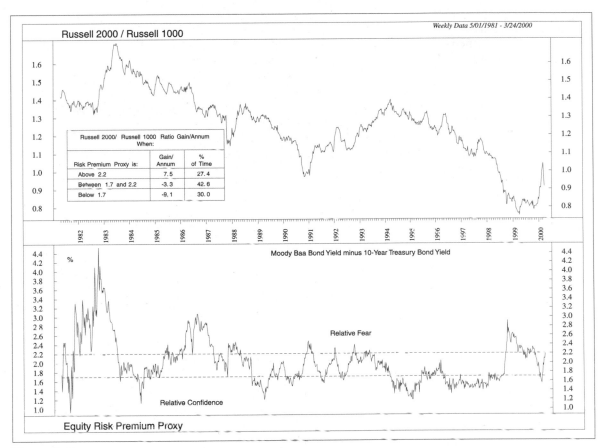

Figure 9–5

tor for small caps. The ratio of the Russell 2000 to the Russell 1000 has dropped at a –9 percent per annum rate when the spread has been below 1.7, indicating complacency. Negative Treasury bond momentum and a relatively low-risk premium were both present at the bull market peaks of 1981, 1987 and 1990, peaks followed by small-cap underperformance. When bond momentum and the risk premium have both been high, small caps have tended to perform better than large caps. The indicators in Figures 9–4 and 9–5 both favored the Russell 2000 at the onset of the index's run of outperformance starting after the bear market bottoms of 1982, 1987, and 1990.

On top of the indicators based on interest rates, the economic indicators themselves show that the Russell 2000 tends to perform poorly late in an economic expansion and well in anticipation of better growth ahead. The ratio of the Russell 1000 to the Russell 2000 has risen at a rate of 5 percent per annum when the Index of Lagging Economic Indicators has been well above its two-year average, and the ratio has dropped at a –9 percent per an-

T A B L E 9–3

Ratio of Ibbotson Small Companies Total Return Index to
S&P 500 Total Return Index versus Economic Turning Points

High Preceding Expansion Peak			Low Preceding Recession Trough		
Ratio High	Peak	Months	Ratio Low	Trough	Months
01/51	07/53	30	07/49	10/49	3
03/55	08/57	29	04/54	05/54	1
01/60	04/60	3	12/57	04/58	4
12/68	12/69	12	12/60	02/61	2
03/71	11/73	32	07/70	11/70	4
08/79	01/80	5	06/73*	03/75	21*
06/81	07/81	1	03/80	07/80	4
07/83	07/90	84	08/82	11/82	3
05/96	?	?	12/90	03/91	3

*Low preceded expansion peak.

num pace when the index has been well below its average. More specifically, Table 9–3 uses the ratio of the Ibbotson Small Companies Total Return Index to the large-cap S&P 500 Total Return Index to show that the small-cap/large-cap ratio has tended to peak prior to expansion peaks and bottom prior to recession troughs. This reflects the tendency for small caps to anticipate major reversals in the economy, with the small-cap relative strength often fizzling out well before the end of the economic expansion. As indicated by the lead times listed in the table, the leads from ratio peaks to expansion peaks have generally been longer than they have been from ratio lows to recession lows.

The last three economic troughs can be seen in Figure 9–6, which uses the NDR Economic Timing Model. The chart illustrates how the ratio of the Russell 2000 Total Return Index to the Russell 1000 Total Return Index has tended to rise when the model reading has been low, reflecting the tendency for small caps to lead fledgling expansions. The ratio has tended to fall when the model reading has been high, in keeping with the tendency for large caps to take over in a maturing expansion.

GROWTH VERSUS VALUE

The model can also be used to demonstrate how the economic cycle affects another allocation concern, the relative appeal of growth stocks versus value stocks. Whereas a growth stock is a stock that's appealing for the company's earnings growth prospects, a value stock is a stock that's appealing for its low price.

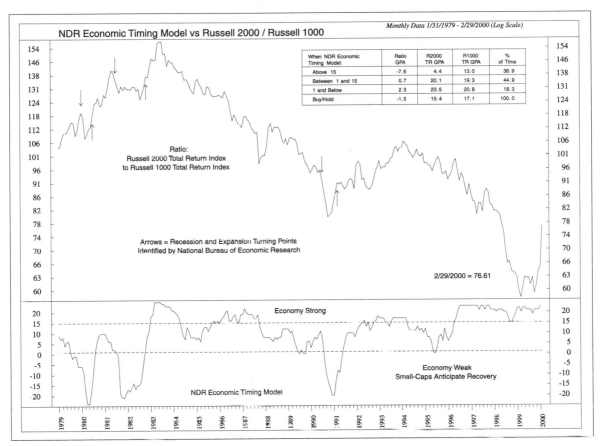

Figure 9–6

But while you might think that growth stocks would do better than value stocks during periods of strong economic growth and strong earnings growth, the historical records show the opposite. Figure 9–7 indicates that when the NDR Economic Timing Model has been positive, the Russell 1000 Growth Total Return Index has tended to underperform the Russell 1000 Value Total Return Index. When weak economic growth has been indicated by a model reading of +1 or lower, growth has outperformed by about five percentage points per annum. Likewise, Figure 9–8 shows that when the year-to-year change of S&P 500 earnings has exceeded 7 percent, the growth/value ratio has dropped at a rate of about −1 percent per annum. When the earnings growth has been −6 percent or lower, the growth/value ratio has risen at a per annum rate of about 6 percent.

In the same way that, counter to what you might expect, the aggressively minded small caps respond poorly when risk premiums are extremely low, relative performance of growth and value has to do with sentiment extremes, the supply/demand balance, and

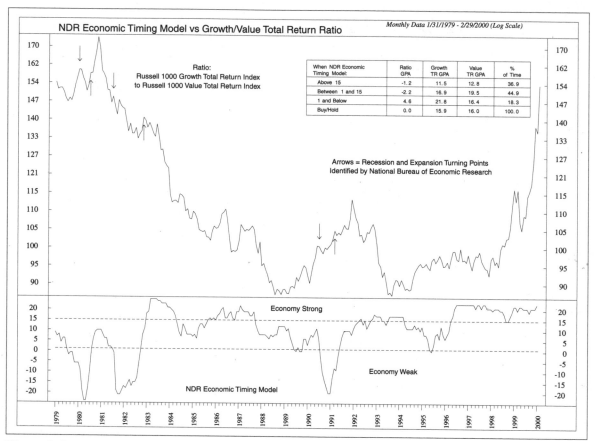

Figure 9–7

the anticipatory behavior of stock prices. An ideal environment for value stocks would include not only extremely strong economic growth and extremely strong earnings growth, but also a peaking stock market, and a steep yield curve, in which long-term interest rates exceed short-term rates in anticipation of economic strength and higher rates ahead. At such times, the good news becomes fully discounted, and value stocks tend to benefit as investors look for stocks that, in contrast to high-multiple growth stocks, are less vulnerable to earnings disappointments. In the midst of the generally high earnings multiples, the supply/demand balance for value stocks is favorable, as they are in demand and hard to find.

But the favorable environment for value stocks is far from ideal for growth stocks. Typically, by the time the economic numbers indicate expansion strength, the growth stocks have already advanced in anticipation of the accompanying earnings growth, they are already widely owned, the economy's performance has swelled their numbers, and their supply/demand balance is unfavorable for continued price appreciation.

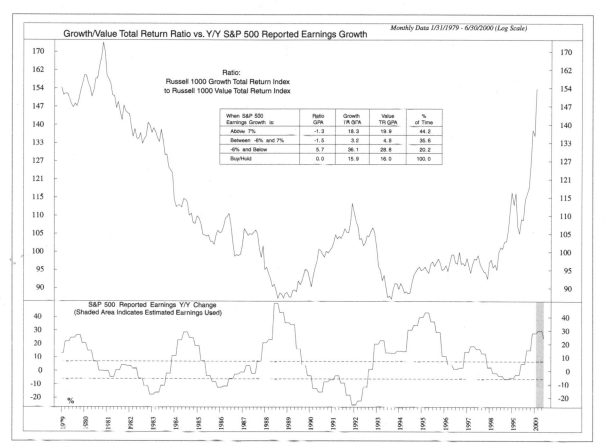

Figure 9–8

Growth stocks are additionally threatened if the late stage of the economic cycle is accompanied by high and rising interest rates. Since high earnings multiples imply optimism toward expected returns far into the future, growth stocks are threatened by rising rates, which can reduce those returns. Value stocks are less threatened by rising rates, as their multiples make less optimistic assumptions about future earnings growth.

At the opposite end of the spectrum, you would watch for growth to start outperforming value after periods of weakness in both the stock market and the economy, when the supply/demand balance would be less favorable for value stocks than it would be for growth stocks. Interest rates are usually low at such times, providing reassurance that there's justification for the relatively high multiples of the relatively rare growth stocks.

You would therefore look to growth stocks during periods of extremely weak earnings growth, extremely weak economic growth, a bottoming stock market, and a flat or inverted yield curve, in which long-term rates are in line with or below short-term rates

in anticipation of economic weakness and declining rates. The bad news would be discounted, and growth stocks would benefit as stock buyers would start looking for stocks
that would stand to benefit most from the expected improvement in the environment for
corporate profits. The relative performance of growth stocks can be expected to improve
when, with the economic numbers still depressed, the bottoming stock market is starting to anticipate a future economic upturn.

The relative performance of growth and value after market peaks is summarized in
Table 9–4, and the relative performance after market bottoms is evident in Table 9–5.
While growth stocks tend to outperform after bottoms, value stocks tend to hold up
better when a peaking stock market reflects expectations for a future economic downturn. After the last seven bull market peaks, the growth/value ratio has been down by
medians of –2 percent 6 months later and –6 percent 12 months later. After the last
seven bear market bottoms, the medians show the ratio up by 3 percent 6 months later,
but unchanged over the 12-month period. By comparison, the median 6-month and
12-month returns for all periods have been 0.2 and 0.6 percent respectively.

T A B L E 9–4

Growth/Value Returns after Peaks

	Median % Change Following NDR-Defined Market Tops			
	3 Months	**6 Months**	**9 Months**	**12 Months**
Growth	–4.1	–5.9	1.0	–1.2
Value	–4.0	–1.9	6.9	7.8
Growth/value	1.0	–2.0	–4.7	–5.9

Note: Based on S&P BARRA growth and value indices.

T A B L E 9–5

Growth/Value Returns after Bottoms

	Median % Change Following NDR-Defined Market Bottoms			
	3 Months	**6 Months**	**9 Months**	**12 Months**
Growth	14.7	27.2	30.8	33.1
Value	14.1	24.0	27.7	30.7
Growth/value	2.6	2.6	0.7	0.1

Note: Based on S&P BARRA growth and value indices.

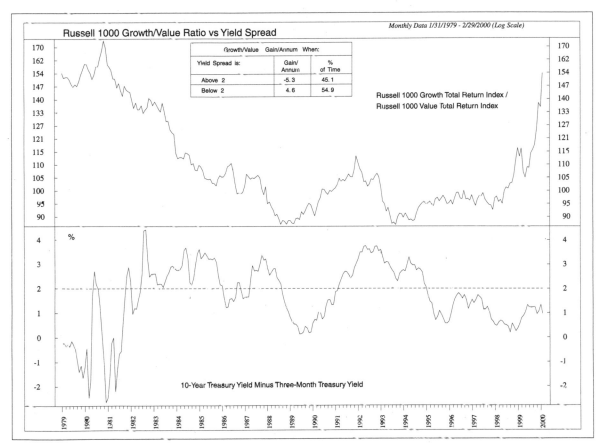

Figure 9–9

But growth has had a better chance of holding up in a down market if the decline has started with the yield curve flat or inverted, as indicated by a narrow or negative spread between the 10-year Treasury bond yield and the three-month T-bill yield. The implicit expectation of declining interest rates helps explain why growth held up relatively well after the market peaks of 1990 and 1998. Figure 9–9 shows that, historically, growth has tended to outperform value when the yield curve has been relatively flat or inverted. Value has tended to perform better when the yield spread has been wide, the sign of a steep yield curve and an indication that rates are expected to rise.

The determination of whether growth stocks or value stocks will perform better is far from simple. The indicators rarely line up in complete agreement, and the extreme conditions that offer the most useful information are infrequent. They are, after all, extremes. The more common state is the economy and the stock market moving midtrend

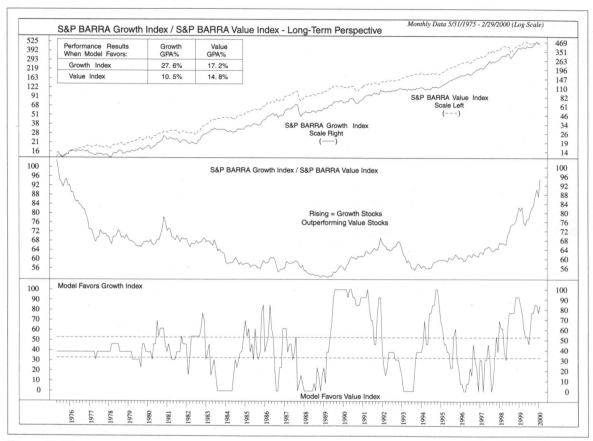

Figure 9–10

somewhere, with a specific sector story driving the growth or value index. It can therefore help to simply watch the technical action of the growth/value ratio, in the same way that, as I suggested earlier, you can watch the trend of the small-cap/large-cap ratio. Figure 9–10, for example, shows a model based on technical indicators for the ratio of the Russell 1000 Growth Index to the Russell 1000 Value Index.

SECTOR APPLICATIONS

Whether the growth/value ratio is midtrend or undergoing a major reversal around a market extreme, the practical matter of how to invest your funds will be affected not only by your outlook for growth versus value, but also by your evaluation of the sectors most responsible for the relative performance of the two style indices. While your assess-

GROUPS AFTER PEAKS AND TROUGHS

To identify the groups that have tended to perform best after peaks and troughs, Table 9–8 uses Standard & Poor's data starting in 1971 to rank S&P groups for their average performance over the first three months of the past eight bear markets, while Table 9–9 ranks those groups for their average performance over the first three months of the past nine bull markets. As most bear markets have been shorter than most bull markets, the three-month period covers a greater portion of the average bear market than the average bull market, in fact encompassing the entirety of the short bear markets of 1987, 1990, and 1998. But the intent is to illustrate which groups have tended to benefit

TABLE 9–8

Median S&P Group Performance in 13 Weeks Following NDR Bull Market Peaks (Eight Cases, 1/11/73–Present)

Group Name	First Three Months of Bear Market (%)	Group Name	First Three Months of Bear Market (%)
S&P Oils Composite	1.0	Multiline insurance	−11.7
Telephone	0.8	Major regional banks	−12.0
Domestic oils	−0.3	Insurance: life/health	−12.3
International oils	−0.4	Containers: metal/glass	−12.7
Tobacco	−1.4	HC medical products and supplies	−13.2
Electric companies	−1.6	Retail: general merchandise	−13.2
Natural gas	−3.8	Aluminum	−13.3
Foods	−6.2	Beverages, alcoholic	−13.7
Computer: hardware	−7.3	Diversified machinery	−13.7
Metals (misc.)	−8.1	Broadcasting: TV/radio	−13.8
Money center banks	−8.1	Retail: department stores	−13.9
Railroads	−8.6	Electronic semiconductors	−14.5
Personal care	−8.7	Aerospace/defense	−14.7
Paper and forest products	−9.1	Footwear	−14.9
Health care drugs	−9.2	Retail: composite	−15.0
Property/casulty insurance	−9.6	Newspaper publishing	−15.2
Retail food chains	−10.1	Publishing	−15.4
Restaurants	−10.8	Entertainment	−17.0
Electronic instrumentation	−10.9	Building materials	−18.2
Automobile	−10.9	Truckers	−19.5
Beverages, nonalcoholic	−10.9	Airlines	−20.3
Electrical equipment	−11.1	Textiles: apparel	−21.1
Containers and packaging	−11.1	Lodging: hotels	−21.4
Chemicals	−11.3	Waste management	−22.3
Iron and steel	−11.6	Savings and loan	−22.9
Retail drugstores	−11.7		

ment of growth versus value will help with certain broad investment decisions, such as whether to move funds into or out of mutual funds that emphasize growth, those that focus on value, or hybrids of these, your analysis will be equally helpful at the sector level. If your indicators favor growth, consider that a plus for the sectors that are dominated by growth stocks. If your indicators favor value, consider that a plus for the sectors that are dominated by value stocks.

To identify which sectors are growth-oriented and which are value-oriented, Table 9–6 considers all of the stocks in NDR's stock-selection universe as of early 2000, breaking them down by sector categories. Listed after each sector are the number of stocks in the sector and the number of stocks as a percentage of the universe. Those figures are then broken down further to identify the number and percentages of large-cap value stocks, large-cap growth stocks, small-cap value stocks, small-cap growth stocks, mixed-style large caps, mixed-style small caps, and those for which style and market-cap data is not available.

The breakdown is based on the definitions of the Frank Russell Co., which, in maintaining its growth and value indices, uses various valuation criteria to maintain lists of stocks that it classifies as growth stocks or value stocks. In some cases, a growth stock contains value characteristics and appears in both Russell categories, and the same applies to value stocks with growth characteristics. In Table 9–6, such a stock would be counted as a large cap or a small cap, but it would not be included in one of the more specific style categories, which include only those stocks that are growth or value stocks exclusively. The Russell indices include the hybrids along with the stocks classified solely as growth or value.

Table 9–7 lists the sectors with a relatively large share of stocks that fall into one of the four style categories, with a 25 percent weighting used as the cutoff. When the environment favors value, and when the Russell 1000 Value Index starts to outperform the Russell 1000 Growth Index, you can focus on the sectors most heavily weighted by large-cap value stocks. With the economy strong at the end of an advance, you might expect to see strength in economically sensitive cyclicals like automotive and transportation stocks, and in natural resource-based sectors like industrial materials and energy. All are on the list of sectors most dominated by large-cap value.

But if you determine that the bull market is ending, you would be best off moving into the most value-dominated sector of all—the utilities. By the time the market starts to believe that the economy's best news is behind it, to the detriment of corporate profits, the market starts its decline. And while the natural resource-oriented energy stocks may still be holding up if commodity inflation is a reason for the market downturn, you would be almost certain to see the high-yielding utilities benefiting from their defensive appeal. Relative strength could also be expected from stocks in the foods sector, a defensive sector with no predominant style.

TABLE 9–6

NDR Sector Breakdown by Market Cap and Style

Sector	No. of Stocks		LCV		LCG		SCV		SCG		LC		SC		N/A	
	Total No. of Stocks	As a % of Universe	No.	%	No.	%	No.	%	No.	%	No.	%	No.	%	No.	%
Aerospace/defense	15	0.8	4	26.7	0	0.0	2	13.3	1	6.7	4	26.7	3	20.0	1	6.7
Automotive	26	1.4	14	53.8	1	3.8	3	11.5	1	3.8	2	7.7	5	19.2	0	0.0
Banking/loans	131	7.0	61	46.6	2	1.5	32	24.4	8	6.1	11	8.4	17	13.0	0	0.0
Broadcast/media	71	3.8	13	18.3	13	18.3	4	5.6	11	15.5	22	31.0	6	8.5	2	2.8
Conglomerates	107	5.7	16	15.0	19	17.8	10	9.3	27	25.2	18	16.8	15	14.0	2	1.9
Capital goods	100	5.3	25	25.0	5	5.0	20	20.0	21	21.0	8	8.0	21	21.0	0	0.0
Energy	64	3.4	20	31.2	0	0.0	12	18.8	4	6.2	17	26.6	9	14.1	2	3.1
Foods	55	2.9	13	23.6	4	7.3	8	14.5	3	5.5	17	30.9	8	14.5	2	3.6
Health care	129	6.8	9	7.0	26	20.2	8	6.2	43	33.3	27	20.9	16	12.4	0	0.0
Housing	49	2.6	15	30.6	2	4.1	6	12.2	4	8.2	5	10.2	17	34.7	0	0.0
Industrial materials	93	4.9	36	38.7	2	2.2	26	28.0	2	2.2	4	4.3	21	22.6	2	2.2
Leisure/entertainment	33	1.8	6	18.2	1	3.0	5	15.2	5	15.2	7	21.2	8	24.2	1	3.0
Nonbank financial	208	11.0	75	36.1	13	6.2	67	32.2	11	5.3	12	5.8	21	10.1	9	4.3
Precious metals	6	0.3	2	33.3	1	16.7	0	0.0	1	16.7	0	0.0	0	0.0	2	33.3
Retail	174	9.2	25	14.4	39	22.4	20	11.5	28	16.1	28	16.1	32	18.4	2	1.1
Technology	315	16.7	11	3.5	90	28.6	9	2.9	118	37.5	52	16.5	33	10.5	2	0.6
Transportation	38	2.0	14	36.8	1	2.6	12	31.6	4	10.5	0	0.0	7	18.4	0	0.0
Utilities	119	6.3	69	58.0	3	2.5	31	26.1	1	0.8	7	5.9	7	5.9	1	0.8

Notes: LCV = large-cap value, LCG = large-cap growth, SCV = small-cap value, SCG = small-cap growth, LC = large-cap (mixed), SC = small-cap (mixed). Based on 18 NDR sectors in March 2000. Foreign stocks sector (8 percent of universe) excluded because of lack of market cap and style designations for all 151 stocks.

TABLE 9–7

Sectors with More than 25 Percent of Weight in Specific Style

Style	Most Heavily Weighted Sectors	Stocks in Sector (No.)	Stocks of Specified Style (No.)	Style Weight In Sector (%)
Large-cap value	Utilities	128	73	57.0
	Automotive	26	14	53.8
	Banking loans	136	61	44.9
	Industrial materials	93	36	38.7
	Nonbank financial	214	76	35.5
	Transportation	41	14	34.1
	Precious metals	6	2	33.3
	Energy	64	20	31.2
	Housing	49	15	30.6
Small-cap value	Nonbank financial	214	70	32.7
	Transportation	41	12	29.3
	Industrial materials	93	26	28.0
	Utilities	128	34	26.6
Large-cap growth	Technology	322	92	28.6
Small-cap growth	Technology	322	121	37.6
	Health care	130	44	33.9

Note: Based on 19 NDR sectors in January 2000.

Late in the bear market, you would watch for the rate-sensitive sectors to re[cover] to the improvement in the bond market outlook, which would most likely becom[e] dent sometime near the end of the decline. With bonds rallying, you would keep on the financials for signs of improving relative strength, perhaps followed by im[provement] relative performance by stocks in the housing sector, a rate-sensitive cyclical se[ctor] tends to anticipate increased economic activity. As discussed in Chapter 5, ra[te-sensi]tive sectors tend to lead the major market trends, and in this case their relative would be a leading indication of an eventual market upturn.

Finally, at the bottom of the market and the onset of a new bull market expect to see improving relative performance from growth-oriented sectors. stocks in particular. As shown in Table 9–7, growth is synonymous with th[e] sector, with small-cap growth especially prevalent within the sector. In fact ogy sector is the only sector with more than 25 percent of its weight in larg and one of two sectors with more than a quarter of its weight in small-ca other is health care, owing to the high number of small-cap growth-orient ogy and drug stocks.

T A B L E   9–9

Median S&P Group Performance in 13 Weeks Following NDR Bear Market Troughs (Nine Cases, 11/23/1971–Present)

Group Name	First Three Months of Bull Market (%)	Group Name	First Three Months of Bull Market (%)
Airlines	30.4	Textiles: apparel	16.1
Waste management	30.0	Health care drugs	15.4
Lodging: hotels	26.9	HC medical products and supplies	15.4
Electronic semiconductors	26.9		
Electronic instrumentation	25.7	Tobacco	14.8
Newspaper publishing	25.3	Multiline insurance	14.8
Footwear	24.6	Metals (misc.)	14.8
Retail drugstores	23.2	Automobile	14.7
Aerospace/defense	22.7	Beverages, nonalcoholic	14.3
Restaurants	22.1	Paper and forest products	13.9
Entertainment	22.0	Foods	13.1
Electrical equipment	21.8	Containers: metal/glass	13.0
Containers and packaging	21.6	Railroads	12.9
Truckers	21.3	Retail composite	12.5
Broadcasting: TV/radio	21.3	Retail food chains	12.3
Publishing	20.6	Natural gas	12.2
Savings and loan	20.4	Retail: general merchandise	11.6
Beverages, alcoholic	20.3	Money center banks	11.6
Aluminum	19.5	Property/casualty insurance	11.5
Building materials	18.8	Retail department stores	11.3
Insurance: life/health	18.4	Major regional banks	10.4
Computer: hardware	18.3	S&P oils composite	9.3
Iron and steel	17.7	International oils	8.6
Diversified machinery	17.0	Domestic oils	6.3
Chemicals	17.0	Electric companies	4.6
Personal care	16.8	Telephone	4.5

from the recognition that the market is heading lower, and which have tended to gain fastest with the recognition that the market has bottomed out.

Table 9–8 shows that in bear markets, foods groups and value-heavy utility and energy groups have best held their value. After bottoms, two of the growth-heavy technology groups have been among the top performers, but so have groups from a diversity of other sectors. You may also notice that the worst performers after bottoms have been many of the same energy, utility, and foods groups that have held up best during the down markets. In fact, five of the six groups that have held up best at the start of bear markets have been the five worst performers in bull markets. This reflects a basic but important point to remember—relative performance has a lot to do with volatility. The utilities, for instance, have tended to be less volatile than other stocks, thus falling less during market declines and rising less during market advances.

Yet, the inverse is less evident. Of the six groups that have performed the best after bottoms, only three are even among the bottom nine for bear market performance. This suggests that bear markets and bull markets should be considered differently. With a bear market developing, your objective should be to reduce volatility by switching into low-volatility groups like utilities or by diversifying out of the stock market altogether, instead increasing exposure to other assets and increasing your cash position. With a bull market developing and the downside risk limited, you can be more confident in buying high-beta stocks that tend to be relatively volatile.

This volatility consideration brings me back to the comparison of growth and value, since a low-risk outlook can enable you to be more confident in buying growth stocks. The Russell growth indices have been far more volatile than the comparable value indices. Since June 23, 1995, the Russell 2000 Growth Index's standard deviation of its one-day rate of change has been 1.26 versus volatility readings of 1.22 for the Russell 1000 Growth Index, 0.95 for the Russell 1000 Value Index, and 0.71 for the Russell 2000 Value Index. These statistics also reflect the low volatility of large-cap value stocks, which tend to perform better than growth stocks in bear markets.

Again, after a market peak, your decisions will revolve around reducing downside risk and heading for cover in alternative assets or defensive stocks with low volatility. But after a market bottom, your goal will be to make savvy selection decisions that will maximize the profit potential represented by the new bull market, capturing stock volatility as it appears on the upside. Said differently, you will want to get on board with the stocks that are showing the greatest upside momentum. Chapter 10 will explain how to do so.

E N D N O T E S

1. Ibbotson Associates, 225 North Michigan Ave., Suite 700, Chicago, IL 60601.

Screening to Enhance Your Buy and Sell Decisions

Chapter 9 addressed the question of how to apply your market outlook to broad asset allocation decisions, featuring indicators that can help you reach those allocation conclusions. This chapter looks at how to use your market view and allocation decisions in conjunction with screening strategies that advise you specifically on what to buy and sell, both in the United States and in the context of global asset allocation.

Once you have gauged the market's risk/reward balance, and what that implies for asset allocation, you can rebalance your portfolio accordingly, reallocating funds among different assets, changing your relative exposure to your various holdings, adding mutual funds or stocks, or weeding them out. If you are solely a stock investor and you have determined that the market has bottomed and that the downside risk is limited, your best approach will be to separate the slow-moving stocks from the stocks that are quickly responding to the improved outlook. But to make that distinction accurately and without delay, and to act upon it quickly, you would need a screening system in which stocks are ranked based on their relative momentum. Such a system tells you that the higher a stock's ranking, the greater its momentum compared to the momentum of all the other stocks in the ranking.

DEVELOPING A SCREENING SYSTEM

But gauging momentum is not as simple as it might seem. You must first determine your stock universe and identify your time frame, as the length of the momentum will be proportional to the amount of movement within the ranking. If your universe consists of 100 stocks and you want perspective on short-term momentum, you might rank the 100 stocks based on their five-day rates of change. But you would quickly find that in many cases, top-ranked stocks would waste little time dropping rapidly toward the bottom of the ranking, before rebounding just as quickly. Acting upon such a ranking would be difficult.

At the other extreme, a one-year rate of change applied to each stock in the ranking would be so slow and lacking in movement that it would offer very little new information from update to update. Acting upon this ranking would be difficult as well.

In addition to the appropriate rate of change, you must establish a methodology for acting upon the ranking, decision rules that will address your diversification needs by specifying the number of stocks that you will hold in your portfolio. If you seek to spread your equity allocation among 10 stocks, for instance, you might use a strategy that remains invested in the top 10 stocks in your ranking.

If you set out to develop a ranking system, it's imperative that your software enables you to test for the system that would generate the greatest returns with an average stock holding period that falls within your desired trading parameters. You would find, for instance, that with a short rate of change and a strategy that holds only a few stocks, you might generate impressive returns but with a very short average holding period. Not only would such rapid turnover be difficult to execute efficiently, but transaction costs would eat away at your returns. Transaction costs will be far less of a factor with a long holding period, but the returns produced by the strategy will be more modest.

You will therefore need to test for a strategy that suits you best, and this will require that you try various decision rules. You might test, for example, strategies that buy stocks when they move into the top 10 and sell stocks when they fall out of the top 10, that buy when stocks rise into the top 8 and sell when they drop out of the top 12, that buy when stocks rise into the top 12 and sell when they fall out of the top 8, and so on. You should make sure that your software enables you to determine the average holding period and the hypothetical per annum gain produced by the strategy in excess of the S&P 500's per annum return.

You will also benefit from statistics on the relative volatility of the strategy, determined by comparing the standard deviation of your universe with the standard deviation of the portfolio produced by the strategy. In addition, you may want to consider a reward/risk barometer called the *information ratio,* which is the ratio of the strategy's return in excess of the S&P 500's return (known as the *excess return*) to the standard deviation of that excess return.

But importantly, when developing a strategy, you should recognize the potential for excessive back-fitting. As with indicators of the stock market, a highly optimized strategy will be prone to deteriorate when used in real time. But you can increase the chances of real-time success by using the approach discussed in Chapter 4, testing in an in-sample period, applying your strategy to an out-of-sample period, and requiring the strategy to succeed in a real-time period as well. After testing over a three-year period, for example, you would select a strategy and then verify its usefulness by applying it to the subsequent three-year period. If you had the time and patience, you might also let it run in real time for a year before using it for actual trading.

With a stock universe, however, you will have to deal with such data issues as company mergers and delistings, which eliminate stocks from the universe. In fact, the evolution of your universe may affect the strategy's effectiveness in the real-time future. But if developing a stock ranking system appears to be a daunting or impossible task owing to the data issues, keep in mind that ranking systems can be developed based on just about any universe of comparable assets, and they are suitable for mutual funds in particular. If your intent is to develop a strategy for mutual fund switching, you shouldn't have much trouble building a universe by obtaining the fund price histories from the various mutual fund companies.

IDENTIFYING THE TOP STOCKS IN THE TOP GROUPS

At NDR, ranking systems have been developed using industry groups, sectors, mutual funds, currencies, and global equity markets, to be shown later. And for stock selection, NDR has demonstrated that the best approach is not simply to identify the top-ranked stocks, but to identify the top-ranked stocks in the top-ranked groups. Consistent with academic studies, the NDR rankings have demonstrated that the group effect is more important than the stock effect. In other words, it's more essential to be in the strongest groups than the strongest stocks, given the tendency for similar performance from stocks of the same stripe.

While relative strength can be gauged using a single rate of change, a generally more reliable approach is to sum three rates of change, and perhaps smooth the composite as well. A single rate of change can be subject to misleading messages since a spike or temporary low in the data at the start of the period can produce a temporary high or low momentum reading. The sum of three rates of change will reduce the impact of a single aberrant change.

You should recognize that if your combination includes a relatively long rate of change, the momentum message will be dominated by that long rate of change since percent changes over long periods tend to be greater than percent changes over short periods. One way to de-emphasize the percent change of the longest momentum is to equal-weight your momentum sum by dividing each rate of change by its momentum period. If you were using rates of change of 10, 20, and 40 weeks, for instance, you would divide the 10-week change by 10, the 20-week change by 20, and the 40-week change by 40 before adding them together.

Ideally, you would use the composite momentum approach to rank stocks, use the same approach to rank groups, and then combine the two messages. An example of such a combined approach is the Trader's Weekly Buy List developed by NDR. It combines a ranking based on 100 industry group models with a stock ranking of about 2000 stocks. For a stock to appear on the list, it must not only rank in the top 15 percent of the stock

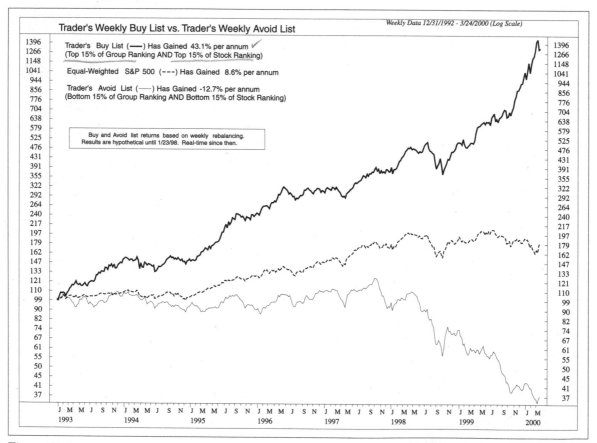

Figure 10–1

ranking, but also be a member of one of the top 15 groups. As shown in Figure 10–1, this list of the top stocks in the top groups has performed impressively since the start of the out-of-sample period in 1993, especially compared to the performance of the Trader's Avoid List. That list of the bottom stocks in the bottom groups comprises stocks in the bottom 15 percent of the stock ranking that reside in the bottom 15 groups.

Since the start of the ranking system's out-of-sample period, the buy list has gained 43 percent per annum, which can be compared to the same-period gain of 9 percent per annum by the equal-weighted S&P 500 and –13 percent per annum by the Trader's Avoid List, as indicated on the chart. But it should be recognized that the results do not account for transaction costs, and you would have needed to stay alert and prepared to trade in order to realize the impressive returns. You would have had to systematically and efficiently rebalance the portfolio, an especially difficult task during periods of rapid group rotation. During such periods, a large contingent of stocks from one group might enter the list, only to exit the list a few weeks later because of a large drop in the group's ranking.

More stable, and easier to execute than the Trader's Buy List, is the ranking process and strategy used to determine the NDR Focus List, the primary ranking system that NDR provides to its institutional clients. Somewhat more involved than the purely momentum-based Trader's Buy List, the NDR Focus List is created by combining the top groups from the 100-group ranking with a stock rank based not only on momentum but also on earnings-based fundamental factors. With the technicals receiving 60 percent of the weight and the fundamentals receiving 40 percent of the weight, these ranks are called *Techno-Fundamental Ranks,* ranging from maximum negative scores of 0 to maximum positive scores of 10. As with the techno-fundamental combination, the group ranks and the stock ranks are combined in a 60/40 mix, with the stock's group rank receiving 60 percent of the weight and the stock's Techno-Fundamental Rank receiving 40 percent of the weight. A stock appears on the Focus List if this combined rank rises into the top 5 percent of all the comparably ranked stocks, and a stock leaves the list if it drops out of the top 10 percent.

The Focus List strategy holds stocks longer than does the Trader's Buy List, yet the strategy has produced strong returns, as shown by the Focus List's out-of-sample record shown in Figure 10–2. As of February 2000, the Focus List's per annum return has been 58 percent since the start of the real-time period on March 13, 1998. That gain is less than the even higher real-time per annum return of 70 percent amassed by the Trader's Buy List, though the strategies have similar information ratios, which risk-adjust the excess returns. And indicating how the Focus List could lend itself to a shorting strategy, Figure 10–2 shows that a loss of –4 percent per annum would have resulted from buying stocks dropping into the bottom 5 percent, and then holding them until they rose out of the bottom 10 percent.

Breaking Down the Focus List

Even though the Focus List is slower than the Trader's Buy List, the turnover is still too fast for many portfolio managers to implement as a system. Yet even if you don't act on their every recommendation, ranking systems can be valuable as screening tools and as focusing mechanisms, helping you keep your eyes trained on the market sectors that are showing relative strength. In fact, one of the greatest benefits of a ranking system is that its composition can tell you a lot about the character of the market itself, with risk and reward implications.

Table 10–1 shows the composition of the NDR Focus List as of late March 2000, breaking the list down by sector, market cap, and style. The left half of the table indicates the extent to which the various sectors are represented on the list, ranked in descending order and excluding sectors without representation. Moving from left to right,

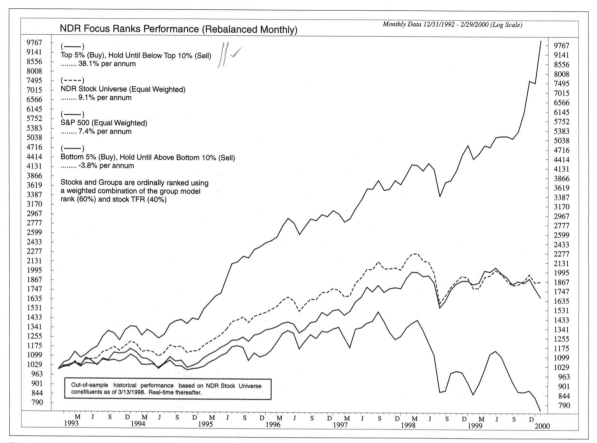

NDR Focus Ranks Performance (Rebalanced Monthly)

Monthly Data 12/31/1992 - 2/29/2000 (Log Scale)

(———)
Top 5% (Buy), Hold Until Below Top 10% (Sell)
.... 38.1% per annum

(----)
NDR Stock Universe (Equal Weighted)
.... 9.1% per annum

(———)
S&P 500 (Equal Weighted)
.... 7.4% per annum

(———)
Bottom 5% (Buy), Hold Until Above Bottom 10% (Sell)
.... -3.8% per annum

Stocks and Groups are ordinally ranked using
a weighted combination of the group model
rank (60%) and stock TFR (40%)

Out-of-sample historical performance based on NDR Stock Universe
constituents as of 3/13/1998. Real-time thereafter.

Figure 10–2

the table includes an indication of whether a sector gained or lost representation with its latest update, the number of the sector's stocks on the list, the percentage of the list represented by that number, the sector's representation in the universe, and the ratio of each sector's stake in the Focus List to its share of the stock universe.

The ratios are useful for comparisons between large sectors and small sectors, indicating whether the Focus List representation is greater or less than what would be considered normal. If the list includes a large percentage of technology stocks, for instance, the percentage won't be impressive unless it exceeds the sector's large percentage of the universe. At the same time, you might be impressed if the list's small percentage of automotive stocks exceeded the sector's even smaller percentage of the universe.

The same breakdown is applied to the market cap and style categories listed in the right half of the table, indicating whether large caps or small caps are dominating the list, and whether a specific style is dominant. At the beginning of a market downturn, you would expect to see growth stocks and small caps heading for the exits, large-cap

T A B L E   10–1

NDR Focus List Components by Sector and Allocation Class

	1-Week Change	No. of Stocks In List	% of List	% All TFRs	Ratio
Sector					
Technology	–	80	64.5	16.7	3.86
Capital goods	+	22	17.7	5.3	3.34
Health care	N/C	13	10.5	6.8	1.53
Energy	+	7	5.6	3.4	1.66
Leisure/entertainment	N/C	1	0.8	1.8	0.46
Nonbank financial	N/C	1	0.8	11.0	0.07
Large-Cap versus Small-Cap Stocks					
Large caps	+	55	44.4	47.3	0.94
Small caps	–	69	55.6	43.2	1.29
Large-Cap vs. Small-Cap, Growth and Value		114			
Large-cap value	+	5	4.0	22.7	0.18
Small-cap value	+	6	4.8	14.6	0.33
Large-cap growth	–	33	26.6	11.8	2.26
Small-cap growth	N/C	48	38.7	15.6	2.49
Mixed	+	32	25.8	35.4	0.73

Notes: N/C = no change. TFR = Techno-Fundamental Rank.

value stocks entering the list, and the defensive utilities and foods sectors gaining sector representation. At the beginning of a market upturn, you would expect to see the representation broadening out, including a notable increase in the representation of small-cap growth stocks and technology stocks.

In late March 2000, technology stocks and growth stocks in general were losing dominance in the Focus List and value stocks were starting to make their presence known, so the development to watch out for was a subsequent defensive shift that would confirm the presence of a developing market downtrend. Taking a closer look at the style category statistics in Table 10–1, the actual Focus List stocks in the four style categories at the time are shown in Tables 10–2 (large-cap growth), 10–3 (large-cap value), 10–4 (small-cap growth), and 10–5 (small-cap value). Additional perspective could be gained by inspecting the broader lists of the Focus List's large caps and small caps, including growth and value stocks as well as stocks of mixed styles.

After major reversals and throughout a market trend, including corrections and trading ranges, a ranking system breakdown can identify major rotational shifts and changing leadership themes that can help you focus your selection efforts. If you trade mutual funds, for instance, such breakdowns can help you determine whether to lighten

T A B L E 10–2

NDR Focus List Ranks–Large-Cap Growth Stocks (03/24/2000)

Ticker	Group (Rank) Stock Name	TFR	Price Bought	Date Bought*	% Change†
	Electronic Semiconductor (1)				
ADI	Analog Devices	10	29.406	11/19/1999	198.41
XLNX	Xilinx	9	45.250	11/12/1999	82.60
VTSS	Vitesse Semiconductor	9	52.750	01/21/2000	72.63
TXN	Texas Instruments	9	107.500	12/23/1999	63.49
RFMD	Rf Micro Devices Inc	9	115.000	02/25/2000	39.35
MXIM	Maxim Integrated Pdts	9	43.688	11/12/1999	64.81
MCHP	Microchip Tech	9	44.458	01/14/2000	47.05
LLTC	Linear Tech	9	89.625	01/14/2000	16.46
JDSU	JDS Uniphase Corp	9	50.000	11/12/1999	165.00
AMCC	Applied Micro Circuits	9	44.000	11/12/1999	240.91
AMAT	Applied Materials	9	53.625	11/19/1999	99.18
ALTR	Altera	9	59.625	01/14/2000	60.80
RMBS	Rambus Inc	8‡	332.938	03/24/2000	0.00
QLGC	Q Logic	8	63.219	11/12/1999	132.43
INTC	Intel	8	97.938	01/21/2000	41.99
PMCS	PMC Sierra	7	74.875	01/07/2000	208.93
	Electronic Instrumentation (2)				
PEB	PE Corp.-PE Biosys	9	83.938	01/21/2000	19.14
WAT	Waters	8‡	89.938	03/24/2000	0.00
MIL	Millipore	8	50.562	02/18/2000	17.55
	Electrical Equipment (7)				
SANM	Sanmina Corp	9	52.688	12/10/1999	25.27
JBL	Jabil Circuit Inc	8	73.062	12/10/1999	12.66
	Biotechnology (9)				
IMNX	Immunex	8	33.292	12/23/1999	101.25
BGEN	Biogen	7	93.125	01/28/2000	−16.71
	Health Care–Drugs (10)				
ADRX	Andrx Corp	9	93.500	03/17/2000	13.44
	Telecommunication Services (11)				
NXTL	NEXTEL Comm	8	83.906	10/08/1999	83.76
ALGX	Allegiance Telecom Inc	7	42.000	10/08/1999	110.12
	Computer Systems (14)				
NTAP	Network Appliance Corp	9‡	100.000	03/24/2000	0.00
	Brokerage Firms (20)				
NITE	Knight/trimark Grp Cl A	10	51.750	03/17/2000	14.13
	Telecommunication Equipment (21)				
ADCT	ADC Telecomm	10	34.781	01/07/2000	58.13
CMVT	Comverse Technology Inc	9	134.938	12/03/1999	46.73
CIEN	Ciena	9	57.750	01/07/2000	181.17
QCOM	Qualcomm	8	73.594	11/05/1999	98.39
	Computer Services (23)				
NSOL	Network Solutions	9	244.531	03/10/2000	−13.43

* = Date stock joined Focus List. † = % Change through 3/24/2000. ‡ = Stock is new to Focus List. TFR = Techno-Fundamental Rank.

T A B L E   10–3

NDR Focus List Ranks—Large-Cap Value Stocks (03/24/2000)

Ticker	Group (Rank) Stock Name	TFR	Price Bought	Date Bought*	% Change†
	Electronic Semiconductor (1)				
NSM	National Semiconductor	8	44.062	12/17/1999	47.80
	Electrical Equipment (7)				
VSH	Vishay Intertech	10	28.375	11/12/1999	98.24
AVX	AVX Corp	10	43.000	11/12/1999	90.70
ARW	Arrow Electronics	9‡	32.062	03/24/2000	0.00
	Telecommunication Services (11)				
FON	Sprint Corp	8	60.500	02/04/2000	−2.07

* = Date stock joined Focus List. † = % Change through 3/24/2000. ‡ = Stock is new to Focus List. TFR = Techno-Fundamental Rank.

T A B L E   10–4

NDR Focus List Ranks—Small-Cap Growth Stocks (03/24/2000)

Ticker	Group (Rank) Stock Name	TFR	Price Bought	Date Bought*	% Change†
	Electronic Semiconductor (1)				
TQNT	Triquint Semiconductor Inc	10	45.500	11/12/1999	96.84
MCRL	Micrel Inc	10	52.000	11/12/1999	111.30
CMOS	Credence Systems Corp	10	57.000	11/12/1999	139.25
BBRC	Burr Brown	10	36.938	01/28/2000	68.19
TXCC	Transwitch Corp	9	48.375	12/31/1999	137.73
SMTC	Semtech Corp	9	49.250	11/12/1999	41.88
PRIA	PRI Automation	9	50.188	11/26/1999	55.92
LTXX	LTX Corp	9	20.625	01/07/2000	110.00
LSCC	Lattice Semi	9	58.750	02/04/2000	25.96
ATMI	ATMI	9	36.500	01/14/2000	47.60
ANAD	Anadigics Inc	9	31.458	12/31/1999	163.84
SIPX	Sipex Corp	8‡	36.500	03/24/2000	0.00
POWI	Power Integrations Inc	8	51.875	11/12/1999	−43.01
DS	Dallas Semiconductor	8	33.375	01/28/2000	25.09
CREE	Cree Resh Inc	8	86.250	01/14/2000	94.57
AHAA	Alpha Industries	8	91.938	01/21/2000	34.06
MIPS	Mips Technologies Inc Cl A	7	48.000	02/18/2000	38.41
ETEC	Etec Systems Inc	7‡	138.250	03/24/2000	0.00

(Continued)

T A B L E 10–4 *(Concluded)*

NDR Focus List Ranks–Small-Cap Growth Stocks (03/24/2000)

Ticker	Group (Rank) Stock Name	TFR	Price Bought	Date Bought*	% Change†
	Electronic Instrumentation (2)				
CYMI	Cymer	10	60.875	02/04/2000	−11.19
CGNX	Cognex	9	43.875	02/11/2000	32.19
MTD	Mettler Toledo Int'l	8‡	41.688	03/24/2000	0.00
	Oil Drilling (5)				
PPP	Pogo Producing	8‡	26.125	03/24/2000	0.00
	Photography (6)				
PCLE	Pinnacle Systems Inc	8	31.125	08/27/1999	82.73
	Electrical Equipment (7)				
AEIS	Advanced Energy Industries	10	41.500	11/12/1999	50.00
SAWS	Sawtek Inc	9	42.625	11/12/1999	41.64
MVSN	Macrovision Corp	9	33.812	12/03/1999	111.83
DIIG	DII Group	9‡	118.000	03/24/2000	0.00
CTS	CTS Corp	9	67.938	11/12/1999	−10.95
CHP	C & D Technologies	9	35.250	12/17/1999	60.99
ZBRA	Zebra Tech	8	60.625	11/12/1999	−15.15
TNL	Technitrol Inc	8	47.500	01/21/2000	26.32
PLXS	Plexus Corp	8‡	69.188	03/24/2000	0.00
	Biotechnology (9)				
MLNM	Millennium Pharma	8	122.000	12/31/1999	14.45
INCY	Incyte	8	128.500	01/28/2000	−16.44
HGSI	Human Genome	8	80.156	01/07/2000	22.03
CEPH	Cephalon	8	34.562	12/31/1999	33.45
ALKS	Alkermes Inc	8	174.250	02/25/2000	−40.71
AFFX	Affymetrix Inc	8	169.688	12/31/1999	−8.21
	Health Care—Drugs (10)				
JMED	Jones Medical Inds	10	44.708	02/11/2000	−19.20
	Telecommunication Services (11)				
MTZ	MasTec Inc	10	34.125	10/22/1999	130.04
0PR	Price Communications Corp	9	25.750	10/08/1999	−13.83
PRTL	Primus Telecomm	8	20.875	10/22/1999	96.41
PTEL	Powertel Inc	7	65.000	10/08/1999	27.69
	Telecommunication Equipment (21)				
HLIT	Harmonic Lightwaves Inc	10	58.625	11/05/1999	76.87
PROX	Proxim Inc	9	43.375	11/05/1999	241.21
PLCM	Polycom Inc	9	65.625	02/04/2000	52.57
AFCI	Advanced Fibre Comm	9	28.188	11/26/1999	194.01
ADTN	Adtran	9	39.188	12/03/1999	76.08

* = Date stock joined Focus List. † % Change through 3/24/2000. ‡ = Stock is new to Focus List. TFR = Techno-Fundamental Rank.

T A B L E 10–5

NDR Focus List Ranks—Small-Cap Value Stocks (03/24/2000)

Ticker	Group (Rank) Stock Name	TFR	Price Bought	Date Bought*	% Change†
	Electronic Semiconductor (1)				
IDTI	Integrated Device	9	19.062	11/12/1999	112.46
CRUS	Cirrus Logic	9	13.781	01/28/2000	51.47
	Electronic Instrmentation (2)				
TEK	Tektronix	8‡	64.750	03/24/2000	0.00
	Oil Drilling (5)				
HP	Helmerich & Payne	8‡	27.938	03/24/2000	0.00
	Electrical Equipment (7)				
AXE	Anixter International	9‡	29.750	03/24/2000	0.00
	Health Care—Drugs (10)				
NBTY	NBTY Inc	9	13.438	03/17/2000	6.98

* = date stock joined Focus List. † % Change through 3/24/2000. ‡ = Stock is new to Focus List. TFR = Techno-Fundamental Rank.

up on a technology fund and increase exposure to a utility fund, or whether to scale back in a growth fund and increase exposure to a balanced fund or a value fund. The applications of a stock ranking system extend well beyond stock selection.

The Focus List and Sentiment

Also when observing a ranking system's changing composition, keep in mind the sentiment concepts discussed in Chapters 6 and 7. When a particular sector becomes widely and even wildly popular, like the technology sector in late 1999 and early 2000, there's a good chance that the sector will dominate a ranking system. When that happens, you must stay alert to the possibility of profit taking and rotation out of the sector into better-valued and less overbought areas of the market. You should also recognize the possibility that since the sector has assumed such a leadership role in the market, a sell-off will have a negative influence on the major averages and the market as a whole.

In late 1999, for instance, the technology sector represented as much as 85 percent of the Focus List, consistent with the concurrent market dominance of the tech-heavy NASDAQ Composite. But almost imperceptibly, as the NASDAQ Composite continued

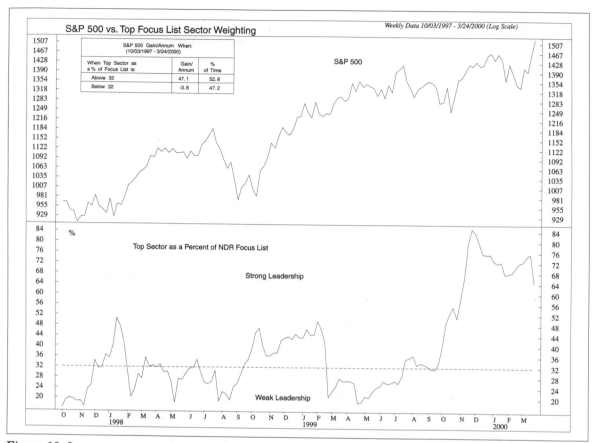

S&P 500 vs. Top Focus List Sector Weighting

Weekly Data 10/03/1997 - 3/24/2000 (Log Scale)

When Top Sector as a % of Focus List is:	Gain/ Annum	% of Time
Above 32	47.1	52.8
Below 32	-3.8	47.2

S&P 500 Gain/Annum When: (10/03/1997 - 3/24/2000)

S&P 500

Top Sector as a Percent of NDR Focus List

Strong Leadership

Weak Leadership

Figure 10–3

to reach record highs, the sector's leadership role began to diminish, with the Focus List's technology stock defection getting under way. This raised a warning flag for both the sector and the general market outlook, considering the tendency for major growth-stock sell-offs to correspond with market weakness.

Since October 1997, the S&P 500 has dropped at a rate of –4 percent per annum when a lack of leadership has been indicated by no sector accounting for at least a third of the Focus List, as shown in Figure 10–3. And for a sector, lost leadership has marked the start of a period of underperformance. After the three previous periods in which a sector represented more than 45 percent of the Focus List, that sector underperformed the S&P 500 for at least eight weeks from the time of the sector's drop below 40 percent of the Focus List, indicating a peak in representation.

The significant point of this demonstration is that as with stock market models, ranking systems should not be followed blindly. For the vast majority of the time, you will do well to let your selection run on autopilot by following your ranking's momentum message. But when the ranking is top-heavy with a specific sector, consider halting your purchases in that sector, don't waste time paring stocks that start to show relative weakness, and consider a more persistent effort to take profits ahead of the sector's inevitable descent. Depending upon the style of the dominant sector and the risk level indicated by your market indicators, you may also want to move into more defensive stocks or assets.

On the other hand, if utilities have been dominant and the market has been weak, you will want to respond aggressively when, in conjunction with improvement in your market indicators, high-beta growth stocks start rising in your ranking. That would signal an excellent opportunity to position yourself to take full advantage of a new bull market. For useful indications of how the market's internal character is changing, and for specifics on which stocks to buy and sell, it's essential to remain cognizant of which stocks are joining your list and which stocks are exiting. Table 10–6, for example, includes the stocks that were entering the Focus List in late March 2000, while Table 10–7 includes the stocks that were dropping off the list. Showing that more technology stocks were leaving the Focus List than were joining it, these tables were, when used together, an additional sign of the diminishing dominance of technology stocks.

T A B L E   10–6

NDR Focus List Ranks–Additions (03/24/2000)

Ticker	Group (Rank) Stock Name	TFR	Ticker	Group (Rank) Stock Name	TFR
	Electronic Semiconductor (1)			*Electrical Equipment (7)*	
SIPX	Sipex Corp	8	MOLX	Molex	9
RMBS	Rambus Inc	8	DIIG	DII Group	9
ETEC	Etec Systems Inc	7	AXE	Anixter International	9
	Electronic Instrumentation (2)		ARW	Arrow Electronics	9
			APCC	Amer Power Conv	9
WAT	Waters	8	PLXS	Plexus Corp	8
TEK	Tektronix	8	LFUS	Littlefuse	8
MTD	Mettler Toledo International	8			
	Oil Drilling (5)			*Oil Well Equipment & Services (8)*	
NE	Noble Drilling Corp	9	SII	Smith International	8
ESV	Ensco International	9		*Computer Systems (14)*	
PPP	Pogo Producing	8	NTAP	Network Appliance Corp	9
HP	Helmerich & Payne	8			
APA	Apache Corp	8			

TFR = Techno-Fundamental Rank.

T A B L E   10–7

NDR Focus List Ranks—Deletions (03/24/2000)

Ticker	Group (Rank) Stock Name	TFR	Price Bought	Date Bought	% Change*
	Telecommunication Equipment (21)				
PWAV	Powerwave Technologies Inc	8	74.625	11/05/1999	112.90
INTV	InterVoice-Brite	8	26.781	01/28/2000	21.12
IATV	Actv Inc	8	35.750	01/07/2000	1.92
DSPG	DSP Group	8	27.594	11/05/1999	120.16
CACS	Carrier Access Corp	8	48.000	11/05/1999	19.01
ASPT	Aspect Communications	8	43.312	11/19/1999	–0.43
BRCM	Broadcom Corp	7	74.625	11/05/1999	212.23
	Computer Peripherals (28)				
SNDK	Sandisk Corp	9	117.000	03/17/2000	13.30
KRON	Kronos Inc	9	47.125	03/17/2000	–5.57
CUBE	C-Cube Microsystems	9	85.000	03/17/2000	0.15
CS	Cabletron Systems	9	46.000	03/17/2000	1.36
ADIC	Advanced Digital Info Corp	9	42.031	02/25/2000	9.44
EMLX	Emulex Corp	8	182.938	03/17/2000	14.25
	Computer Software (33)				
ADBE	Adobe Systems	10	52.500	09/17/1999	106.07
VRTS	Veritas Software Corp	9	168.688	03/10/2000	–3.63
SEBL	Siebel Systems Inc	9	110.500	02/11/2000	30.77
MERQ	Mercury Interactive	9	132.125	03/03/2000	–22.09
ISSX	ISS Group	9	125.062	03/10/2000	11.24
FILE	FileNet Corp	9	40.625	03/10/2000	–17.23
BEAS	BEA Systems	9	18.312	10/08/1999	478.84
VRSN	Verisign Inc	8	52.172	10/01/1999	265.86
ITWO	I2 Technologies	8	25.031	10/15/1999	594.63

* % Change through 3/24/2000. TFR = Techno-Fundamental Rank.

Even if you overlay your risk and reward assessment of the market and the dominating sector, it's essential to keep in mind that a ranking system will be of limited use without an objective set of decision rules. In addition to testing for a strategy of buying at a specific level of the ranking, you may have luck in testing for a strategy of buying based on a specific amount of improvement in the ranking. Such a strategy might, for instance, buy if a stock rises 20 ranks or by 20 percentage points in the ranking. If you plan to sell short, of course, you should test for strategies that indicate poor subsequent performance. But you may also want to do so for the purpose of identifying an avoid list, a list of stocks that you definitely do not want to own.

EXTERNAL INFLUENCES

In addition, keep in mind that a ranking system need not be based on rates of change alone. You could try, for example, ranking stocks or other assets based on their levels relative to a common moving average, with one stock or asset ranking above another if it is higher above its moving average. Alternatively, your system might call for holding all the stocks in your universe that are above their 50-day or 200-day moving averages, while avoiding those that are below the smoothings. Whatever you develop, it will need to suit your tolerance for turnover and not overwhelm you with a list of stocks that you cannot hope to manage efficiently as you rebalance your portfolio.

It can also help to keep an eye on external factors that tend to influence specific sectors or groups. The performance of bank stocks, for example, can be affected by the yield curve, as represented by the spread between the long bond yield and the T-bill yield. Bank stocks tend to anticipate improving profitability when bond yields are well above T-bill yields, since banks tend to loan at the long end of the curve and borrow at the short end. If the T-bill yield is above the bond yield, indicating that the yield curve is inverted, bank stocks tend to anticipate worsening profitability since the cost of borrowing is high relative to loan revenues.

As shown in Figure 10–4, the S&P Major Regional Banks Group has tended to perform very well when the ratio has indicated a steep yield curve, and the group has tended to decline when the ratio has indicated a relatively flat or inverted yield curve. With bank stocks rising or near the top of your rankings, you would be more confident buying them if you were seeing the yield curve steepening, whereas caution would be in order if you were starting to see the yield curve flatten on its way to a possible inversion. If the yield curve has been flat or inverted but then starts to steepen in conjunction with the rate declines that the condition had called for, the banks would benefit from the trend of declining rates as well as the improving profitability message. If the yield curve has been steep but then starts to flatten in conjunction with the rate increases that had been expected by the steepness, the banks would be threatened by the new rate uptrend as well as the worsening profitability outlook.

Moreover, in assessing bank stocks, you would be keeping an eye on loan demand, bond momentum, and factors that affect interest rate trends in general. While flat or inverted yield curves reflect the market's view that rates will drop in the future, their presence is usually accompanied by tight monetary conditions and an overall interest rate landscape that is unfavorable for financial stocks in general. While steep yield curves reflect expectations for higher rates in the future, they are usually present when monetary conditions are relatively accommodative and the current interest rate land-

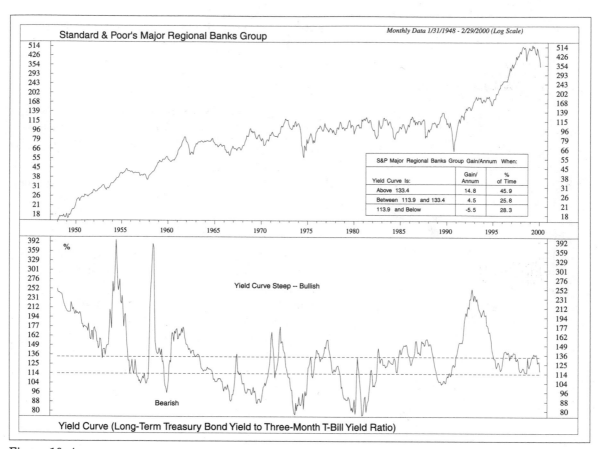

Figure 10–4

scape is favorable for financials. With the exception of yield curve extremes, the macro message of the broad interest rate trend is usually as great or greater an influence on financials, and the market in general, than is the micro message of differences among different rates.

   In fact, your overall assessment of monetary conditions will be especially relevant to all of the sectors that are most sensitive to interest rates. Rising rates are, for example, a negative influence on the housing sector, made up of the home building group and others. When assessing the environment for home building stocks, you would consider the monetary environment along with such factors as the momentum of new home sales, shown in Figure 10–5, and such data as building permits and housing prices.

   For stocks in commodity-based sectors, the monetary environment is less significant, and you will benefit more by focusing on the trend of the underlying commodity. The energy sector, for example, is sensitive to changes in the price of crude oil. As illustrated in

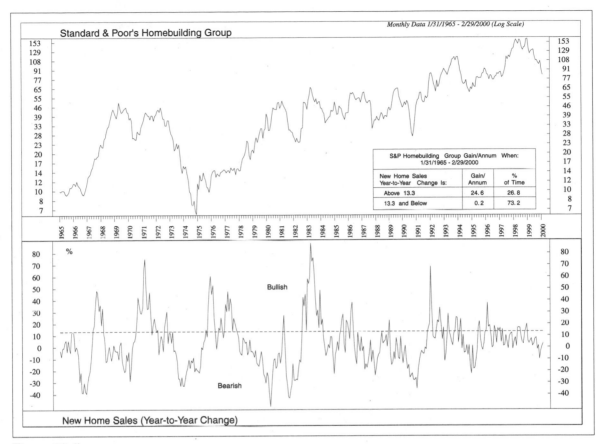

Figure 10–5

Figure 10–6, the S&P Oil Domestic Integrated Group has tended to outperform the S&P 500 when the 13-week rate of change of crude oil futures has indicated strong oil price momentum, and the group has dramatically underperformed when crude oil momentum has been decisively negative. In watching the rankings of energy stocks, you would thus keep an eye on crude oil momentum, and you would also assess the supply/demand balance, OPEC policies, and data on such factors as drilling activity and oil rigs.

GLOBAL SECTORS AND REGIONAL RELATIVE STRENGTH

In the case of energy and several other sectors, an additional benefit of your external factor examination is that the factors will often have global implications. The bullish implications of rising oil prices, for example, will be similar for U.S. -based energy companies and European firms alike. And to the extent that interest rate trends tend to be global in

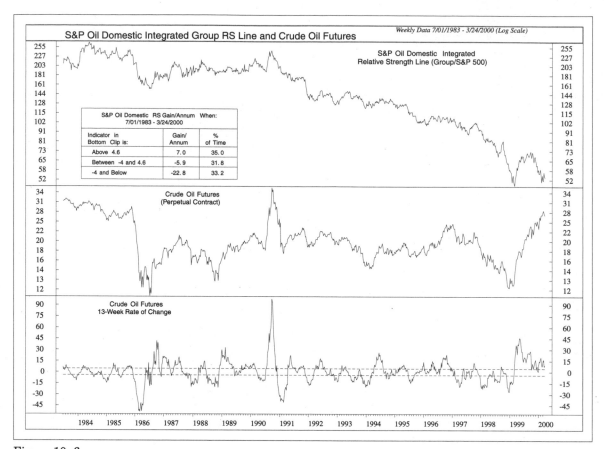

Figure 10–6

scope, rising rates will have a similar negative impact on rate-sensitive stocks in one part of the world as in another. One of the most pronounced examples of the global reach of sector trends was the technology sector outperformance in late 1999, when telecommunications stocks and others involved with information technology were market leaders around the globe, and equally at risk of selling off from their overvalued and overextended levels.

There are many reasons for the growing globalization of market sectors, including cross-border merger and acquisition activity; the establishment of the eurozone as well as increased regional emphasis elsewhere; a rising public interest in equities in Japan and Europe; the increased accessibility of market news and trading vehicles via the Internet; and more broadly, the increased efficiency and breadth of the global information flow. As part of this worldwide convergence, global portfolio managers have started to take a closer look at the relative strength of the global sectors to enhance returns, thus complementing their assessment of relative strength among countries and regions. In global bull markets, there are sizable relative strength differences among countries, warranting relatively high exposure to the strongest countries, and returns can be further enhanced by maintaining relatively high exposure to the strongest sectors in those countries. Above and beyond your strategy of buying the strongest U.S. stocks in the strongest U.S. sectors, the ideal global approach would entail purchasing the strongest stocks that are in the strongest global sectors and in the strongest regions of the globe.

But in taking a top-down approach to your global allocation decisions, a good starting point is an assessment of relative strength among countries and regions, an assessment that can, once again, be accomplished through a ranking system. Table 10–8 shows NDR's Global Equity Ranking, which uses a composite of three rates of change to rank 42 markets. This ranking's strategy calls for overweighting a market when it rises into the top three and maintaining the high exposure until the market drops out of the top 13. The strategy calls for underweighting a market when it drops into the bottom three and maintaining the low exposure until the market's ranking rises above 30. Figure 10–7 illustrates how this strategy has fared since the start of the out-of-sample period in 1996.

But in addition to its evaluation of which markets to overweight and underweight, the ranking provides a more general illustration of relative strength among regions. In the same way that the Focus List can be broken down into sector, market cap, and style categories, the Global Equity Ranking can be broken down to indicate which region has the greatest proportion of overweight markets, which region has the greatest proportion of underweight markets, and whether developed markets or emerging markets are the most highly represented among the overweight or underweight markets. If you are unable or unwilling to buy stocks in Sri Lanka, for example, and would rather use mutual funds that buy stocks in specific regions, you could use the kind of information shown in Table 10–9 to help you determine which regions to emphasize. And if you are interested in only a few markets, you might use the ranking to check on the relative strength of those markets and the regional breakdown to confirm that your preferred market is in a strong region.

The regional breakdown is especially useful for incorporating the global sector assessment, since Dow Jones and other services track not only global sectors, but also the sectors within various regions. Figure 10–8 shows 3 of the 10 Dow Jones sectors for the world (including the United States), while Figure 10–9 shows the same sectors within the Asia Pacific region. You would be interested in these two charts if, for example, you were enthused about the prospects for financial stocks globally and if your global market ranking argued for weighting the Asia Pacific region most heavily. You would want to confirm that the global financial sector was showing relative strength versus other global sectors and that the Asia Pacific financial sector was showing relative strength versus financial sectors for other regions of the world. As of late March 2000, however,

T A B L E   10–8

NDR Global Equity Ranking (03/24/2000)

Rank	Previous Week	Four Weeks Ago	Market	Composite Reading	Position Entry Date	Entry Price	Current Price	Current Gain/Loss (%)
Overweight								
Ranked 1–3—Buy/Overweight								
1	1	1	Helsinki HEX General	275.50	07/24/1998	5458.45	17579.20	222.05
2	2	3	Stockholm Affarsvarlden	146.77	12/17/1999	5192.50	6646.00	27.99
3	3	4	São Paolo Exchange Index	146.61	12/31/1999	17092.00	18674.53	9.26
Ranked 4–13 after Reaching Ranks 1–3—Hold/Continue to Overweight								
6	6	5	Budapest Exchange Index	97.74	01/21/2000	9794.06	10126.69	3.40
8	7	2	BSE 100	94.34	08/13/1999	1990.10	2937.31	47.60
Underweight								
Ranked 30–39 after Reaching Ranks 40–42—Continue to Underweight								
35	36	36	NZSE Capital Top 40	−3.36	09/10/1999	2124.02	2071.44	−2.48
36	35	39	Brussels Bel–20 Index	−8.90	04/16/1999	3284.59	2919.33	−11.12
37	37	38	Austrian Traded Index	−10.83	12/03/1999	1164.05	1127.37	−3.15
38	40	40	Jakarta Exchange Index	−16.62	02/25/2000	568.55	581.47	2.27
Ranked 40–42—Sell/Underweight:								
40	39	31	Colombo Exchange Index	−19.25	03/24/2000	515.81	515.81	0.00
41	41	41	Bangkok SET Index	−27.75	02/18/2000	408.35	404.16	−1.03
42	42	42	Manila Exchange Index	−64.07	11/12/1999	1991.01	1681.71	−15.53

Full Rank

Rank	Previous Week	Four Weeks Ago	Developed Markets (**)	Market	Country	Composite	Current Price
1	1	1	**	Helsinki HEX General	Finland	275.50	17579.20
2	2	3	**	Stockholm Affarsvarlden	Sweden	146.77	6646.00
3	3	4		São Paolo Exchange Index	Brazil	146.61	18674.53
4	5	6	**	Frankfurt Xetra DAX	Germany	102.79	7932.42
5	4	15		I.P.C.	Mexico	102.51	8093.58
6	6	5		Budapest Exchange Index	Hungary	97.74	10126.69
7	12	14	**	Toronto 300 (TSE)	Canada	95.89	10052.68
8	7	2		BSE 100	India	94.34	2937.31
9	8	10	**	Paris CAC 40	France	88.69	6364.26
10	14	12		Prague PX-50 Indes	Czech Republic	83.99	691.00
11	16	11	**	Hong Kong Hang Seng	China	80.84	17784.57
12	11	16	**	Copenhagen SE Overall	Denmark	80.03	884.11
13	9	8	**	Milan MIBtel Index	Italy	77.71	32946.00
14	13	7		Warsaw WIG Index	Poland	70.82	22387.90
15	10	9		Mishtanim 100	Israel	59.44	529.45
16	15	13	**	Madrid General Index	Spain	51.28	1107.28
17	17	20	**	Amsterdam ANP-CBS General	Netherlands	47.53	965.80
18	18	17		Kuala Lumpur Composite	Malaysia	44.64	970.27
19	19	35	**	S&P 500 Stock Index	United States	42.27	1527.46

T A B L E   10–8 (*Concluded*)

NDR Global Equity Ranking (03/24/2000)

Full Rank

Rank	Previous Week	Four Weeks Ago	Developed Markets (**)	Market	Country	Composite	Current Price
20	23	30	**	ISEQ Overall Index	Ireland	34.52	5,512.50
21	21	22	**	Oslo General Index	Norway	33.47	1,375.33
22	24	18		Taiwan Trade-Weighted Index	Taiwan	32.87	9,482.64
23	20	25		Indice D.C. Bursatil	Venezuela	32.20	5,838.19
24	22	21	**	Nikkei 225 Average	Japan	29.82	19,958.08
25	25	23		Johannesburg Overall Index	South Africa	27.76	8,209.10
26	28	27	**	All Ordinaries	Australia	22.62	3,247.40
27	29	34	**	London FTSE 100	U.K.	20.43	6,738.50
28	26	28		IGPA Index	Chile	18.56	5,196.59
29	31	33	**	Zurich Swiss Market	Switzerland	16.36	7,440.40
30	33	29	**	Straits Times	Singapore	11.18	2,146.20
31	30	24		Buenos Aires Exchange Index	Argentina	8.86	21,041.70
32	27	19		Athens Exchange Index	Greece	4.47	4,685.17
33	38	32		Seoul Exchange Index	South Korea	4.22	889.24
34	32	26		Lima Exchange Index	Peru	1.73	1,715.05
35	36	36	**	NZSE Capital Top 40	New Zealand	−3.36	2,071.44
36	35	39	**	Brussels Bel-20 Index	Belgium	−8.90	2,919.33
37	37	38	**	Austrian Traded Index	Austria	−10.83	1,127.37
38	40	40		Jakarta Exchange Index	Indonesia	−16.62	581.47
39	34	37		Bogotá Exchange Index	Colombia	−18.52	935.44
40	39	31		Colombo Exchange Index	Sri Lanka	−19.25	515.81
41	41	41		Bangkok SET Index	Thailand	−27.75	404.16
42	42	42		Manila Exchange Index	Philippines	−64.07	1,681.71

Notes: Out-of-sample performance results 2/9/1996–3/24/2000 (weekly rebalancing). Top category has gained 41.5 percent per annum, equal-weighted universe has gained 14.0 percent per annum, bottom category has gained 5.6 percent per annum.

the middle clips of these charts reflected a lackluster trend in financials, especially in the Asia Pacific region.

As discussed in Chapter 9, global diversification is a sound asset allocation strategy, and there have been periods, such as 1985 through 1988, in which the U.S. investor would have benefited by shifting exposure to markets outside of the United States. In the Global Equity Ranking, such a period would be indicated by a low and falling U.S. market rank, and especially a decline to underweight status. You should recognize, however, that the relative strength message is less valuable in bear markets, since markets tend to correlate a lot more closely on the downside than on the upside. When a bear market is at hand, you can count on it being global in magnitude, which means that your best approach will be to emphasize the most defensive sectors around the globe or to move out of equities and into bonds, cash, and other assets.

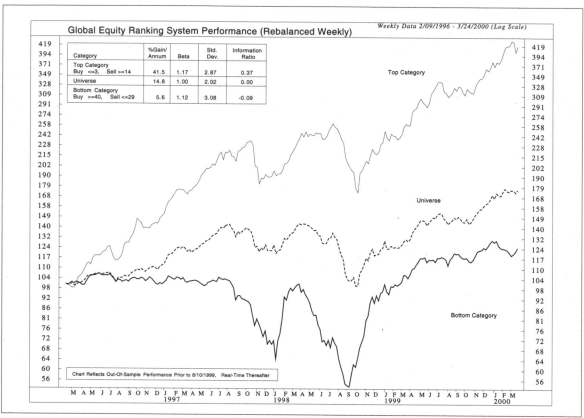

Figure 10–7

T A B L E 10–9

Regional Breakdown of NDR Global Equity Ranking
(Number of Markets Overweight, Market-Weight, and Underweight)

Market	Overweight	One-Week Change	Market-Weight	One-Week Change	Underweight	One-Week Change
Europe	3	nc	13	+	2	–
Asia Pacific	1	nc	7	–	5	+
Latin America	1	nc	6	nc	0	nc
North America	0	nc	2	nc	0	nc
Developed	2	nc	16	+	3	–
Emerging	3	nc	14	–	4	+

Note: Regions include all countries shown in Figure 10–8 except Israel and South Africa. All countries classified as developed (21) or emerging (21). nc = no change.

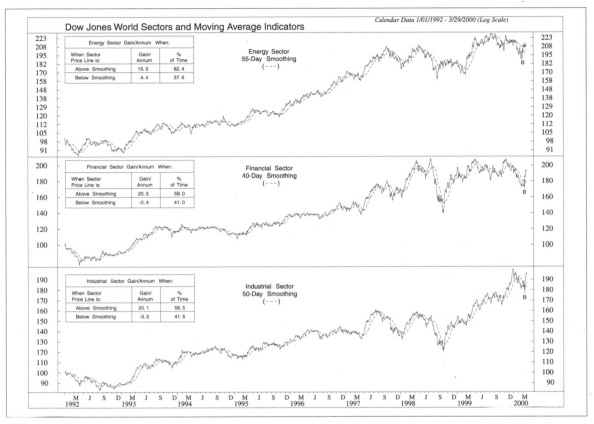

Figure 10–8

In addition, when considering your relative foreign and domestic exposure, you should consider currency relative strength, since dollar weakness will generally increase the appeal of adding exposure to unhedged investments based in other currencies. And dollar strength will generally decrease their appeal. Again, an excellent barometer is a relative strength ranking, exemplified by the NDR currency ranking in Table 10–10.

No matter how clear and accurate your view of what lies ahead for the markets in the United States and around the world, your outlook will be of little use to you without a strategy for acting upon it. But your effort to develop and implement a profit-generating strategy will be easier and more effective if you make use of indicators and rankings that compare assets, regions, sectors, and individual stocks. In the process, you will be able to use the asset allocation and selection tools to confirm your market outlook. In the final chapter, I will use current conditions as an example of how to develop a market view and put it to use.

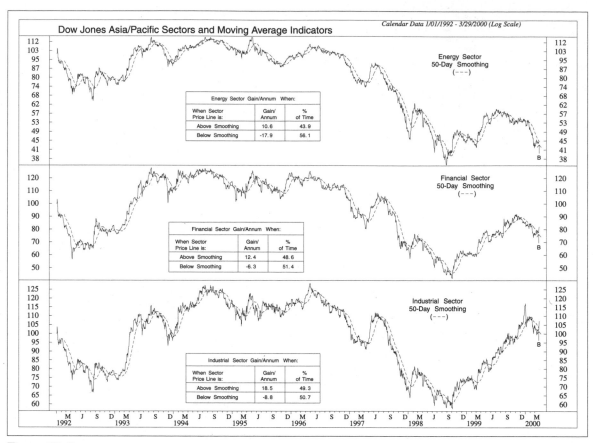

Dow Jones Asia/Pacific Sectors and Moving Average Indicators

Calendar Data 1/01/1992 - 3/29/2000 (Log Scale)

Energy Sector
50-Day Smoothing
(– – –)

Energy Sector Gain/Annum When:		
When Sector Price Line is:	Gain/ Annum	% of Time
Above Smoothing	10.6	43.9
Below Smoothing	-17.9	56.1

Financial Sector
50-Day Smoothing
(– – –)

Financial Sector Gain/Annum When:		
When Sector Price Line is:	Gain/ Annum	% of Time
Above Smoothing	12.4	48.6
Below Smoothing	-6.3	51.4

Industrial Sector
50-Day Smoothing
(– – –)

Industrial Sector Gain/Annum When:		
When Sector Price Line is:	Gain/ Annum	% of Time
Above Smoothing	18.5	49.3
Below Smoothing	-8.8	50.7

Figure 10–9

T A B L E 10–10

NDR Currency Relative Strength Ranking

Rank	One Week Ago	Four Weeks Ago	Currency Market
1	1	1	U.S. dollar
2	2	3	Japanese yen
3	4	4	Swedish krona
4	6	8	Swiss franc
5	5	6	British pound
6	3	2	Canadian dollar
7	7	5	Australian dollar
8	8	7	Euro

Current Applications, Long-Term Implications

This book has shown how your investment decision making can be enhanced with indicators and screens that use clean data and sound quantification methods to place current conditions in the context of history. I have also stressed that longer-term trends are cyclical, with history repeating itself in form, if not in substance. The same kind of emotional fervor that made Dutch tulip bulbs the hot investment of the late seventeenth century sent silver above $40 and gold above $800 in 1980, and it fueled such stock market manias as the electronics boom of the early 1960s, the Nifty 50 era of the late 1960s and early 1970s, the biotechnology craze of the early 1980s, and the Internet frenzy of the late 1990s. The subject of the speculation was different in each case, but the drivers were the same. Unrealistic expectations led to widespread and growing greed, culminating in a peak upon the inevitable realization that the expectations were, in fact, unrealistic.

Examples of the latest craze were numerous at the end of the 1990s and start of 2000, with almost anything related to the Internet and information technology benefiting from expectations that the new IT revolution would bring perpetual riches to all participants. But in keeping with past manias, it was inevitable that at some point in the near future, the realization would become widespread that the stratospheric earnings multiples, or price-to-sales ratios of the many dot-com outfits without earnings, were discounting unattainable goals. A severe shakeout was inevitable. And only then, with paper profits dwindling, was it likely to become widely obvious that the hype of the speculative blow-off had enticed buyers to purchase the latest "new era" stocks based on stories alone, without any regard for fundamentals.

In all likelihood, it would become increasingly clear how stock prices had been driven by rumors appearing on Internet message boards and circulating in on-line chat rooms, and how the day trading outfits helped fuel the Internet frenzy by turning investing laypeople into nonstop traders, influencing the unknowing much like the "boiler rooms" that hawked precious metals in the early 1980s. Typical for the final stages of an investment, those with the least investment experience provided the liquidity for the final move up. And for many buying into the hype, Wall Street had taken on the appearance of Las Vegas Boulevard, and that careless casino mentality contributed to the dangerous uptrend in volatility discussed in Chapter 7.

As money poured into the IT-related winners during this period, the rest of the market languished, as indicated by the statistics shown in Table 11–1. Based on a universe of more than 6000 stocks, the average stock was down by about –5 percent during the bull market year of 1999, and about 55 percent of the stocks posted losses. Among S&P 500 stocks, 51 percent declined. And among the NASDAQ stocks, 49 percent ended the year lower. Since the S&P 500 and the NASDAQ Composite are both capitalization-weighted indices, they were propelled by the relative strength of their largest-cap components, primarily stocks with a substantial stake in the IT boom.

One could argue that compared to the smaller-cap dot-com stocks and Internet-related IPOs more popular with the short-term traders, the largest-cap technology stocks would represent a safe alternative for taking part in the boom. But this argument might also have been heard in discussing the Nifty 50 of the early 1970s or the energy stocks of the late 1970s. Those stocks achieved the large market caps as a result of their past market performance, in much the same way the energy stocks dominated at the end of the 1970s. Table 11–2 shows that by end of the 1980s, the energy-stock dominance had

T A B L E 11–1

Price Gains of U.S. Common Stocks 12/31/1998–12/31/1999

	Median Gain, %	% of Stocks Down for Period
S&P 500 Components (500 issues)	–0.6	51.0
S&P 500 Index gain	19.5	
NASDAQ-listed companies (3746 issues)	1.3	49.3
NASDAQ Composite Index gain	85.6	
All U.S. common stocks in NDR database (6210 issues)	–4.6	54.5
Wilshire 5000 Index gain	22.0	

Notes: Indices are capitalization-weighted, price-only returns. S&P 500 index tracks the value of 500 leading large-capitalization stocks. NASDAQ Composite Index tracks the value of all stocks traded on the NASDAQ stock market. Wilshire 5000 Index tracks the value of all U.S. companies listed on U.S. exchanges (approx. 7500 issues total).

T A B L E   11–2

Largest 20 S&P 500 Stocks by Market Capitalization

		As of 12/79		As of 12/89		As of 12/99
1	T	International Business Machines	E	Exxon Corp.	T	Microsoft Corp.
2	E	Exxon Corp.		General Electric Co.		General Elec Co.
3	E	Amoco Corp.	T	International Business Machines		Cisco Sys Inc.
4	E	Schlumberger Ltd.	E	Royal Dutch Petroleum Co.		Wal Mart Stores Inc.
5	E	Mobil Corp.		Philip Morris Cos Inc.	T	Intel Corp.
6		General Electric Co.	TC	AT&T Corp.	T	Lucent Technologies Inc.
7	E	Royal Dutch Petroleum Co.		Merck & Co Inc.	E	Exxon Mobil Corp.
8		General Mtrs Corp.		Bristol Myers Squibb Co.	T	International Business Machines
9	E	Chevron Corp.		Du Pont E I De Nemours & Co.		Citigroup Inc.
10	E	Atlantic Richfield Co.	E	Amoco Corp.	T	America Online Inc.
11	E	Shell Oil	TC	Bellsouth Corp.		American International Group Inc.
12	E	Texaco Inc.		Coca Cola Co.	TC	Sbc Communications Inc.
13		Eastman Kodak Co.	E	Mobil Corp.	TC	AT&T Corp.
14	E	Phillips Petroleum Co.		Wal Mart Stores Inc.	T	Oracle Corp.
15	E	Gulf Corp.		Procter & Gamble Co.		Merck & Co. Inc.
16	TC	AT&T Corp.	E	Chevron Corp.		Home Depot Inc.
17		Procter & Gamble Co.	TC	GTE Corp.	TC	MCI Worldcom Inc.
18	E	Getty Oil Co.	TC	Bell Atlantic Corp.		Procter & Gamble Co.
19		Du Pont E I De Nemours & Co.		General Mtrs Corp.		Coca Cola Co.
20		Dow Chem Co.		Ford Mtr Co.	TC	Nortel Networks Corp.

Notes: *E* = energy, *T* = technology, *TC* = telecommunications.

dwindled, and the technology and telecom stocks grew to almost entirely replace them by the end of the 1990s. During that decade, 17 of the top 20 performing stocks were technology or telecom stocks. As 2000 got under way, it remained to be seen whether, and for how long, the momentum would persist. And in any event, the greater challenge was to identify the market sector with the most potential to grow into a dominant position, perhaps dethroning the current leaders down the road.

As discussed in Chapter 10, a momentum-based screening system should help you identify emerging themes and those that have persisted for so long that they may be in a manic phase. In the latter case, you should overlay a contrarian perspective by resisting the urge to buy and instead weeding out the stocks that are showing signs of momentum loss. The difficulty is making the determination of when a momentum move has in fact reached its final stages. If you ignore the momentum message and start selling too early, you could cost yourself enormous potential profits.

You should therefore view the momentum message in the context of a top-down perspective. When the market leadership is narrowly focused after an extended market move, with your indicators describing a high-risk environment, the cautious contrarian approach is warranted. When a sector exhibits dominant momentum early in a new uptrend and your indicators describe a low-risk environment, you should have good luck in responding actively to your momentum message.

A NINE-INDICATOR MODEL

Accurately describing the environment is thus crucial. And as I have discussed, the most reliable approach to assessing the environment is to rely on the composite message of reliable market indicators, which will keep you from getting caught up in the current hype and short-term sentiment that "this time is different." A composite model gives you the consensus message of what the objective indicators are saying about how, historically, the market has responded under similar circumstances.

But as discussed in Chapters 3 and 4, your indicators will be of use to you only if they provide accurate real-time messages, which is why it's a good idea to test your indicators in actual or simulated real time before putting them to use. Among the indicators featured in this book, the vast majority have been running real time for at least a few years. To present an example of how a composite model could be constructed, I selected nine indicators with real-time records suggesting that they can be counted on for value-added input, all with real-time records starting in October 1996 or earlier. In the case of indicators with records based on buy and sell signals, I gauged the indicator's performance based on the number of accurate real-time signals and the per annum gain generated by those signals. In the case of indicators that use modes, I made the assessment based on the real-time per annum gain generated with the indicator in its upper mode versus the per annum gain produced with the indicator in its lower mode.

Table 11–3 lists each indicator, its chart identification in this book, its bullish and bearish parameters, and its real-time starting date. As you can see, the nine indicators are representative of the indicators discussed in Chapters 5 through 8, including a relatively heavy dose of tape indicators. Two indicators are based on market breadth entirely—weekly new lows divided by issues traded and net new highs (new highs minus new lows) divided by issues traded. The market's trend and momentum are gauged by the indicator based on the S&P 500's percentage reversals. And an overbought/oversold indication is provided by the 40-day TRIN, which uses breadth and volume data.

Representative of right-money sentiment indicators, the New York member short ratio indicator is included. And relative valuation is assessed by the indicator based on the ratio of the composite long bond yield to the S&P 500 earnings yield. The important influence of interest rates themselves is gauged with the indicator based on reversals in the composite long bond yield, representing long-term interest rate trends, and with the

T A B L E 11–3

Composition of Nine-Indicator Model

Indicator	Type	Figure	Bullish Parameter	Bearish Parameter	Real-Time Starting Date
Issues-adjusted NYSE weekly new lows	Breadth	5–22	1.95%	7.2%	October 1996
Issues-adjusted NYSE net new highs	Breadth	5–25	8.8%	–3.6%	April 1996
S&P 500 reversals	Momentum	5–28	Rise by 8.4%	Fall by 7.2%	October 1991
40-Day TRIN	Contra-trend	7–10	Rise to 112 or reverse below 97.7	Fall to 79.8 or reverse above 90.9	April 1994
New York member short ratio	Sentiment	7–5	Rise above 97.75	Fall below 102.7	June 1992
Bond yield/earnings yield change	Valuation	6–9	–8%	12%	October 1996
Composite bond yield reversals	Interest rate	8–8	Fall by 8.7%	Rise by 11.7%	February 1995
Prime rate reversals	Interest rate	8–6	Fall by 3.9%	Rise by 7.5%	November 1987
CRB index change	Inflation	8–13	–4%	8.2%	January 1996
Nine-indicator model	Composite	11–1	67%	50%	October 1996*

*Based on earliest real-time starting date common to all nine indicators.

indicator based on prime rate reversals, representing the impact of short-term rates. Rounding out the list is the indicator based on the year-to-year change of commodity prices, a gauge of inflationary pressure.

For a composite model, the indicator signals are added together. The buy/sell signal indicators contribute +1 if they are on buy signals and –1 if they are on sell signals. Those indicators include the S&P 500 reversal indicator, the TRIN indicator, the member short ratio indicator, and both interest rate indicators. The mode indicators contribute +1 if in on a buy signal, 0 if neutral, and –1 if on a sell signal. Those indicators include both of the breadth indicators, the relative valuation indicator, and the commodity price momentum indicator. After the signals of the nine indicators are added together, the composite can be presented on a percentage scale from 0 to 100 percent. As shown in Figure 11–1, the model stood at a neutral 56 percent in late March 2000, indicating that a net of five of the nine indicators were positive.

Over the period of nearly 3½ years from October 1996 to early 2000, the period in which all nine of the indicators were operating real time, the composite has been effec-

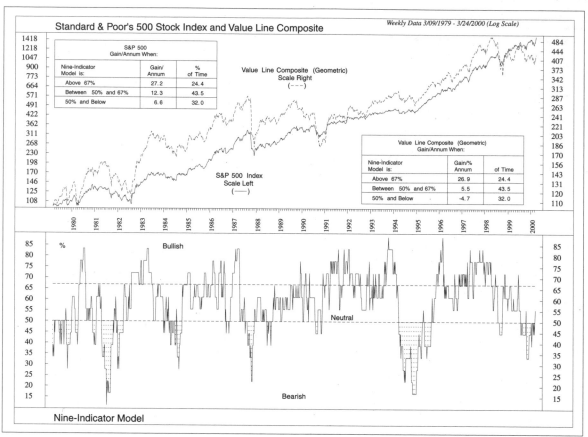

Figure 11–1

tive in advising a bullish outlook when the consensus message has been decisively positive, as indicated by a reading of more than 67 percent. It has effectively advised a bearish outlook when the model reading has been 50 percent or lower. During the real-time
period, the S&P 500 has gained 42 percent per annum when the model has been above
67 percent, and it has gained just 11 percent per annum when the model has been 50 percent or lower. The real-time gain in the neutral mode has been 21 percent per annum,
similar to the S&P 500's per annum gain of 25 percent over the entire real-time period.
The upper box of Figure 11–1 shows results that include the in-sample period starting in
1979. Those results can be compared to the S&P 500's per annum return of 14 percent
from March 1979 to March 2000. The lower box quantifies the model's success when applied to the geometric Value Line Composite, showing results that can be compared to
the Value Line Composite's per annum return of 7 percent over the 21-year span. The
composite has gained 5 percent per annum during the real-time period starting in 1996,

and that can be compared to the composite's real-time gain of 29 percent per annum with the model above 67 percent, 5 percent per annum with the model neutral, and –23 percent per annum with the model at 50 percent or lower.

As is often the case with a composite model, this model has an idiosyncrasy, in this case a tendency to whipsaw. To compensate, you could add a time filter, in which you might require the signal to last for at least two weeks before acting upon it, or you could apply a moving average. In either case, you would want to test to see how the additional decision rule would have affected the results.

LISTENING TO THE MODEL'S MESSAGE

But the key point is to remember why you have a model in the first place. A model's greatest value is that it provides an objective assessment of the consensus message of the indicators, preventing you from developing a market outlook based on the message of a specific pet indicator or based on a preconceived assumption of what the market should be doing. If you would follow the nine indicators independently, you might find yourself ignoring or placing little weight on the indicators that didn't agree with your view, while giving disproportionate weight to the indicators that agreed with your view. You would be using the indicators to support your view, rather than using the indicators for developing your view.

At a client conference in 1987, Ned Davis illustrated this point by wearing a green tie to give a bullish speech supported by bullish indicators. At the halfway point, he announced that he had brought the wrong speech, went backstage, emerged with a red tie, and gave an equally convincing bearish speech supported by bearish indicators. The more indicators you have at your disposal, the greater will be the number of indicators that do not agree with the consensus message, and the greater will be your ability to support almost any argument. You will be able to data-mine with your indicators until reaching the desired conclusion.

The temptation to abuse indicators is at its greatest if you have made a forecast and feel compelled to justify it as time passes. If you would announce in January that you expected the DJIA to rise 20 percent for the year, and it had risen 10 percent by the end of June, you might be tempted to find bullish indicators that would support the prospect for another 10 percent over the next six months, even if the indicator consensus was decisively bearish. By placing greater weight on a model than a forecast, however, you would be more inclined to admit that the environment had changed and that it was time for a more cautious approach than you had forecast.

The greatest danger of forecasting is that it can lock you into a mindset that can be difficult to change. The value of a good model is that it tells you about the current risk and reward, which is what affects your investment decisions. The progression of a model's messages over time enables you to scale up and scale down in your market exposure as you manage your asset allocation. To buy or sell based entirely on, for example, a forecast DJIA level is little different from buying a lottery ticket, except that with a forecast you're less likely to recognize the slim odds of being right.

Forecasting can, however, be useful if conducted not for the purpose of convincing yourself that specific levels will be reached, but for the purpose of establishing upside reward levels and downside risk levels. Rather than say that you expect the market "to rise 20 percent by year-end," a valuation-based risk/reward assessment (discussed in Chapter 6) would enable you to say that "the upside potential is 20 percent if the model continues to describe a favorable environment and the downside potential is –10 percent if the model describes a hostile environment." In that way, your model will remain the primary driver for your investment decisions. Forecasting procedures can be used to place current developments in the context of long-term probabilities if they are used in conjunction with objective models and screens that enable you to maintain flexibility in responding to changing market conditions.

You can also apply forecasting approaches to a time horizon that extends well beyond your investment time frame, as you address the top tier in the top-down process by developing expectations for long-term macro factors that stand to affect market performance. As explained in Chapter 1, the top level of a top-down approach will include the development of long-term expectations for demographic trends, economics, investment flows, and the influence of cyclical tendencies.

A CURRENT APPLICATION

To exemplify how the top-down process can be implemented to apply the macro assessment, interpret the model's message, incorporate allocation and selection themes, and develop an investment strategy, let's assess conditions and probabilities as they stood in early 2000. Starting with demographics, you may recall that as suggested by Figure 1–1, the population of 45- to 54-year-olds is expected to rise throughout the decade, based on the high birth rate after World War II. And that prospect bodes well for consumer spending and investing, including equity investing. Also favorable is the general trend of the global economy, which started the new century in better shape than it had been in several years.

As discussed in Chapter 5, 1997 was the year of a major breadth peak in the United States, with weekly new highs exceeding 1000 in July of that year. It was no coincidence that at about the same time, the seeds of the Asian economic crisis were sown with the devaluation of the Thai baht, which Thailand unlinked from the U.S. dollar. As economic crises spread across the region, the divergent U.S. breadth statistics appeared to reflect expectations for global economic troubles, which in fact became pronounced and widespread by mid-1998. During the bear market that followed, the U.S. financial markets represented a global safe haven, with the U.S. stock markets maintaining relative strength versus markets in other regions.

In October of 1998, the Fed cut interest rates in what was perceived as the antidote that would put an end to the so-called Asian contagion. The U.S. market took off, as did other markets around the world. And in keeping with the tendency for market strength to precede economic strength, improving economic numbers in 1999 confirmed the end of the crisis, with Far East markets showing impressive relative strength and the especially impressive performance of Japanese small caps summarizing the improved outlook for that region's stock markets and economies. By 2000, it was clear that in the Far East as well as Latin America and Europe, the early stages of economic expansion were under way, accompanied by rising interest rates. In the United States, rates were rising as well. But they were doing so in conjunction with a mature economy that, in contrast to economies elsewhere, had reached a milestone for longevity, having surpassed its previous record streak in the 1960s. And in contrast to 1998, the U.S. market was losing relative strength, suggesting that it would lead the world into the next bear market.

So while the century started with a demographic outlook that appeared to be encouraging for the U.S. market, global comparisons were suggesting that the United States would take a back seat to markets that would benefit from the profit expectations that tend to occur early in an economic cycle, markets just starting to benefit from the growth in the kind of mergers and acquisitions activity and public participation that had long been props for the U.S. stock market. It remained to be seen if other regions would experience a wealth effect caused by rising stock market profits, an effect that encouraged excessive confidence and uninhibited spending among U.S. consumers. But there was increasing evidence that German and Japanese investors, among others, were gaining interest in stocks.

In Germany, the revival could be seen in mutual funds sales, in the growing popularity of discount brokerages, and in plans to establish an electronic communications network (ECN) similar to those in the United States that had encouraged the proliferation of day trading. A Salomon Smith Barney estimate showed that by 1999 German equity holdings as a percentage of German household disposable income had risen to 22 percent, more than double its level in the early 1990s. And in Japan, individuals accounted for 29 percent of the trading value of Japanese stocks in 1999, double its percentage in the previous year, according to the Tokyo Stock Exchange. Overseas investors accounted for 39 percent of the trading, reflecting renewed global confidence.

At the same time that equity investing was gaining the public's fascination in Europe and Japan, the U.S. public's affinity for stocks appeared to be reaching a saturation point by 2000. Among other indications, households were allocating a record 43 percent of their assets to equities at the end of the decade (Figure 6–2), and Federal Reserve statistics indicated that as of 1998, 49 percent of all U.S. families owned stock, up from 40 percent in

1995 and 32 percent in 1989. But while the median value of stock holdings climbed to $25,000, up from $15,400 in 1995 and $10,800 in 1989, debt rose as well, with 13 percent of families owing at least 40 percent of their income as debt in 1998, up from 11 percent in 1995 and 10 percent in 1989. And the percentage of families that had missed a debt payment by at least two months reached 8 percent in 1998, up from 7 percent in 1995.

While others were just warming up to equities, the U.S. investor was leveraging based on paper profits, consistent with the record levels of consumer confidence (Figure 8–17), accelerating margin debt, the willingness to buy stocks at exorbitant valuations, and the speculation toward Internet-related stocks. The increased impatience with poor stock performance, combined with the unprecedented ease and efficiency of trading that had developed with advances in on-line brokerage services, encouraged rapid turnover, a big influence on volatility.

According to statistics from Sanford Bernstein, investors held stocks for an average of eight months in 1999, down from a holding period of two years in 1989, while the average NASDAQ stock holding period dropped to five months, down from two years in 1989. The average mutual fund holding period dropped to 4 years, down from 11 years ago a decade earlier. And share turnover, a measure of trading activity, reached its highest levels since the 1920s, as 79 percent of the shares traded on the New York Stock Exchange changed hands in 1999. The turnover figure was 221 percent for NASDAQ stocks, indicating that all of the NASDAQ-listed shares turned over more than twice during the year.

With so much paper profit, so much leverage, and so much short-term trading emphasis, a top-down analysis could identify substantial risk as the decade began, the risk that the long-term uptrend in U.S. market volatility would culminate in U.S. investors heading for the exits, quickly and en masse, upon signs of their paper profits dwindling into losses. The risk was that the U.S. market would underperform on the downside and that U.S. investors, still licking their wounds, would be slow to participate in the subsequent bull market. In contrast to 1998, when investment flows into the United States helped keep the U.S. market relatively strong, the relative market improvement elsewhere stood to attract equity flows out of the United States and into those markets. The prospect for contrasting relative strength was supported by long-term momentum trends, and Figure 11–2 shows the 1990s ending with the United States market's momentum looking less and less impressive compared to the momentum of the Japanese and European markets.

So as the new millennium got started, it looked as though the U.S. stock market would underperform versus markets in countries with more to gain economically, with those markets benefiting from expectations that their respective economies would contribute increasingly to global economic growth. In contrast to those markets, the U.S. market would have to contend with the contraction of the wealth effect, which stood to bring on disproportionate weakness in the U.S. market, and in turn the economy. It ap-

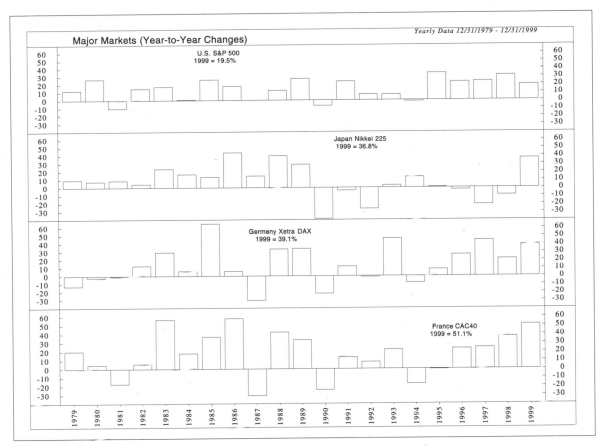

Figure 11–2

peared likely that after a probable global bear market in 2000, the U.S. market would remain vulnerable to underperformance and a premature top during the subsequent global advance.

In the same way that it took several years for the market to complete a long-term topping process and begin to correct the long-term illiquidity and excessive optimism, it seemed probable that for the pendulum to swing back to a pessimistic state with high liquidity, more than one cyclical bear market would be needed. Perhaps the process started in 1998. Perhaps in retrospect the period would look like the choppy period of the late 1970s. Perhaps after a period of overall weakness, including several big swings over the first few years of the decade, the market would move back into a steady uptrend, though without the kind of huge gains that had become commonplace in the 1990s.

As many noted at the time (myself included), the 1990s ended with the U.S. market holding many similarities to the markets of 1929, 1973, and 1989 in Japan. Each was followed by market disaster. Yet, the risk of one or more normal cyclical bear markets turning into a multiyear downside calamity appeared to be limited by better economic management by the Fed and the world's central banks, including a recent record of success in keeping inflation in check while enabling productivity to expand and keeping money supply growth sufficient to maintain economic liquidity.

An economic depression, or even a severe recession like the one that started in 1973, looked like long shots, as did the prospect for the kind of liquidity trap that rendered interest rate indicators useless during the 1930s in the United States and the 1990s in Japan. In those cases, the falling interest rates failed to stimulate economic growth, since consumers were not willing to borrow despite the minuscule lending rates. In contrast to the 1930s in particular, the global economy appeared to be on sound footing, with markets around the world benefiting from public participation in equity markets, cross-border merger and acquisition activity, and other signs that economic isolation would be far less likely than increasing globalization.

This kind of long-term demographic and economic evaluation is a useful and necessary exercise. The long-term evaluations keep your eyes open to long-term trend shifts that may affect your allocation, getting you ready to act aggressively or defensively, and directing your attention to the opportunities in foreign markets when the relative strength prospects are poor for the U.S. market. But the problem with this type of analysis is the need to use terms like "perhaps" or "it looked as though" or "is likely to" or "could be expected to." The longer the look-ahead period, the greater the guessing, and the greater the chance that things won't work out as you had expected.

In the bond market, yields on long-term bonds are greater than the yields on short-term bonds to compensate investors for the greater future uncertainty. But there is no compensation for acting on a long-term stock market forecast, despite all the unexpected political, economic, and even social developments that can trigger short-term market moves or set off chain reactions with longer-term implications. By staying focused on the here and now, you will have far better investment success.

THE MODEL'S BOTTOM LINE

This brings me back to the value of a good model for describing the current level of market risk. While keeping the long-term outlook in the back of your mind, the model's reading should be the basis for your investment decisions. If the model is bearish, for example, it is always possible that conditions will change, that a major decline will be averted, and that the model will start to improve again. But you shouldn't make a habit of second-guessing your model or trying to predict its future levels. Instead, if the model indicates that the market outlook is risky, you should respond by maintaining a defensive investment approach. When the model starts to indicate that the skies have cleared and that there is little risk on the investment horizon, you can again be confident in taking an aggressive approach.

Once you have determined whether to invest defensively, aggressively, or somewhere in between, you can apply the top-down approach to the levels of asset allocation and selection. In early 2000, the reading of the nine-indicator model called for a cautious view, having deteriorated steadily since the 1997 breadth peak. And the risks were highest for growth stocks, especially the technology stocks that had diverged from the rest of the market in pushing the NASDAQ Composite to repetitive record highs. Not only were many of the dominant stocks overvalued even by the standards of growth stocks, which normally carry high earnings multiples, but several fundamental indicators were negative for growth stocks relative to value stocks, many of which were undervalued even by value stock standards.

As discussed in Chapter 9, growth stocks tend to perform worse than value stocks when earnings growth is high and economic growth is in its mature stages, suggesting that despite the defiance of those tendencies as 2000 got under way, the growth outperformance would be short-lived. The model's decline itself was a bad omen for growth stocks, given the tendency for growth to perform worse than value in bear markets. The high level of market risk also argued for holding large-cap stocks rather than the more volatile small caps, which would be more vulnerable during a market decline.

As the market started to languish, technology stocks began to exit the NDR Focus List and the momentum-only Trader's Buy List, signaling that it was time to start selling those stocks. And the need to emphasize defensive stocks, large caps, and value called for a look at large-cap utilities, the epitome of defense and value. Using the NDR Focus List, the Trader's Buy List, or any other screening system during this kind of transitional phase of the market cycle, you would be watching for those defensive stocks to enter the list, and you would buy accordingly. You might also watch for the list to include stocks from the defensive foods sector, or the energy sector in an environment of high and rising oil prices.

But the best approach in early 2000 was to address the pervasive market risk by simply getting out of the market altogether and establishing a heavy cash position. Not only were money market funds and other cash proxies appealing as shelters from capital losses, but their returns had become more attractive owing to the short-term interest rate increases that had occurred as a result of the Fed's rate hikes. The rising short-term rates had helped cause an inversion of the yield curve. And when the yield curve has been flat or inverted, the returns from cash have been far better than the returns from bonds, and especially the returns from stocks, as shown in Figure 9–3 in Chapter 9.

At the time of the yield curve's inversion, it was still too early to make a decisive move into bonds. But they warranted close scrutiny given their attractive valuation at the high yield levels and given the probability that interest rates would stabilize and start to recede once the stock market decline had raised economic concerns. Bonds would then stand to benefit from their safe-haven appeal and from the mounting worry that the stock market weakness would be followed by a slowdown in the economy.

While a risk-averse, low-risk approach appeared warranted as 2000 progressed, there was no way of knowing if an unexpected development would change the environment and call for an aggressively bullish approach. But if that were to occur, the model would move to bullish and it would be time to reassess your strategy. Of equal importance, it would be time to abandon any preconceived notion of how you had expected the market to perform in the context of your long-term view. Whereas adherence to a forecast inhibits flexibility, adherence to a model enables you to respond efficiently to a change in the market environment, regardless of whether or not you expected the change to occur.

A model's reading also serves as a reminder that historical norms do not shift overnight. If an indicator level has been a consistent negative influence in the past, it's unlikely to be a bullish influence in the future, even if that appears to be the case at the end of an advance. In response to the chart in Figure 8–17 quantifying the bearish implications of extremely high consumer confidence, a client claimed in early 2000 that the indicator wasn't working since the major indices were still rising despite the record levels of confidence. But the message of the indicator's apparent failure "to work" was that the market's performance was truly abnormal in the face of the excessive optimism. It only reinforced the warning of the other indicators based on sentiment, liquidity and valuation, the warning that a return to normality was inevitable. And that reversion was bound to occur in conjunction with a market decline.

Also at the start of 2000, it might have seemed that growth outperformance was normal, despite the historical tendency for value to perform just as well, if not better. Excessive levels had been reached in the mania surrounding growth stocks as well as in the extreme neglect in value stocks.

The contrasting extremes were illustrated by an anecdote of abnormality at the end of 1999. In November of that year I paid a visit to a client whom I had visited two years earlier. During the earlier visit, we had discussed the excellent 20-year track record that he had been able to maintain through a disciplined style of value investing. But during the second visit two years later, he lamented over the deterioration of his performance and the defection of clients, which had forced him to put his business up for sale. Adding insult to injury, his office rent had tripled, and most of the building's other occupants were now dot-com start-ups, in keeping with its location just up the road from growth-stock hotbed Silicon Valley. In contrast, I learned shortly after that visit that a colleague in our computer department, who admitted to knowing next to nothing about investing, had hit the jackpot with a hot growth stock, as her investment club had gotten her into an Internet stock that had risen 800 percent in just a few weeks. When the gain was pointed out to her, she promptly sold the stock.

Clearly, something was out of whack and abnormal when a seasoned value manager with a proven record was on the verge of losing his business at the same time that a novice was able to make such a huge profit with so little effort. Inevitably, abnormalities become widely apparent in retrospect, and it was likely that at some point early in the new millennium, it would again be viewed as normal to buy attractively priced stocks with strong fundamentals and risky to buy into a speculative bubble by loading up on stocks with little or no earnings.

In keeping with the human mass mood swings between fear and greed, the market and its various style categories and sectors inevitably revert to their normal rates of growth. To the extent that the market trends upward in keeping with the advancements of society, the market's cycles take it higher like a helix or a spiral, rather than a circle that brings it back to its starting point. The human emotions that create peaks and troughs are the same from cycle to cycle, but the transitions from bull market to bear market are different in identifiable ways. By understanding how investors have responded historically to various circumstances, you will better understand the market implications of the current spectrum of conditions.

As I stated at the start of this book, to beat the market, you must first understand it. Ideally, you would endeavor to do so by establishing a clean and extensive historical database, building quantifiable indicators, and combining them into a model to be used in conjunction with asset allocation indicators and screening systems. But even if you apply the approach in a very basic way, perhaps keeping a scorecard of bullish and bearish influences on the market, your investing should be enhanced. By keeping yourself objective and focused based on historical norms and abnormalities, you won't get caught up in the fervor of the moment, and you will have a clear perspective on risk and reward. You will be well on your way to investment success.

The
Research Driven
Investor

INDEX

Advance/decline line:
  bias of, 94–95, 96 (table)
  and confirmation, 111
  defined, 93
  leading tendency of (*see* Leading indicators of the stock market)
  and moving averages, 95–97, 98–101 (figures), 113–115
  See also Market breadth
Advisory service sentiment, (*see* Sentiment indicators)
American Association of Individual Investors, 186–187, 188 (figure)
Appel, Gerald, 115
Arms, Richard, 173
Asset allocation, 2
  benefit of, 71
  bonds and, 231–235
  and economic cycle, 231–233, 237–244
  and portfolio mix, 231, 232 (table)
  and top-down approach, 7
  See also Bonds; Global investing; Large-cap stocks; Small-cap stocks
Automated trading systems, 48, 51

Barron's Online, 35, 39
Bear markets, 80
  and asset allocation, 231
  defined, 14, 15 (table), 80
  duration of, 14, 20, 136
  and economic cycle, 223–225, 230, 233
  and economic recessions, 11–12, 224
  group performance during, 250–252
  and indicator testing, 54
  and interest rates, 195

Bear markets (*Cont.*):
  magnitude of, 14
  rallies within (*see* Rallies)
  and valuation levels, 219
Bernstein, Richard, 21
Big Charts, 32, 39
Big Mo (*see* Models)
Black, Fischer, 47
Blind simulation, 58
  See also Out-of-sample performance
Bloomberg, 29, 35, 39
Bollinger bands, 74, 76*n*, 186
  See also Standard deviation; Trading bands
Bonds:
  and asset allocation, 231–235
  composite long-term Treasury bond yield, 204–206, 207–208 (tables)
  credit spreads, 196–197
  momentum of, 184, 209–210, 237–239
  price index, 207–211
  See also Interest rates; Leading indicators of the stock market
Bottom-up approach, 6, 13, 13, 27–28
  See also Top-down approach
Breadth of Market (*see* Market breadth)
Buffett, Warren, 8
Bull markets:
  and asset allocation, 231
  corrections within, 14, 18 (table), 80, 112, 161, 207–208 (tables), 259
  defined, 14, 16 (table), 80
  duration of, 14, 20
  and economic cycle, 223–225, 230
  group performance during, 250–252, 259
  and indicator testing, 54

Timothy Hayes is the global equity strategist for Ned Davis Research, where he writes the weekly Stock Selection Focus, International Focus, and other market advisory publications. A chartered market technician (CMT), Hayes has written for the *Market Technicians Association Journal* and other financial periodicals. His commentary appears often in the financial media, including regular appearances on CNBC and CNN's Moneyline and quotations in *The Wall Street Journal, Investor's Business Daily,* and others. He is a winner of the Charles H. Dow award, sponsored by Dow Jones Telerate, the Market Technicians Association, and *Barron's* for groundbreaking research in technical analysis.